Social Theory after the Internet

Social Theory after the Internet

Media, Technology and Globalization

Ralph Schroeder

First published in 2018 by
UCL Press
University College London
Gower Street
London WC1E 6BT

Available to download free: www.ucl.ac.uk/ucl-press

A CIP catalogue record for this book is available from The British Library.

ISBN: 978–1–78735–124–0 (Hbk.)
ISBN: 978–1–78735–123–3 (Pbk.)
ISBN: 978–1–78735–122–6 (PDF)
ISBN: 978–1–78735–125–7 (epub)
ISBN: 978–1–78735–126–4 (mobi)
ISBN: 978–1–78735–127–1 (html)
DOI: https://doi.org/10.14324/111.9781787351226

Acknowledgements

I have taught this topic for many years, and so my first thanks must go to my students, from whom I have learned so much. I am also grateful to former colleagues at Chalmers University and current colleagues at the Oxford Internet Institute (OII) for many great conversations. At the OII, they include Grant Blank, Eric Meyer, Jonathan Bright and Bill Dutton. Outside the OII, there are far too many to list, but I want to thank especially Rasmus Nielsen, Kerk Kee, Tim Groeling, Jack Qiu, Angela Wu, Cornelius Puschmann, Andreas Jungherr and Sahana Udupa. The usual disclaimers apply. The research for this book was partly undertaken while I was Distinguished Visiting Professor at the Departments of Communication and Sociology during the winter term at UCLA in 2016 and an Erskine Visiting Fellow in the Department of Media and Communication at the University of Canterbury in February and March of 2017. Several of the chapters here are based on previous publications and these are indicated in the relevant places in the text. Finally, the biggest thanks go to my family, who have taught me how to use a mobile phone and social media: as they know, I'm still a tyro.

Contents

List of figures

1
The internet in theory

1.1 Theories of media, new and old

Digital media have been responsible for some of the most wide-ranging changes in society over the past quarter-century. At the same time, there is little agreement in the social sciences about how these changes should be understood. One reason is increasing disciplinary specialization. For example, media and communication studies concentrates on specific areas such as the news or influencers on social media – without a broader analysis of what people do online. Other disciplines such as sociology have, with few exceptions, left the study of new media to the discipline of media and communications. Or again, political science has tended to concentrate on specific questions, such as the role of media in election campaigns or for social movements. The sociology of science and technology, meanwhile, has adopted a stance whereby generalizations across particular contexts of uses of technology are deemed impossible. The same applies to anthropology. And there is a further problem that cuts across disciplines: that theories which were suited to mass media and interpersonal communication are no longer suited to digital media – since new media often have elements of both.

A few brief examples about how the use of 'mass' versus 'interpersonal' is misleading for digital media can suffice at this point.[1] First, there is the growth of user-generated content, which goes beyond passive 'audiences' and 'senders versus receivers'. Second, news and other content is often shared among groups on social media rather than being accessed by individuals or broadcast one-to-many. Third, the way in which we seek much online information, for instance, via Wikipedia, is subject to new gatekeeping mechanisms such as search engines. A search via Google that leads to a Wikipedia entry, for example, means that the gatekeeping mechanism works differently from traditional gatekeepers, such as professional journalistic fact-checking norms or control by publishers of encyclopaedia volumes. One of the aims of this book is to provide a theory of the internet and social change that goes beyond 'mass' and 'interpersonal' – and which at the same time overcomes disciplinary divides by arguing that a single theory can be applied throughout the social sciences.

There is another problem that the book must address: research about the internet tends to focus on what is new, without recognizing that traditional media still often dominate,[2] for example, during election campaigns. Yet it is also true, among younger people and in some countries such as Sweden and America at least, that digital media have largely displaced – even if they also complement – traditional media for news. One proposal for coping with this simultaneity of 'old' and 'new' is to talk of 'hybrid' media (Chadwick 2013), which postulates the side-by-side existence of both, in this case for the political realm. But this sweeps under the rug the very problem that needs to be solved: unless there is a clear sense of how old and new relate to one another, 'hybridity' does not overcome the need for a theory of digital media since it leaves open the balance between the two and the differences in how they work.

The few theories that have tackled the changing media landscape all have shortcomings. Castells' theory of network power (2009) has two main elements: an ontology whereby all media are best understood as working via networks, and a theory of power whereby power is increasingly concentrated in a few global transnational media conglomerates but which at the same time always generates resistance. Both ideas are flawed since there are countries in which the capitalist imperatives of media conglomerates play a far lesser role, such as in China, where the party-state exercises much control over media, or Sweden, where public-service media continue to be dominant. Put differently, national 'media systems' (Hallin and Mancini 2004), which can be grouped into regional types, still outweigh the dynamics of global capitalist concentration, and nation-states also place strong boundaries around how media operate, as well as the bounds within which popular political inputs – public opinion and civil society organizations (or 'resistance', if we want to use Castells' term) – shape the political agenda via media, as we shall see.

The second major theory, mediatization theory (Hjarvard 2008), takes these national differences into account and proposes that people's relationship to society is increasingly mediated. This is a theory that, suitably modified, I will build on here. Yet as it stands, the theory lacks analytical precision about which particular areas of social life are being mediatized: mediatization is defined as 'the process whereby society to an increasing degree is submitted to, or becomes dependent on, the media and their logic'; media become 'integrated into the operations of other social institutions' and are also 'social institutions in their own right', and 'as a consequence, social interaction – within the institutions, between institutions, and in society at large – take place via the media' (Hjarvard 2008, 113). However, as we shall see, it is important to distinguish between cultural, economic and political power, or their respective spheres, and to understand how media or mediatization operate quite differently within them. We can think here of the difference between the scarce attention for which political leaders and parties compete (in a zero-sum game) – as against how cultural products compete for consumer attention (in a more open-ended market). Further, while new media add to the mediatization of social life, it is also possible to argue that disintermediation takes place, as when people produce and consume content directly, outside of institutions.

Actor–network theory is yet another theory that has been applied to the internet. Although it is more about new technologies than about media specifically, it has had a wide influence in media studies (for example, Chadwick 2013; Couldry 2012). This theory puts the emphasis either on the agency of individuals or of non-humans (in the latter case, there is a kind of back-door technological determinism, which the theory otherwise rejects). Yet individual 'agency' cannot account for structures, and the non-human physical environment does not engage in volitional acts. Actor–network theory has also, like other theories of science, technology and society (STS), been dominated by the idea that science and technology are constructed or shaped by specific local social contexts, thus making it impossible to generalize about the role of media or technology beyond individual contexts of constructedness or shaping. Yet general patterns are essential if theory is to guide research, and structures are essential to uncovering asymmetries of power.

There are other media theories, but these three strands currently dominate. There is also research in subfields such as political communication, where particular theoretical concepts, for instance, the 'public sphere', are used (which will be discussed later). It is also important to add that much empirical media or communications research operates below the level of the general theories mentioned so far, with theories of the 'middle range'. These include agenda-setting, gatekeeping, framing, uses and gratifications, and rational choice or collective action. These theories all presuppose that research can take place without an overall or macro theory of social change – except perhaps insofar as they implicitly take the stance that the main aim of research should be to counteract excessive control or bias by some groups at the expense of others. In doing so, they presume – again, implicitly – a pluralist view or a theory of ideologies that compete in the marketplace of ideas (Neuman 2016).

The notion that ideas or ideologies compete in the media is an important one, as we shall see. However, with few exceptions (some key examples will be discussed), this research programme focuses on individual media, making it impossible to understand, for example, how agenda-setting works across traditional and new digital media. Moreover, this type of research typically focuses on media at the national level and for particular domains and periods. Yet there may be important lessons from comparisons (Esser and Pfetsch 2004), from longer-term trajectories, and again, from analysing the range of media. And it will be argued that it is necessary to identify structural constraints to the competition of ideas or ideologies instead of an open-ended market – at least in the political realm. Finally, yes, research should counteract asymmetries of power or control, but to do so it is also necessary to start from the top down: where do these asymmetries originate – at the global level, the national level or somewhere else?

The alternative put forward here rests on three starting points: first, national differences matter for the implications of digital media just as they did for traditional media. This entails that 'media systems' theory (Hallin and Mancini 2004) is an essential starting point, although there are also globalizing patterns that cut across nationally bounded media systems. Second, while new digital media add to and complement traditional media, old and new media must be encompassed within a single framework that enables an understanding of how, for example, the political agenda is shaped across both. As we shall see, it is useful to posit a limited attention space or a dominant agenda across different types of media. Third, this limited attention space – as well as the limits on individuals' connectedness to each other and to information – operates differently in relation to political communication, popular culture and online markets. For politics, the agenda that dominates the limited attention space has consequences. For culture, as long as there is diversity and reliability in certain types of information, there is also scope for taking the approach that 'anything goes' – that the description of different ways of life can suffice for social science. And online markets are open-ended, but data-driven targeting of consumers, among other forces, also shapes the growing diversity (or otherwise) of entertainment and other content.

Apart from these three points, another more general one is that the validity of theories of media rests on evidence about how new technologies are integrated into everyday life. This 'bottom-up' approach to analysing the role of the media is the strength of domestication theory (Haddon 2004; 2011; Silverstone and Hirsch 1992). Media should be gauged by how they are used, and with what effect in terms of social change, which overcomes the disciplinary divides mentioned earlier. Understanding everyday life must not exclude macro-dynamics, however, and particularly politics and wider longer-term and cumulative changes and discontinuities. These macro-changes also include divergences between and convergences across societies. Asymmetries of power or control can be unearthed by making comparisons, both on the levels of everyday life and how they fit into macro-changes, and contrasting what has changed between traditional and new digital media. This will be done here for four countries – Sweden, America, India and China – in order to (again) ground the argument in specific evidence. As will become evident, however, the argument may apply beyond these four.

Ultimately, the question that this book seeks to answer is this: at what point must a contemporary theory of society take into account that the internet plays a significant role in social change? The answer can be briefly previewed: in politics, certain new forces, here mainly exemplified by right-wing populists and nationalists but also by other new groups from below, are enabled by circumventing traditional gatekeepers. However, they also struggle against established media and rival elites or ideologies to dominate the attention space. Second, digital media tether us more closely to each other and to information. Within the realm of culture, a more mediated way of life creates new digital divides, and these are particularly important where reliable information, cultural diversity and social isolation are at stake. Third, big data is at the leading edge of a new research front based mostly on digital media. Apart from generating new academic knowledge, a major consequence is that private-sector media companies, and to some extent political and policy campaigns, have more powerful tools to target and manipulate publics. But big data analytics mainly pertain to consumers, so the implications are primarily in the economic realm.

As we shall see, these three changes – in politics, in culture and everyday life, and in the media economy – follow their own logics and interconnect only partially. But each entails a significant change attributable to the internet. A common thread among all three is that they are part of a larger process whereby technology penetrates more deeply into social life. Yet in contrast with other theories that speak of revolutions caused by the internet and the like, this increased mediatization must be put in its place: the internet is not responsible for a wholesale change in society, as Castells and others claim. There are other, deeper and more long-term transformations that confront society and which affect the political, economic and cultural systems. These include limits to expanding citizenship rights, climate change and financialization, and they have little or nothing to do with the internet.[3] The internet has brought about more specific changes in politics, culture and markets that are at best indirectly connected to these transformations. Still, social theory must take specific internet-related changes into account since together they amount to new and lasting ways in which we have become subject to more targeted political messages and ways to engage with them (politics), more tethered to each other and to information (culture) and to more online consumption (economy). In short, the internet has caged us and provides us with a more powerful exoskeleton, a mainly Weberian understanding of technology that will be elaborated further. These are profound ways in which digital technology has shaped our life – more specific than, but on a par with, the broader changes that were just mentioned. This brief hint at some of the main arguments and the overall conclusion of the book can now be expanded in more detail before we begin with an overview of the chapters to come.

1.2 Summary of the argument

As already mentioned, there is currently a gap in theories of the role of the internet, and I am not the first or only one to point this out (see, for example, Neuman 2016). Digital technologies – as already mentioned – do not fit into theories of either mass (or broadcast) or interpersonal media. However, rather than explain the role of the internet or media in society as such, it is necessary to separate out its role in three different parts of society – or, if the reader prefers, types of power (Mann 2013) or social orders (Schroeder 2013). In the end, of course, the relation between them must also be explained. But to understand the role of the internet (and social change generally), it is simply the case that different parts of society work differently: politics, where legitimacy and inputs are bounded and authoritative; markets, where sellers and buyers are connected via diffuse and extensive exchanges; and culture, with its plural worlds of symbols and sources of information (but also with one unified or cohesive part – science). These differences are one part of the argument; another is that technology shapes society – or technological determinism. This theory entails that the effects of new technologies should be the same across societies. I shall argue that this is indeed the case; the internet extends the reach and intensifies the penetration of media into society, but in doing so it shapes these orders or powers and is shaped by them. It can be added that the distinction between these orders or powers is not just analytical, but also applies to how media, including the internet, work – in practice.

This book will tackle global processes; however, partly because the evidence is most powerful at the level of different countries and partly because media systems are different, it will examine four countries: the United States, Sweden, India and China. I have chosen these four because they are useful cases from the point of view of the comparative method: the first two are at opposite ends of the spectrum among advanced democracies, the latter two provide alternative models of developing countries. The cases also represent a very wide range since they have quite different political systems (liberal democracy, social democracy, elite-skewed democracy and authoritarian). Still, across all four, the internet and media are becoming more market-oriented, although again, the internet remains shaped by different types of media systems (Hallin and Mancini 2004; 2012). This shaping matters above all for the role of media in politics, and especially for the autonomy of media – or the lack thereof. The internet extends the mediation of politics, from above, such that political elites can target and respond more directly to their publics, and from below, such that people or citizens (or civil society) can engage in more diverse ways with politics. From above and below, there are also possibilities to circumvent traditional gatekeepers, as with Donald Trump's tweets in America, as well as with populists in the other three countries. But the internet – and especially social media – also plays a greater role in India and China (as we might expect from rising powers) because in these two countries, traditional media are more skewed towards maintaining the hold of powerful elites while the internet is newer and less gatekept. The political impact of the internet, or of smartphones, is also greater in these two countries because it is closing the urban–rural divide more quickly. Finally, the impact is different for China and India: there are more possibilities for state control but also for resistance to authoritarianism in China (Yang 2014), whereas in India there is greater scope for civil society activism but also more manipulation by elites.

The argument thus extends mediatization theory (Couldry 2012, building on Meyrowitz 1985), whereby social life is increasingly mediated, and this process is intensified by the internet in all four countries.

More extensive political mediation is shaped by media systems, but mediatization also applies to markets and to culture: entertainment services and more diverse sources of information are driven by media competition and consumer (or audience) demands. Greater mediatization of markets and culture entails convergence, but this does not imply a homogenization of societies: in terms of content, digital media may often operate on a near-global scale ('global' always, for our four cases, with qualifications for China), but there is no zero-sum loss of diversity if content flows across borders. Instead, societies become more homogeneous inasmuch as media become more diverse. The increasing mediatization by means of the internet also allows more powerful targeting and reach into society, as with analytics that can tailor content to specific audiences. But this increasing mediatization is constrained by the limits of attention, with media experiencing ever more competition as the online realm expands into consumer markets and into culture or everyday life.

Culture is shaped by the internet mainly in terms of the micro level of everyday routines. Here the internet (and especially social media) makes for more dense and frequent relations of connectedness – or rather tetheredness, in keeping with the caging/exoskeleton idea already mentioned – to people and to information. The most widely experienced changes stemming from the internet, at least from the perspective of people's everyday lives, are that it provides more mediated engagement with others and with information. These changes, however, have no dramatic repercussions at the macro level; they are changes in people's way of life, their rituals and routines. There are exceptions to the absence of significant repercussions: there is a subset of online material that provides more and less reliable information and is important for everyday practical purposes. The main access to this information is via search engines, and the Web is the main source of these materials. This new digital infrastructure extends and displaces traditional media and information sources, and it is vital to provide enhanced access to this infrastructure and ensure its reliability and non-skewedness towards limited sources (or diversity) for a well-functioning society. Similar arguments apply to those for whom online access to others is an important lifeline.

From the perspective of long-term social change, the most important consequences of the internet are in relation to politics. The internet pushes media towards greater differentiation, caging people in mediated relations from above, including more targeting and greater responsiveness from elites, and from below, enabling more input and engagement. Again, increasing mediation faces the constraint of limits of attention, as with gatekeepers setting agendas. Populists, as we shall see, circumvent gatekeepers of traditional or mainstream media by allowing leaders and parties to get across their messages online, and enabling their supporters to access and share these messages, but in quite different and nationally specific ways. Big data also intensifies this caging, but as before, this is both a general process and depends on the setting: in India and China, smartphones are becoming the dominant way to access the internet, which means that different services are enabled by big data approaches. Or again, smartphones increasingly tether people to information and to each other, but technology matters, and in the case of smartphones, it can also limit engagement in comparison with access via computers (Napoli and Obar 2015). For online markets, where the targeting of populations relies on people's increasingly online activities, there is also competition for attention, but without a zero-sum limit.

The arguments presented here depart from the main alternative theories of media and the internet: the public sphere is not becoming more commodified but it is also not just a space for potential rational consensus or agreement (Habermas 1982); indeed, to avoid this normative view I shall refer to a public arena, which is contested because there are counterpublics that challenge the status quo (Fraser 1990) – again, in a limited attention space. Nor does increasing online content production lead to greater political liberalism or pluralism (Benkler 2006), as we shall see; and the internet does not generate more resistance in an increasingly globalized network society that is becoming borderless (Castells 2009). However, the internet does cause structural changes beyond those suggested by empirical studies of individual topics, as with much of American social science, which restricts itself to theories of the middle range, such as opportunities for collective action or gatekeeping and agenda-setting in particular media. Unlike European 'critical' social theory, however, which takes the position that theory comes before or outweighs evidence, the argument here is that theories must be open to evidence. And theory is needed. Research claiming to do without theory inevitably relies on an implicit theory of society; better to foreground it than to be subliminally guided and perhaps misled by it.

So far, I have presented a sketch of the argument, and several theoretical arguments have already been mentioned that will be used throughout the book. It will be useful to elaborate four key issues in more detail in advance to specify where I depart from existing theories. These are: how the media are autonomous but only a subsystem; how the role of the media is separate in the three social orders or powers; how there is a limited attention space for media; and technological determinism or shaping.

1.3 The autonomy of the media (sub)system

I have argued that there is increasing mediatization, but I have mentioned (and I will elaborate on this shortly) how media operate differently in three social orders or spheres of power. This leads to the question: are media yet another, separate social order or power? I will argue that media are autonomous – that there is an autonomy of the media system – but media are only a subsystem. This may seem a highly theoretical point, but much will hang on it, so it is worth spelling out. We can start by contrasting it with other theories. The lack of autonomy of the media system is particularly evident in Marxist theory (McChesney 2013), where the media are the glue that keeps capitalism intact and capitalist control of the media determines their political content or how the media shape politics. This idea is misleading, as some of the prima facie evidence that has already been mentioned from the four cases to be considered suggests (this will be elaborated on in later chapters): Sweden, and in a different way India, have public-service media, and in China, the state, not the market, most strongly controls the media. In China, journalists have also, though not without tensions, imbibed the ethos of American journalistic impartiality (Zhu 2012), which is key to autonomous media, and in America, this ethos and the watchdog function of media, as elsewhere, play a large role (Schudson 2011). Still, the alternative to the Marxist view must be theoretically anchored.

One reason that the media are autonomous, as Hallin and Mancini (2004) argue, is that they have institutions such as the journalistic profession with its own norms of impartiality and objectivity, furthered, for example, through professional education and associations. But more than these separate norms, autonomy is also 'vertical', from political elites above and from people below, including how they are represented within the political system, and from the economic and cultural systems 'horizontally', for example, being independent via regulation about media ownership (or, in the case of public service, regulation about media functions). This will be detailed further below, but there are different types of autonomy of media systems in different regions of the world, even if it is also the case that market forces have deepened everywhere in recent decades and thus weakened this autonomy. Comparisons, as we shall see, can help to establish how the role of the media varies between societies, for example, how media institutions have more or less independence in the context of different political and economic systems. Many accounts of media do not address this systemic nature of media, or they overlook or take as given their autonomy. In American social science in particular, there are theories of the middle range (agenda-setting, gatekeeping, uses and gratifications, framing), but they do not explain the macro-dynamics (or larger structural changes) of media and the variation in autonomy as between different systems, or the varying strength of media over time within a system or country.

To complicate matters further, and against the idea of autonomy, there are also, as we shall see, examples of some media losing autonomy, as when digital media bypass the gatekeeping mechanisms of traditional media. This means that traditional media partly lose autonomy; for example, when the media's ability to input the interests of civil society or of elites in an impartial way is diminished at the expense of the greater agenda-setting power of those using digital media. Another example is if data analytics for online audiences push journalists to be led by what audiences want rather than representing the interests of society beyond these audiences. Losing autonomy thus entails de-differentiation – though the process can be even more complex, as when there is further differentiation: digital media can also act as watchdogs on those new media that bypass traditional gatekeepers; new watchdogs then play a role as a 'fifth estate' (Dutton 2009; Graves 2016).

So the media system is autonomous in the sense that it has its own institutions and acts as a watchdog in politics, attempting to be a transmission belt between governing elites and people or civil society, and a mirror of social concerns.[4] Yet it is only a subsystem because, except insofar as it translates into political – or cultural or economic – change (put differently, in that it makes political, cultural and economic changes in these three systems), it does nothing on its own, except to grow and become more differentiated. In other words, the subsystem connects, for the political system, the people (or civil society) to the political elite, but it does not connect political elites or people to social development as a whole: the political system does that. Similarly, as we shall see, information ties people to the social environment, so media are a kind of (non-political) subsystem connecting people to their everyday social or cultural tasks. However, people's relation via information is to their immediate social environments, and again, this mediation is not related to social development as such. This is similar to how markets relate to consumers. In short, social development is driven by the three main systems, not by media per se.

This subsystemic nature of the media and their autonomy can be considered together, via the notion of differentiation: how can the media be both autonomous and 'only' a subsystem? The reason is because they are independent of parts of these systems that they connect, and which together make for larger changes. Media have thus become differentiated so they are an autonomous subsystem. Yet sometimes new media can circumvent the existing subsystem of traditional media and foment changes propelled by connecting elites and people in new ways. However, this only 'reinserts' the autonomy of media (even while it takes away the autonomy of traditional media) in furthering change in a new way; it does not alter the nature of media as a subsystem.

This leaves one question: the media subsystem translates between people and elites in politics, and between market producers or services and consumers or audiences in the economy. What about media in the sphere of culture? But technoscience is part of culture, and so it is also a subsystem between (non-commercial and non-political) cultural content (such as information) and everyday users of information. This question can be resolved when we recognize that technoscience produces and advances the tools or technologies of mediation as part of technoscientific advance, and so it affects the political and economic media subsystems, as just discussed. Yet when these tools of mediation are introduced within the cultural order, they also add complexity (or differentiate and de-differentiate) to mediatization, translating cultural content of *all* types, including scientific and non-scientific parts of culture (the latter include practical information and other non-commercial and non-political symbolic exchanges, such as the arts). There is therefore a general effect of new technology on the media subsystem in all three orders or powers, and a specific one that pushes new technology into the other two orders but also into the cultural sphere itself, adding to how cultural content (including scientific communication) is mediated, which includes the growing place of scientific knowledge in society and the increasing everyday uses of media technology in everyday cultural life as part of an overall cultural development.

This section (and especially the preceding paragraph) has made a complex argument; again, it is crucial to what follows, and also to the overall aim of offering a comprehensive theory of the role of the internet (including traditional media) in society and which also overcomes disciplinary specialization. Luckily, the complexity can be reduced by means of figure 1.1, which also serves as a bridge to the next sections. What figure 1.1 illustrates is how media are both autonomous and only a subsystem: media have a dashed line around them (indicating a 'sub' system rather than a 'system' with solid lines), but they are also expanding with mediatization, and changes take place 'through' them. Figure 1.1 also shows how the role of media technology is both part of culture but also – as technoscience – drives change within culture and the other two

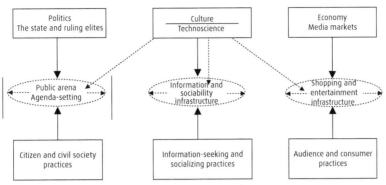

Fig. 1.1 Three spheres or powers (politics, culture, economy) and the increasing mediation between dominant institutions and people's everyday practices (dashed arrows).

spheres, via dashed arrows: technology (or technoscience) is a separate force. Further, it shows how media operate differently within the three spheres: within politics, the arrows that expand come up against the zero-sum limited attention space of agenda-setting. (As we will see in figure 7.1 in chapter 7, the differences between these realms also mean that changes in digital media work in different ways in and through them.) What figure 1.1 illustrates is how the subsystem of media connects politics, culture and the economy to changes in people's lives. This leads to a final point, which is what I have labelled in the bottom row in figure 1.1 (and 7.1) as 'practices', but I could equally have talked of the people's social role as citizens or members of civil society, or as socializers and information seekers, or as consumers and audiences: nothing in the argument hangs on the difference between two ways of labelling the bottom row.

1.4 The role of the media in politics, culture and the economy: separate and different

A key argument is that the political, cultural and economic implications of media are separate: for politics, there are macro-changes, changes in how the media system translates between political elites and civil society. For culture, the main change is at the micro level, changes embedded in everyday routines or ways of life, and for the most part without macro-repercussions. In the economy, a major change is how markets tailor media content to consumers and how consumers, in turn, need to manage their media consumption. The theory proposed here divides media – including digital media – uses into three realms: politics (defined broadly, as issues related to the state); culture, which includes socializing and information seeking (or the everyday realm of sociability and practical tasks); and consumerism, including entertainment, with this third realm again dealt with from the point of view of audiences and online markets (the economics of production, and also work, will be dealt with only in passing, or insofar as they relate to the main focus here; one theory and book can cover only so much).[5]

A simple and overlooked difference can be illustrated by reference to the first two. This is that political communication is zero sum and culture is not (or at least not in the same way). For media in politics, gatekeepers dictate what publics or citizens focus on, and the agenda is set by ruling elites and by the public's input as mediated by media elites. For mediated culture too, there is competition for attention, and there are gatekeepers shaping the content produced and received. However, this is not zero sum in the sense that information seekers, for example, access different types of content, sometimes overlapping, without the further ramification that this content sets the agenda for societal change (as with politics). Further, they can spend more time with more information sources, adding new digital ones, whereas in the political realm, there are no signs of an overall expansion of attention. Gans (1999) has argued that popular culture is plural, and where it is not, it should be more so, so that diversity and non-zero-sum openness matter. There can of course be overlaps between politics and culture, as when culture is politicized to include or exclude certain groups. But this then is a question of openness and diversity within a zero-sum space and a political rather than a cultural issue.

Put differently, culture can be skewed towards certain groups, but with respect to everyday life or culture (or also to markets and consumers or audiences), it is also diffuse and unbounded, while political communication is authoritative and largely bounded. Furthermore, news and political participation are focused within the nation-state. For socializing, the question of dominance within a bounded territory does not arise: everyday routines and rituals are at the micro level of interaction. There are wider macro-patterns of changes in everyday life, such as the strengthening of rituals of everyday sociability. But their significance for societal development is a matter of analysing different ways of life, which are partly converging globally with increasing mediatization. The implications for the role of media in politics, on the other hand, is that this (sub)system has a limited attention space that mediates between the state and people where this mediation is zero sum (except at the margins, with new technologies). The role of the media in culture, on the other hand, is more open-ended, even if there may be political attempts to control it. And the same kind of open-endedness applies to online markets and consuming audiences.

1.5 A limited attention space

The argument will be made that there is a limited attention space dominated by a few actors (the 'law of small numbers') across all media, online and offline. Unlike theories of the middle range (agenda-setting and gatekeeping), this idea provides a theory of the role of media because it can account for the *range* of media, old and new. It also posits (as already discussed) a different kind of limited attention space for mediated politics and for the mediated cultural and economic orders. The point in all cases is to examine all media, old and new, together, distinguishing their effects but also identifying the interplay between them – without evading the question of the strength of the combination of media in the (sub) system as a whole.

The idea of a limited attention space in politics is akin to Gans' idea of a 'national newshole' (2004, 319) or Carey's point that 'reality is ... a scarce resource' (1989, 87), though these ideas were never developed as part of a systematic media theory or social theory. It can be likened to agenda-setting and gatekeeping – as long as the media agenda that passes through the gate, as a whole, translates into changes in social development. Gatekeeping and agenda-setting have been a part of different research paradigms, but they overlap: the 'gate' constrains the agenda, and the agenda is the content that gets past the gate, to which could be added the media theory whereby the media 'frame' different agendas. But again, there is a dominant frame – at least in the political system. The dominant frame consists of prevailing political ideologies, including those of the counterpublics that challenge it, and these shape politics, which is nowadays almost entirely mediated.[6] What both theories leave out is the overall structure of the gate or the agenda or the frame – or, whether these mechanisms have changed over time, also in terms of the structure of how new inputs shape politics; for example, via new media or with new forces such as populism, and how these are translated into (or not) – and so provide a direction-giving impetus to – the state and ultimately social development. Put differently, there are media agendas that dominate, pushed by elites or people, at least in politics. The idea of the newshole captures this, allowing the newshole to constrain the limited attention space and thus shape new ideologies. But a limited attention space, via a newshole or other media inputs, can also include content that, for example, circumvents traditional gatekeepers and so sets a new news agenda or ideological course.

Unlike mediated culture or markets, political communication is zero sum. Put differently, there is a sense in which limited media attention space is important only in the political realm. The idea of limited attention space in relation to media has also been put forward by Neuman (2016), drawing on Collins (1999), and it will be useful to contrast Neuman's ideas with those presented here. Neuman argues that, as long as there is a well-functioning marketplace of ideas (or competition for attention), political communication functions as well as it might. This is an America-centric view, based on the dangers that American communication and political science scholars have fretted over, such as that this marketplace is distorted by polarization or echo chambers or skewed by unequal political participation or a declining interest in politics or the pressures of media ownership. These concerns may be important, but they overlook the fact that the American media system is unique: first, because the American polity is uniquely fragmented or logjammed by many interests without a strong state, and its media system reflects this fragmentation.[7] The second is that, in comparison with other media systems, America's is more market-oriented. This has implications for a limited attention space, which is more commercially competitive in America, unlike media systems where, for example, public broadcasting plays a major role. However, in terms of political ideologies, for instance, a multi-party system effectively also has a 'market' of the ideologies of several parties. In any event, a limited attention space here will mean that there is not an open (non-zero-sum) market, at least for politics: instead, there is competition for ideologies to dominate in the media.

Neuman's book details how American communication research has struggled over the course of its development to pin down the effects of media empirically. It explains how it has yo-yoed back and forth between finding major effects of media on what people think – for example, in the era of propaganda in the wake of the totalitarian regimes of the mid-twentieth century – as against showing minimal or no effects in a pluralistic America where ideas compete freely in the media and media reflect a healthy competition in the marketplace of ideas (even if this healthiness may need improvement, which is Neuman's view). This state of communications research – and communications and media research is dominated by the United

States – I argue, is itself not healthy: it bases our ideas of how media work on agonizing among American academics about what is wrong with American media, for example, bias in this marketplace.[8] The same America-centric nature of media debates is evident outside of politics too; for example, with Turkle's (2012) ideas about the loss of togetherness, which will be discussed in chapter 4. But again, American media are unique among media systems, and this uniqueness can be highlighted by comparison.

Neuman's solution is to plead for engagement with European traditions of 'critical studies'; but this idea, too, is problematic, since, as mentioned, European theories, including media theories, often reject objectivity, or fail to engage with evidence, and remain diffuse without cumulation. The idea of a limited attention space that is not based on an open-ended market, but posits a public arena in which ideologies compete to dominate, can cope better with the fact that politics is about legitimation across media. This makes it possible to take a 'critical' stance without losing sight of objectivity or evidence, and with the limitations of what social science can achieve via 'critical' knowledge, as will be detailed in the final chapter. In mediated culture and online markets, too, the attention is limited but not zero sum: there is competition among many different types of content, and although there are winners and losers, no coercion follows.

An example of competition for attention without zero-sum competition in online markets will be useful: advertising has recently shifted online, with Google and Facebook taking a large share of this market (outside China). But they compete for a limited though not zero-sum share of attention. While Facebook has been obtaining a growing share of advertising revenue because more of its users have been getting their news through their Facebook feeds (with content based partly, as will be discussed in chapter 6, on their Facebook friends), Google has started to have a news feed based on its users' search history and their location (thus, with more individually based content). This competition is simply the latest example of competition for limited attention, which has shifted to digital media where advertising revenue is increasingly concentrated and where media companies are forced into ever-fiercer attempts to capture users' eyeballs. However, competition is for a limited but not zero-sum attention space: digital media take away from traditional media advertising revenue, but consumers can also expand (within constraints) the attention devoted across both, in time and resources devoted via both.

1.6 Who's afraid of technological determinism?

There have been many breathless accounts of how the internet has changed society, not least in the use of labels such as the 'network society' or the 'information society'. Here the argument will be more modest: for example, the internet has changed politics, bypassing traditional gate-keepers and weakening the autonomy of media. This change is bounded by the nation-state, with similar but also specific implications in the four countries examined here. Apart from this political effect, which takes different forms but also has similarities across countries or media systems, there is a more general global effect of new media technology whereby it tethers people more to information and to each other. This is a change in terms of culture rather than politics, without larger macro-social implications, though there are some aspects of cultural change – how information needs to be open and diverse and reliable, and connect those that are isolated – with wider and important implications. And digital media have also tied consumers more closely via media to online markets, with content targeted at populations and consumers (or audiences) having to manage a high-choice environment. So social theory needs to take the internet into account, in understanding how politics and ways of life and markets have changed. New media have transformed society, but only within certain bounds, even if some of the changes have also been globalizing. This is a complicated picture, but also one that identifies major changes and remains based on evidence while avoiding exaggeration.

Thus there are global changes inflected by the systems in different countries and by the different orders or powers, all attributable to new digital media technology as opposed to traditional media technology. This implies a technological determinist view, which is mostly invoked in the social sciences only to be dismissed out of hand. But the terminology in the debate about 'technological determinism versus social shaping' is also misleading: first, it should be about technological shaping versus social shaping, since the debate is about which shapes which. Indeed, it could be called technological shaping versus social determinism. This immediately points to the fact that what is not liked is 'determinism', since it implies inescapable forces. But social forces shape or determine. And shaping – or determining – entails not just constraining but also enabling certain actors, always within structures and often but not always at the expense of other actors. As we shall see, this enabling includes, for example, populists that gain more visibility, or commercial actors that use analytics to target audiences, or people who orient themselves with new information sources. This book will argue for a technological determinist perspective on the internet, but I will not spend much time on this debate since I have argued for this perspective in relation to science and technology generally elsewhere (see Schroeder 2007; 2013). Instead, this book will concentrate on how the internet has changed society, though we will come back to these debates in the conclusion.

Although a full account of technology (or science and technology – technoscience) and social change is beyond the scope of this book, the argument here is that new media technology shapes society – or rather, shapes the three social orders or powers. It is worth briefly elaborating this argument. In my account of technology and social change (2007; 2013), I build on the work of Ian Hacking (1983), a realist in the philosophy of science, and Randall Collins' (1994) idea of how technologies migrate out of the laboratory and into the everyday world and become consumer devices. These ideas are also based on Weber's idea of rationalization, or the translation of technoscience into social change, 'disenchanting the world' and creating an 'iron cage' (or, to put it not only on the side of constraining but of enabling, an 'exoskeleton'). Gellner argued that this is too pessimistic; in a consumer society, there is a 'rubber cage' of user-friendly technologies (1987, 152–65). These elements make for a general account of technoscience and social change. As applied to digital media, what these ideas entail is that digital technologies, compared with traditional media, tether us more to each other and to information; they target us more powerfully and engage us more closely with tailored messages; and they enable new political actors to bypass gatekeepers – a cage and an exoskeleton alike.

All of this can be put differently: technoscience leads to increased power over – or more control or greater effectiveness in mastering – the social environment; again these are the characteristics of technoscientific advance or rationalization in all three realms. More specifically, political leaders and parties and social movements have a new power outside established media, but so, too, do publics, which are represented more outside of established media. Companies can target people more effectively, but consumers are also closer to more information, and can, for example, challenge services with negative publicity. And people have stronger mediated relations to each other, but they are also more bound to or surveilled by others.

In all of these cases, caging and a more powerful exoskeleton are easy to recognize, as is the fact that caging and an exoskeleton go hand in hand; the uses of online media technology enable and constrain. There is new and more diverse economic activity that changes consumption activity towards being driven by online attention. Everyday life is occupied more by online socializing and information seeking. And there is more online engagement between populist leadership and their publics or supporters. Equally easy to recognize then is that this account of technoscience and social change is neither utopian nor dystopian, as are so many accounts of the internet or media and social change. And it is also worth stressing that this account focuses on technology in use, never technology on its own. Furthermore, technological shaping or determinism does not rule out and can go hand-in-hand with social shaping: I shall argue, for example, that in all four country cases, populist forces circumvent traditional media by means of new technology (determinism), but they also do so in quite different ways, depending on the four political systems (social shaping).

The conclusion about technoscientific advance in the form of mediatization – which of course remains to be shown in the chapters to come – can therefore be summarized as follows: First, it is an extension of an existing process of mediating politics, but, combined with new political forces, it has transformed politics in a populist direction, and harnessed politics more to elites' and people's agendas via online media. Second, it has yoked media content more closely to audience attention based on their online behaviour. Third, it has tethered people more closely to each other and to information. These all depend on an underlying process that combines them (or a fourth one, represented by the downward arrows in figure 1.1 emanating from 'technoscience') as already alluded to earlier. This is how technoscience extends mediatization in all three realms, which is also an independent shift whereby technology increasingly suffuses social life built upon previous media and extends them. The causal arrow therefore goes from more technology to the developments in markets and politics and culture, but not the other way round.

The change brought about by technology is conceptually difficult because in all three domains, only a subsystem (media) is affected, including culture with its increasing mediation of everyday life. But the part of culture that is science or technoscience also technologizes the other two domains, and so imposes a more mediatized 'culture' (or rather technoscience) upon them. So the domain of culture is both affected subsystemically as one part of culture, but, as technoscience, it also affects politics and markets. All three domains are therefore more technologically mediated, but the political and economic subsystems have become more 'cultural' via their subsystems (insofar as mediatization imposes a technoscientific culture), and the cultural subsystem is also more mediated. Technoscientific advance is thus the ultimate cause of change towards greater mediatization, and in this book we will focus on how this happens with the uses of new media technologies.

It is worth previewing one other related debate about the role of science, which has re-emerged with 'big data', and which will be discussed in chapter 6. There, it will be argued that scientism (or positivism) and the 'realist' view of science that goes with it raises anew a key question about how big data contributes to scientific advance (or not). In chapter 6 it will be argued that big data does indeed contribute to technoscientific advance ('advance' should be regarded here neutrally, in the sense of 'moving forward'). Yet this view goes together with technological determinism or shaping, and a view that can nowadays be associated with a right-wing or conservative stance (leaving no room for 'agency' – although agency is always shaped by or takes place within structures). Yet this alignment is quite recent: there have been periods when a scientific social science was on the side of progressive politics and, with big data, the role of social science is sure to be rethought along these lines again. Here, I will take the position that advancing valid or objective or value-free social scientific knowledge is needed regardless of politics or norms or ideologies; this is a position shared by many social theorists and also consistent with a realist and technological determinist account of science.[9]

1.7 Chapter overview

At this point, an overview of the book will be useful. One point to note before proceeding is that the three main topics covered: politics (chapters 2 and 3), everyday life (4 and 5) and big data (6) can be read independently. They concern how digital media relate to existing media systems (2), enable right-wing populism (3), connect to others (4) and to information (5) and the implications of big data (6). They can also be read, depending on the reader's interest, independently of the introduction and conclusion. But the argument – briefly, again, that digital technology causes change in the political directions in the four countries, in people's social and 'informational' lives, and in knowledge based on digital media data and how it is used – is also greater than the sum of its parts; there is an overall argument about technology and social change. That argument has already been sketched, and its implications will be drawn out, having put flesh on the bones at that point, in the conclusion.

One task of chapter 2 is to compare the media systems in the four countries. This contextualization, as already argued, is necessary for understanding the implications of digital media for political communication in advanced democracies (the United States and Sweden) and in developing countries (China and India). Are there also commonalities between traditional and digital media? Some studies have found that new digital media set different agendas from traditional media. For example, blogs and microblogs (Twitter), according to Neuman (2016), shift the political agenda away from the priorities of elites in traditional media such as economic and foreign policy – and towards issues that are closer to people's concerns such as crime and abortion. At the same time, since people's activity on digital media can be captured, political election campaigns (among other forms of political communication) can use these digital data traces to measure and predict the public's views, and hence target voters in a more fine-grained way and make politicians more responsive to online sources.

Many other revealing comparisons can be made, including among countries where public broadcasting has played a major role (all countries except the United States), or looking at how elites exercise control over media – the party in China, corrupt politicians colluding with media tycoons in India – which is where the bulk of citizens get their news. Some other differences, such as which media are most common, will be dealt with in later chapters, but it is clear that the difference between, for example, newspaper-centric (India, Sweden) and TV-centric (America and China) countries is rapidly being eclipsed by the difference between younger and older people, or the difference between those who are likely to access news via smartphones as opposed to via TV or in print. Finally, of course, the political systems matter, and China's isolation from the digital media used elsewhere stands out in particular.

One example of how new media bypass traditional media in all four countries are right-wing populist movements – the subject of chapter 3. But in Sweden and America, despite some similarities, circumventing gatekeepers is also shaped by the two historically different media systems: populists such as the anti-immigration Sweden Democrat party go up against the strong tradition of public-service broadcasting in Sweden, whereas Donald Trump's anti-immigrant tweets were readily picked up during the election campaign by mainstream American commercial media competing for audiences. Research also shows that the Swedish public broadcasting system has consequences for how politics is presented and for the levels of knowledge about political affairs compared with the American system. At the same time, in both countries, as in India and China, the growing role of markets is attenuating the distinctiveness of the two media systems.

In India and China, new digital media are also enabling right-wing populism, as with Indian prime minister Narendra Modi's use of

Twitter and Chinese nationalists' use of social media to mobilize support on behalf of ethnic and civilizational assertiveness. In these two countries, the two populations have rapidly come online via smartphones rather than computer-based uses of the internet. In India, there are also important examples of political mobilization by means of non-smart mobile phones; for example, during state elections in Uttar Pradesh, when Dalits (untouchables) coordinated their voting and this contributed decisively to the victory of their party (Doron and Jeffrey 2013). And mainstream Indian media are still controlled by (often) corrupt elites, whereas in China, media control is exercised by the party state – again, two quite different media systems. And in China, again uniquely, digital media are widely used as an alternative to the much more state-controlled traditional media. In this case, there is a growing tension between authoritarian control and bottom-up pressure.

Chapter 4 moves from the public arena to personal uses of information and communication technologies (ICTs). As already mentioned, an understanding of media that goes beyond studying them in isolation or within a disciplinary specialism must be grounded in changing patterns of everyday life. And, in keeping with the argument about media technology here, technology never has an impact per se, but rather impacts in terms of how people use it. Everyday practices are captured best by the 'domestication' approach, which has been applied to television and mobile phones, but rarely to new digital media (de Reuver, Nikou and Bouwman 2016 is an exception). Taking this approach further, Ling (2012), for example, has discussed mobiles in terms of 'interaction rituals' and 'taken-for-grantedness'. To this must be added what has become 'taken-for-granted' – that is, the constant 'tetheredness' to others and to information. This chapter applies these arguments to the four countries that are compared throughout – the United States, Sweden, China and India. It also addresses a problem that has not (to my knowledge) been foregrounded in social science: why are these changes in everyday technology uses important? I will argue that the vast bulk of these everyday changes do not have wider societal repercussions; put briefly, cultural relativism rules. Our changing ways of life can thus be treated much like changes in fashions in clothes or tastes in music – they need to be documented, but they do not create social problems, and nor do they have further implications for macro-developments. Only a small subset of these changes do matter, and it is important to identify them.

Chapters 4 and 5 also deal with two quite different everyday practices: socializing and information seeking. For both, new technological – media – infrastructures have come to play a central role in everyday life on a mass scale and over the course of more than a century, but they have also recently been extended with digital technologies. If we are interested in the types of information people seek, for example, then search engines have become such an infrastructure. Yet studies suggest that the vast bulk of Google searches are for consumption, with only a tiny proportion (1–2 per cent) devoted to political information and other 'serious' types of information. Even more surprisingly, what people search for is very similar across the world, and cuts across how populations are stratified in terms of economic and status groups (Waller 2011a). The implication is that it is important to focus on the small proportion of information for political, health, education and research – or what I will single out as 'serious' – uses.

These two chapters will provide an account of how digital media are used for various everyday purposes such as searching for information online and using digital media for sociability. Everyday life is becoming thoroughly mediatized. At the same time, the vast bulk of media and new media uses are for entertainment and for the maintenance of interpersonal relations. These two uses have led to an important cultural shift – Baron (2008) calls it 'always on', but it is more accurately captured with 'tetheredness'. At the same time, again, only a small subset of this new – increasingly mediated – way of life is important. This includes unequal access to – especially reliable – information and possibilities to shape an open and diverse cultural agenda, and social support. New social divides are thus emerging, but it is important to pinpoint where they play an outsize role, as with an urban–rural divide in India and China, or the divide between smartphone-only internet users and those who have access via a range of devices.

New ICT infrastructures work partly (for social network sites) by means of lock-ins or network effects that translate into a few companies dominating the share of attention. But there are also examples of other sources that dominate the attention space, as with Wikipedia, mainly via Google searches. Yet again, it is essential to put these infrastructures into a broader perspective, charting the differences between the 'media systems' of the four countries considered here. Facebook, for example, within a very short period displaced Lunarstorm, a social network once dominant in Sweden (and pre-dating Facebook). And again, several non-Western social network sites dominate China, and India's infrastructure centres on the mobile phone market. Globalization has limits, but these chapters also show that there are certain commonalities across the four countries examined here, including the increasing importance of everyday access to information and the use of social media.

Apart from socializing in chapter 4, chapter 5 focuses on information behaviour and how it fits into everyday life. Information seeking, by many accounts, makes up half of our uses of the internet. 'Information' has been researched in library and information science, but this research is of limited use if we are interested not in library users or researchers and students but in the broader population-at-large. The chapter provides a definition of information from a broader social science perspective, as a 'difference that makes a difference', and applies this to how, in everyday life, people cope with their physical and social environment. It also argues that a distinction must be made in terms of information for needs (serious information) and information for wants (everything else, and mainly consumption and entertainment). Search engines, and above all Google, have taken on a gatekeeping function in this regard, and the chapter discusses how search engines, along with the Web, have become major infrastructures.

Wikipedia is a good example of how a small proportion of information can be critical for the purpose of being an informed citizen or coping with essential everyday needs. It is also the single most popular (non-commercial) online information source. We know about how, for certain areas such as health, people access Wikipedia pages compared to other online sources. We also know in some cases who produces Wikipedia entries (for health, it is often medical professionals) and about its reliability. And Wikipedia is prominent around the world, though China is an exception because there, Baidu Baike, a rival, is dominant (again, media systems matter here too). And Baidu Baike has been developed under the auspices of the dominant search engine in China, Baidu, which is close to the government (Liao 2009). The difference between open and restricted or controlled infrastructures of information – as in China – mostly accessed via search engines, also illustrates (again) how gatekeepers to information play a new role in everyday life.

Google (or search engines) is not the only infrastructure that has become important as a gatekeeper. So, too, have a number of other infrastructures such as Facebook, Twitter and Amazon. They are also not just (public) infrastructures as such, since they are commercial, so they can additionally be labelled large technological systems. Both terms are preferable to 'platforms', which, among other things, fails to capture their similarity to other large technological systems. But one new feature of these systems is that they collect 'big data' about users, and that is the subject of chapter 6. The 'newness' of big data has itself been the subject of debate, but I argue that newness can be defined in relation to the type of knowledge that is created. At this point a distinction will be necessary between scientific or reliable knowledge, which has been made possible due to the availability of new sources of data, as against knowledge in the private sector and other applied contexts, where these new sources are also available but where knowledge is (mostly) not scientific and subject to practical limits. Yet practical applications of big data are nevertheless increasingly used to target and tailor information to specific populations, and in this way have an effect on everyday life, mostly via advertising but also through political campaigns.

Big data is at the leading edge of the rapidly advancing research front in the social sciences, and especially in communication research. But this research is partly limited by the sources of data, which often, though not always, come from commercial media platforms. Another impediment is that this research is pushing in many directions, based on data sources but without integrating the new-found knowledge into overall accounts of the role of media in social change. And most of this knowledge is not being produced within the social sciences at all, but rather in the private sector and to a lesser extent in policy settings. This knowledge can be yoked to aims such as marketing, targeting populations and tailoring messages to individuals with greater accuracy. More powerful knowledge thus plays a role in everyday life, but it remains largely invisible, as when digital media users are unaware of how information is filtered for them. Big data raises certain issues in new guises, such as privacy, but the public is also adapting to the ways in which media uses are being harnessed for advertising and marketing.

The conclusion (chapter 7) draws these chapters together and also returns to the theoretical debates that have been introduced in this introductory chapter. Exaggerated hopes and fears about new media are in large part due to the 'sociology of the last five minutes' (a phrase coined by Michael Mann), whereby recent technological trends are seen as beckoning huge transformations. A longer-term comparative perspective shows how limited – but also how in specific ways significant – new media and the internet are, in everyday use and also in contrast with mass and interpersonal media. One feature that is common throughout the four countries discussed – and beyond – and that is overlooked in existing media theories, is the role of elites and their gatekeeping and agenda-setting power. Neither the capitalist concentration of media power nor idealism about bottom-up forces captures how the content produced for new media remains the preserve of political elites and media professionals. Second, Twitter, Facebook, Google and other infrastructures play a gatekeeping role since they are dominant around the globe – though in China a separate set of infrastructures is dominant (Tencent, Alibaba and Baidu).

The concluding chapter retraces the argument about the nature of media, technology and globalization, and also the arguments about the different roles of media in different societal domains, the autonomy of media, and the implications of a limited attention space across media. Apart from how these fit together, the theory presented in this book has stayed clear of norms and values. Are there implications for the options ahead? To start with, in developing societies such as India and China, it is necessary to foster a diversified and free and widely accessible set of old and new media to counteract the imbalance of power between political and economic elites on one side and publics or civil society on the other. This argument applies to many developing societies and especially to certain divides within them, such as urban–rural divides. The outlook here also cannot be divorced from the larger questions of the democratizing and globalizing influence of new media in these two countries. In Western democracies, too, the ability of new media to shift the agenda more closely to people's concerns has been a shift away from the autonomy of traditional media, here (among other things) giving more weight to forces from below, with some negative consequences (right-wing populism). Still, the dominance of traditional media, and the ability of elites to use digital media to gauge and shape the agenda in new media, should not be underestimated.

Apart from urging a more plural and open media system that enables greater scope in the realm of politics for bottom-up input, a similar case can be made in media theory for cultural change, promoting more diversity and inclusiveness and access to information. Here one obstacle – and this is also where the implications of the internet in the economic and cultural realms partially overlap – is an increasingly market-driven (and data-driven) consumerism. In both realms, digital media are subject to competition for attention and make certain types of content – including cultural content – more prominent. This is similar to social networks that lock users in. An increasingly tight feedback loop exists now between how user data is harnessed and how people's information and communication needs can be targeted. This targeting presents challenges for citizens and pluralist societies. New technologies-in-use have made a difference to social development, and for this reason the internet and how it has displaced traditional media cannot be dealt with within the silos of disciplinary specialization or empirically investigated with theories of the middle range. Instead, it also requires a theory of increasing mediatization, and its separate effects in the political, everyday and economic realms – including the limits of these effects.

2
Media systems, digital media and politics

This chapter will analyse how digital media have changed politics in four countries. To do this, we will first need to revisit the theoretical approach developed in the introduction (chapter 1). Next, we will compare Sweden and the United States, examining their respective traditional media systems and then turning to digital media in the two countries. The same comparison will then be made for India and China, again starting with their pre-digital media systems and then looking at how they have been transformed – especially through the use of smartphones. Against this background, chapter 3 will then focus on one area where digital media have played an especially important role in all four countries: the rise of online right-wing populism.

2.1 Theories of digital media and politics

Media, and digital media, as argued in chapter 1, are an autonomous subsystem, a transmission belt between citizens and elites in the political process. 'Citizens' provide aggregate inputs into this process, but it would be equally appropriate to use the labels 'people', 'civil society' or 'publics' (indeed, these labels will be used interchangeably). The term 'public arena' is used, as mentioned in chapter 1, in order to avoid Habermas' normatively laden 'public sphere' (see chapter 1), and this also points to the contestedness within this common but limited attention space. To understand the media and politics, the public (or publics) can be counterposed to political elites (which include civic activists, and also economic elites insofar as they are politically relevant actors). Media elites translate the agenda of political elites, plus 'people', into the media agenda. These political elites consist not just of powerful leaders, as Schudson (2011) has pointed out, for the vast bulk of sources of news are government officials. But elites that rule must also set and be responsive to the agendas of the public. And apart from this responsiveness on which the legitimacy of ruling elites is based, there are counterpublics (Fraser 1990), publics that challenge the status quo via media.

The measure of political change is the responsiveness of the political apparatus to citizens, mainly via the media as a transmission belt. For politics, only politically relevant communication and information should be considered, and the yardstick for this is whether they provide a representative and plural set of inputs into the political apparatus.[1] In a democratic society, these inputs should not, as much as possible, be skewed towards powerful elites or towards particularly powerful groups since they should be representative (Dahl 1998). Note, however, that the yardstick of responsiveness can also be applied to non-democratic China, though in this case there is a single, all-powerful elite (the party), which exercises strong control over the media agenda, and publics or counterpublics are kept within bounds.

At this stage we can briefly define 'communication' as comprising two-way one-to-one or one-to-many messages, whereas 'information' means the one-way obtaining of knowledge or data that makes a difference – in this case to how citizens cope with the political environment (or more broadly, makes a difference to how they cope with the physical and social environment – we will come back to this in the discussion of information seeking in chapter 5). 'Media' encompass both information and communication. In focusing on how media constitute the transmission belt of political responsiveness and politically relevant inputs then, an implicit premise – this argument was sketched out in chapter 1 – is that the political system can be separated from the economic and cultural systems (or political power separated from economic and cultural power). This separation is not controversial in mainstream political and social theory (Schroeder 2013; Mann 2013, especially 154–66), and makes sense of the idea (as Hallin and Mancini 2004 have argued) that media systems have become autonomous from market forces and from the political system.

Here we can come back briefly to the idea from chapter 1 that media are a 'subsystem', the transmission belt *within* the political system (even if media subsystems also separately serve the cultural system, as with socializing and information seeking, or the economic system, as with consuming entertainment, for example): their autonomy is from the public, from elites and from the political apparatus – but media serve to promote (or not) political change. This is why, although Williams and

Delli Carpini (2011), among others, have pointed out that what is considered 'political' has widened with digital media beyond what it was with traditional media, they also say that it is nevertheless still important to delimit what falls within politically relevant media (and responsiveness and input), and I will follow them in this respect. As we shall see, this has implications for being able to delimit the *aggregate* political mediated responsiveness and input across all media, traditional and new or digital, in terms of the overall limits of attention or visibility – and thus for gatekeeping and agenda-setting.

In chapter 1, I discussed the problem that digital media no longer fits the models of mass versus interpersonal communication. This problem has also been discussed specifically with regard to the role of media in politics (for example, Bennett and Iyengar 2008; Neuman 2016). Many studies have analysed individual digital media or examined single countries, but studies to date have failed to contrast traditional and digital media in a holistic way. A possible exception is Castells (2009), who argues that networks have become pervasive, with the central conflict between globally dominant media corporations ranged against resistance by often transnational social movements. This theory crucially leaves out the nation-state within which politics is primarily bounded. Media systems are shaped by nation-states (Hallin and Mancini 2004) and the various economic systems. Further, Castells hypostatizes a 'network society', which, apart from not allowing for different media systems, also subsumes the difference that new technologies make under various types of networks.

However, even if much of political communication and information is moving online, it is worth bearing in mind that the vast bulk of political responsiveness and inputs still take place via traditional media, newspapers and television, rather than through new digital media. Chadwick argues that politics and the media (in the United States and the United Kingdom) are currently in a 'hybrid' transition from old to new: he says there is a 'hybrid media system' that 'exhibits a balance between the older logics of transmission and reception and the newer logics of circulation, recirculation, and negotiation' (2013, 208), with the balance still skewed towards the older logics (2013, 209). But this argument fails to pinpoint how the newer logics depart from the older logics in terms of their effects and workings. Second, Chadwick concludes (for the United States) that 'political communication... is more polycentric than during the period of mass communication that dominated the twentieth century... the opportunities for ordinary citizens... are on balance greater than they were... [though it] is primarily political activists and the politically interested who are able to make a difference with newer media'(2013, 210). This overlooks, first, the way in which political and media elites (not just 'ordinary citizens') are also able to make more powerful uses of new media to monitor and respond to the public, and second that new media change not just those who are active and interested in politics, but can also shift attention and the agenda to new political forces, including political 'outsiders', who can use new media to circumvent traditional ones – as we shall see in the next chapter.

Another theory that potentially overcomes the focus on individual media is agenda-setting theory (McCombs 2013), where at least some studies have begun to examine how the agenda changes with the shift from old to new media (for example, Neuman et al. 2014). Agenda-setting provides a means of understanding the topics that are foregrounded by the media – not what media make people think, but what they make them think about. But while this theory can gauge agenda-setting across media, it leaves open the question of how the aggregate political agenda is translated between elites and citizens; in other words, it is a theory of media rather than of the media in society (as here). Further, and again as sketched out in chapter 1, this theory leaves out the fact that there is a limited attention space across all media, such that only certain topics become prominent enough to translate into political change. Bimber says that 'competition for political attention [is] growing more aggressive, against a background of largely unchanged habits of political knowledge and learning' (2003, 230), which leaves unanswered the question of what the effect of this greater competition might be.

Thompson (1995) speaks of a 'struggle for visibility', which comes close to the idea of a limited attention space. However, there is no sense of whether there is more space for visibility in this struggle with new media, and visibility overall is open-ended. Yet even if new media expand the diversity and volume of politically relevant information, there is a limited window across all media for fostering political change: on a rolling basis, this is a zero-sum window, unless new social forces – counterpublics – enter politics, or if new technologies generally broaden the input of citizens. As we shall see, they can do so, though within limits, with the rise of new political forces. In any event, even if some agendas cut across countries with different media systems, these systems are the main unit for analysing political communication and allow us to gauge this limited attention space. We can now turn to these.

2.2 Media systems in Sweden and America

The media systems of the United States and Sweden make for a useful comparison since the two countries have similar levels of technology adoption but they lie at the extremes of the continuum among advanced societies in terms of their politics and economies.[2] They also exemplify two quite different media systems in Hallin and Mancini's (2004) scheme, which contrasts democratic corporatist countries (such as the Scandinavian countries and Germany) with liberal countries (foremost is the United States, although Canada and the UK – partly, because of some public-service broadcasting – also fall into this category).[3] There are many facets to Hallin and Mancini's scheme, but the main contrast for our purposes is between a market-dominated system in the United States and strong state intervention and a tradition of public-service media in Sweden.

We can turn first to the United States, where the impact of the media on politics has been studied in more detail than anywhere else. What gets lost in the research on recent changes is the fact that, apart from a more market-oriented media system, the role of the media in American politics is shaped by political gridlock in a two-party system. The implication is that political news concentrates on the horse race between two antagonistic political ideologies on the one hand and on the antagonism between the president and Congress on the other. Recently, there has been a discussion on whether the media have contributed to the polarization of ideologies and its adherents within this two-party system (Baum and Groeling 2008). Yet this polarization has to be put into the larger context whereby the two parties will continue to dominate, and they must therefore also continue to appeal to the middle ground in order to win elections, no matter how polarized the media and ideology have become.[4]

One analysis related to polarization and the American media system nevertheless deserves detailed discussion: Prior (2007) has made the case, which seems paradoxical at first, that increased media choice results in less political knowledge – at least among a portion of the population. This argument rests on a long-term perspective on American media. As Prior notes, television news made political information more accessible to a broader American population in the 1960s and 1970s since it no longer required the literacy skills needed by newspapers on the one hand and because the news on the three dominant TV channels was the only content available in certain time slots during 'prime time'. In this way, broadcast TV levelled the playing field.

This levelling ceased to be the case from the late 1970s onwards, when cable TV – and more recently the internet – increased viewer choice, which meant that some viewers turned away from news and to entertainment: 'Summing across all media, the total amount of news and political information that Americans read, watch, and hear has, if anything, increased recently (even on a per capita basis). With regard to all elements of political involvement … – news consumption, political knowledge, and turnout – the mean has been remarkably stable, while inequality has increased. The latter is the crucial effect of greater media choice' (2007, 265). By 'inequality', Prior means that some watch more news while others prefer non-news content. Put differently, the result of choice is that some watch as much if not more news, but others prefer entertainment and watch less news, becoming less interested in – and less knowledgeable about – politics in the process.

For Prior this is important because those who prefer entertainment are also less partisan about their politics, which in America means, in view of their lesser likelihood to vote, that they are also less likely to curb those who prefer more news and who are more partisan, thus contributing to polarization in elections. Irrespective of this polarizing effect, we can focus on the argument that greater choice leads to parts of the population becoming less politically interested: Prior says that this does not entail a technological determinist argument, but he contradicts himself on this point. He says that technology is not the only factor because it matters how technology is regulated, how it is shaped by the economy, and its uses (2007, 24), but he also says that 'rising inequality in political involvement' is 'a result of voluntary consumption decisions … technological progress is the ultimate cause of this rise'(2007, 281). However, consumption decisions depend on the choices that technology makes available in the first place, and in this case clearly it was the advent of cable TV and the internet that enabled these choices (and Prior admits as much when he talks about the 'ultimate cause').

With this in mind, we can turn to Sweden, since the increased choice environment is, of course, not limited to the United States. But the implications might be different in media systems that also have public broadcasting – Sweden has a public broadcast system and the state has also subsidized newspapers, policies that aim to enhance diversity and promote the public interest. An important change nevertheless took place in this media system with the introduction of competition by commercial TV in Sweden in the 1980s. Thus we can ask whether similar changes have taken place in Sweden to those identified for America by Prior. To be sure, there has been growing competition among commercial media in Sweden, as in the United States, and this has meant that marketization increasingly overrides the differences between Hallin and Mancini's two types of media systems. Westlund and Weibull (2013) also document similar changes arising from a more market-led 'high choice' environment (as did Prior): using surveys that capture several generations (those growing up before the Second World War, the post-war baby boomers, 'Generation X', and the recent generation growing up with digital technologies), as well as changes in media use over the life course of individuals, they document and analyse changes in news consumption between 1986 and 2011 across all media.

What Westlund and Weibull show is that although the earlier generations stick to public-service media (similar to something we will see with China), there is a shift away from public service to commercial TV and radio among the younger generations. The same applies to print newspapers, with the younger generations shifting to digital versions. Recently there has also been a shift away from paid-for quality newspapers to free ones (Metro) and to mobile news consumption.[5] And their analysis also shows that among 16–29 year olds, a higher percentage read newspapers on mobile devices than in any other format, digital or print (Weibull and Wadbring 2014, 327). So while newspapers and public-service media still dominate among the population as a whole, this is not the case among the younger generation and those at an earlier stage in the life course. Westlund and Weibull point out that this is not a question of complete displacement: the earlier generations add to their repertoire of news consumption with commercial broadcasters and online versions. Nevertheless, there is an unmistakeable shift away from print newspapers and public-service news to more diversified sources of news and online news among the younger generations and for those at an earlier stage in life.

Despite similar shifts towards more market competition and more diversity, the two media systems thus remain distinct: Sweden is a more newspaper-centric society, the United States a more television-centric one (Norris 2000, 85; Norris and Inglehart 2009, 58–9; Aalberg and Curran 2012). In Sweden, public service remains dominant, and in the United States, the three networks still have a large audience share even if people spread their viewing hours rather evenly, including those who watch Fox News or CNN, for example, across many channels in an environment of several broadcast and many cable channels (Webster 2005, 378). However, the two systems have also converged: there is increasing competition for audiences, not just with the rise in choices in Sweden but also in America, with its increasing deregulation. This market orientation has attenuated the differences in Hallin and Mancini's typology, but so has the proliferation of technologies – not just satellite and cable, but also online news consumption.

Overall then, in both countries, there is a continuing diversification: in America, away from the three main broadcast news channels and away from local and print newspapers; in Sweden, away from public television and away from local and print newspapers. These changes are taking place slowly, but even if the shift towards digital visual and textual news consumption is furthest along among younger people, it is a shift that will continue. Mass media, print and broadcast, will fade. The implication is that audiences select their news and political information intake more. However, as argued earlier, there is a limited attention space for mediated politics, so this diversity pertains primarily to *how* material is accessed rather than what content is accessed.[6] Increased selection could lead to an intensification of the 'Prior' effect, but it also means (as we shall see) that elites must cater more to the diversified sources whereby citizens become informed on the one hand, and citizens must take a more active part in managing their needs for political information on the other.

2.3 Digital media and politics in Sweden and America

With digital media, there is an increase in the mediation (or mediatization) of politics: there are more formats, such as disseminating news events via Twitter, sharing content on Facebook, commenting on politics in blogs, and accessing online-only news websites. There is also far more content available. But while the addition of digital to traditional media is not zero sum in terms of consuming media entertainment, there are limits to the effects of digital media on politics: more diverse inputs from society must become part of an overall input into the political apparatus, and this overall input must be managed more in the sense of 'governing with the news' (Cook 2005) from above as well as by citizens. The inputs via media must compete in the 'marketplace of ideas' (Åsard and Bennett 1997), but with the addition of digital media, there is also competition for attention. Political elites and media professionals therefore increasingly, more so than in the broadcast era, actively manage political and media messages. Further, there are structural limits to this attention space, as with the two-party system in the United States or the way the party system has evolved in Sweden, to which can be added the counterpublics and new political forces that shape and challenge them.

In Sweden, as already mentioned, public-service TV continues to have a large (36 per cent in 2007) audience share (Aalberg et al. 2012, 18). But Swedish public media are also going online (as are American public media, the Public Broadcasting Service and National Public Radio, with much smaller audience shares). A number of studies have examined digital media use among Swedish politicians and journalists. Larsson and Kalsnes (2014) analysed the use of Twitter and Facebook by politicians and found that Twitter is more popular than Facebook, which they see as a mismatch because Twitter is mainly used by media-savvy urban elites whereas Facebook enjoys a wider popularity. They also found that both of these digital media are used more by politicians who are 'underdogs' and who 'tend to be younger, non-incumbents' and outsiders rather than prominent insiders (2014, 12). As for Twitter use during elections, Larsson and Moe (2012) showed for the 2010 elections that the conversation was concentrated among journalists, politicians and political bloggers, with few conversations involving the public and few replies to tweets. This is similar to the finding by Hedman and Djerf-Pierre (2013) that journalists mainly use Twitter for self-branding rather than engaging in conversations with their readers or viewers. The same applies to tweeting in relation to talk shows that feature politicians and current affairs guests: Larsson (2013) examined a whole season of a popular talk show and noted that the top tweeters were all journalists whereas a broader public did not become involved in the programme.

Another perspective is Gustafsson's (2012) study of party and political interest group members (and non-members) on Facebook. He found that Facebook was seen as a useful tool for political engagement in terms of coordinating action, recruiting new members and communication among members. At the same time, he also noticed a reluctance to engage in politics on Facebook because of worries about revealing political preferences to potential employers or friends. As for Facebook use by Swedish political parties, Larsson (2014) measured this in 2013, counting the number of posts and shares and likes as indicators of levels of use. He found that although Facebook use was limited, it nevertheless (again) favoured the smaller parties that might otherwise not receive as much media attention as the major parties.

To these accounts of the uses of new digital media by media and political elites, we can add that more than half of all Swedes aged 26–55 use the internet for news on a daily basis, that all ages do so occasionally, and that those under 46 regard the internet as the most important source of news – with TV far behind (Findahl 2014, 65, 66; Findahl and Davidsson 2015, 82). Yet the total amount of time devoted to reading news, both on paper and online, has remained rather constant since the 1980s (Findahl 2014, 66).[7] There are no figures for overall news and political media use, but we can see (from the Westlund and Weibull findings discussed earlier) that there is some displacement and some complementing of traditional media. However, with the exception of the Sweden Democrats, to be discussed in the next chapter (as well as the Feminist Initiative party), there has been no entry of major new political groups into formal political representation as a result of new media, nor a major broadening of the agenda.

For the United States, as mentioned earlier, one of the major debates in relation to digital media has been whether they contribute to political polarization. Analysing Twitter during the 2012 American presidential election campaign, Barberá and Rivero found that 'political discussion in Twitter is mainly driven by citizens with extreme values in the ideological scale, a situation that certainly favors the level of political polarization of the political discussion on Twitter' (2015, 11). Along similar lines, Baum and Groeling (2008) found some time ago that political blog websites (Daily Kos on the Left and Free Republic on the Right) featured far more partisan news stories than the news stories that were top-ranked on the news wires (Associated Press and Reuters, which could be regarded as presenting a balanced set of stories). The polarization thesis remains contentious, however: Messing and Westwood (2014) showed that endorsements of news items via social network sites (such as Facebook likes) could prompt more people to read these items. Hence – since people's social networks are likely to be diverse and their recommendations for news items cut across partisan political lines – these endorsements could help to overcome rather than to increase political polarization.

As in Sweden, the use of Twitter in politics is mostly confined to elites and does not generally lead to more involvement or conversations with a broader public. Golbeck et al. (2010) found that members of Congress used Twitter mainly for self-promotion rather than for engaging with the public. Similarly, having a Facebook site, which had become the norm among candidates for the national election in America in 2012, mainly means that they push information about their activities to their publics (Gulati and Williams 2013). In any event, the most widely discussed use of digital media in politics has been in relation to presidential election campaigns. Bimber (2014) argues that the Obama campaigns of 2008 and 2012 were the most advanced to date in terms of the use of digital tools, including using data analytics or big data to target particularly critical voters (see also Chadwick 2013, 137–58). Obama's campaign team also analysed, among other things, people's social networks, including on Facebook and Twitter. Bimber says that this strategy took personalized political communication to a new level, that it has been copied by Republicans, and will be taken even further in future election campaigns in America and elsewhere. Again, we will come to a new political force, populism, and the use of social media (and Twitter in particular), which changed the picture during the 2016 election, in the next chapter.

These findings can be put in the contexts of Americans' use of the internet for politics. Social network sites are becoming increasingly widespread among all generations in America (Duggan et al. 2015), and according to Pew (2015), 61 per cent of millennials, for example, received their news from Facebook.[8] Ideally, as argued earlier, the input from society into the political apparatus should reflect society in an increasingly democratic way, representing its interests more inclusively or accurately. Yet Schlozman et al. (2010, 501) found that higher socioeconomic status groups are more likely to use the internet for various kinds of political participation than lower ones. This finding for the United States can also be put into a broader and comparative perspective: the divide between higher and lower socioeconomic groups applies to news media generally, but it is more acute in the United States than in Sweden. At the end of a study that systematically compared news and political knowledge in the United States with Northern Europe, Aalberg and Curran say that 'the American system, ultimately geared to optimizing high earnings expectations, makes little attempt to shrink the knowledge gap between the privileged and the underprivileged' (2012, 199). In other words, the media system, and in particular its public-service component, makes a difference to how well-educated citizens are in public affairs.

In terms of the internet, there is also an age divide: young people use the internet more for political participation than do older people, but it is unclear whether this is a generational effect or a life-cycle one (with the implication that it will fade over time). It is true, as Nielsen and Schrøder (2014) document, that Americans and Danes (who, in terms of the nature of the media system, are similar to Swedes) have not shifted wholesale to using digital media as a vehicle for news. However, the proportion who share a news story or who comment on a news story in an average week via social networking sites is more than 20 per cent in the United States and more than 10 per cent in Denmark (though in the 15–35 age bracket, digital media have 'surged' as a source of news, to over half; Schrøder 2015, 66).

There have also been a number of studies that compare the content of the two media systems. Some of these confirm that the differences between the two types of media systems have persisted into the era of digital media. So, for example, Dimitrova and Strömbäck (2011; see also Strömbäck and Dimitrova 2011) compared election news in America and Sweden, and found that Swedish public television is more issue-focused, while American television (and Swedish commercial television news) frame elections more as a horse race. They also found that election news content is governed more by a media logic in the United States, which foregrounds the role of journalists, whereas in Sweden the political logic is more pronounced and thus more prominence is given to politicians. In both systems, however, both public and commercial news used an 'interpretive' and a 'descriptive' journalistic style equally (though it should be noted that the analysis included only 'functionally equivalent' major news programmes – ABC, CBS and NBC – and excluded round-the-clock news such as CNN and Fox News). In sum, the Swedish and American systems continue to be different, but in both systems, commercial media overlap more.

A different way to compare the two systems is from the side of what audiences take away from the media – rather than what is provided. In this vein, Curran et al. (2009) compared the American market-driven media system with the Scandinavian public-service model. They measured the kinds of TV and print news produced by these systems for a certain period and then gauged public knowledge at the end of this period. They found, among other things, that 'the public service of broadcasting gives greater attention to public affairs and international news, and thereby fosters greater knowledge in these areas, than the market model' (2009, 22). Furthermore, as we have seen, there is less of a gap in knowledge between different socioeconomic groups in Scandinavia compared to the United States.

Much has also been written about the use of digital media for political activism, and this can be briefly mentioned here. It is to be expected that these uses are similar across both media systems (and beyond) since this depends mainly, once digital media are widely used, on a lively civil society. There is agreement among scholars that the internet has changed digital activism somewhat: Earl and Kimport (2011, 10) argue that the main advantages of political online activism are reduced costs and also the aggregation of actions without physical co-presence. And Bennett and Segerberg add that online activism need not be about organized mobilization; digital media also provide 'personal action frames' (2013, 36–40) whereby people can participate in activism on their own terms, sharing issues with distant others beyond boundaries of groups or ideologies that may be required in offline activism. These changes in political activism are similar to the broader changes that have been discussed so far: political communication becomes more personalized in a media environment that is more diversified. In addition, there are enhanced possibilities for coordinating activism. But this enhancement is a marginal addition because the media environment (in these two countries at least) is already saturated; activist inputs only add to an already crowded set of media inputs, and within the overall aggregated inputs, there is a limited attention space and competition for visibility. Even so, gatekeeping can be expanded somewhat when new media can circumvent or provide new inputs into traditional ones, as we will see in the next chapter (chapter 3) with other 'marginalized' actors.

The differences between the two media systems thus persist, but apart from marketization, new media have made for an incremental extension of political communication – more mediation – that adds to, displaces and complements traditional media. Hence there is a gradual increase in the density of political communication between political and media elites on one side and citizens on the other in both – and indeed, as we shall see, in all four – countries. But this leads to social change only inasmuch as forces on both sides take advantage of the openings that new technologies provide, which have so far mainly consisted of elites using media more and targeting them better on one side – and more diversified access and lower costs of engagement on the side of citizens or civil society. The difference this makes to the political system is a greater responsiveness to the expanded aggregate inputs from the media system, plus citizens managing their media more. Hence, too, there needs to be more responsiveness to how the agenda is shaped by the public via media. The change is incremental – adding to and complementing traditional media rather than constituting a break with them – because a radical break would require new media to expand and diversify political engagement from either or both sides. As we shall see, right-wing populists meet this criterion since they constitute a new social force that is less visible in traditional media, and new media are used to bypass traditional gatekeepers.

Still, one way to highlight that the change is only incremental in media-saturated societies (or where there is a limited attention space) is by contrasting this with the situation in non-media-saturated societies. In societies where media adoption is still limited or constrained by an authoritarian political system, new digital media can reshape the flow between publics and the political system (Howard 2010). We will see how this applies to China and India shortly, where new media play more than an incremental role (at least potentially, insofar as they are not curbed) because they add to inputs to the media subsystem, which is otherwise constrained for traditional media. The question in these two cases, however, will be whether the autonomy of media is expanded by escaping party or elite control.

In Sweden and the United States, again, there is limited scope for new digital media to make a difference – given that an increased flow would need to significantly enhance political informedness or engagement or the responsiveness of the political system to citizens. But this enhancement is limited, since macro-sociology also tells us that, overall, political change from below has been constrained in advanced democracies in recent decades (Mann 2013; Schroeder 2013). And in certain respects, as we have seen, new digital media diminish news consumption and political knowledge. Digital media thus allow some degree of circumvention of gatekeeping institutions everywhere, but in a political communication environment with many channels and formats, and where the balance of media power between political elites and people is relatively stable, large-scale changes cannot be expected, even with greater density of mediated politics.

Further, even if responsiveness is changing incrementally, the result is also that this responsiveness can be used by political elites to enhance their legitimacy, unless citizens can express their political demands more forcefully. The importance of this limitation can be highlighted: politics plays the central direction-giving role in society, and citizen inputs into this process take place mainly via media. As Luhmann put it, in a claim that is only slightly exaggerated, 'what we know about our society, or indeed about the world in which we live, we know through the mass media' (2000, 1). If this seems a trivial point, it can be noted again that in countries such as China, where digital media have rapidly become a more powerful vehicle than traditional media for expressing forceful demands, the implications are different: in countries like these, unlike in developed democracies, the political system has to be much more active in managing these demands in order to contain them. Further, as Tang (2016) points out, in democracies, once elected, rule is guaranteed until the next election, whereas in China, the party-state must be constantly attuned to public opinion. In other words, in these countries, the role of digital media is more important – both on the side of more forceful inputs or demands and on the side of the need to contain them, unlike in developed democracies.

This point can be put differently: as mentioned in chapter 1, the idea of a limited attention space, or competition for visibility (Thompson 1995), provides the constraint for how politics is communicated. More diverse sources of political information and engagement do not necessarily make a difference unless they expand the scope and forcefulness of inputs vis-à-vis the regime. However, if we think about where we can find such expansion, it is where digital media have rapidly become more important than traditional media and where, at the same time, politics is most unsettled. In Sweden and America, as we have seen, this expansion has been incremental but significant. We shall see that when new actors such as populist right-wing forces come onto the scene, reshaping politics, they do so by taking advantage of new digital media to circumvent traditional media, though again, this effect is shaped by the respective media systems (public media in Sweden, audience competition in the United States). Communicative responsiveness has become somewhat denser, but it is still subject to a limited attention space.

A limited attention space pertains not just to the political agenda set by elites, but also to the inputs that feed from the public or from citizens into the political apparatus via media. Denser mediated relations mean that political elites, including media elites, have to become more responsive to greater input. Insofar as these inputs have expanded beyond traditional media, this expansion demands a response to a more complex set of media inputs. But it is not just politicians who can better target the electorate, nor just citizens who can select more news and other politically relevant information and provide more differentiated and more mediated inputs into the political apparatus. It is also the case that news media and politically relevant information sources can target their audiences more accurately, as we shall see in chapter 6.

To give just one striking example of this media targeting: Bright and Nicholls (2014) have shown, in the case of five major UK news websites, that the 'most read' articles stay on the front page longer than the 'less read' articles, which is an indication of a new 'populism' (in the sense of audience-drivenness) whereby editors cater to the wishes of their audiences. This closer yoking of content to audience demands is in tension with a 'patrician' view of the media, which has been particularly associated with public-service media, whereby the media should tell the public what is most important, but it is also in tension with the autonomy of the media system, whereby journalists rather than audience metrics shape the news agenda. At the same time, the idea that the media should promote the common good is more pronounced in systems with public media (and as we have seen, public media also produce greater political knowledge). Yet this yoking could also be seen as allowing greater responsiveness to citizens, in this way benefiting democracy, as long as citizens are becoming more aware of – and engaged in – political issues.

However, there is little evidence of such an overall increase in political engagement due to internet-related changes in media (in addition to the references discussed so far, Hindman 2008 also makes this point). And the effect could also be the opposite: monitoring the public could lead to a skewing or misrepresentation of the public because what is being monitored represents a more mediated digital realm than the aggregated realm of all (traditional media and offline) inputs (so that users of mainly traditional media could be underrepresented, for example). In other words, the increasing reliance on the measurement of publics via digital media rather than on votes or surveys and the like produces a new type of responsiveness (again, within the constraints of being shaped by various media systems).

A final point is that limited attention and visibility apply not just to content produced and agendas purveyed, but also to content consumed. 'Selection' (or 'self-selection', a term used by Castells 2009) is misleading in the sense that it implies unlimited content. But news consumers or audiences are also limited by the time they devote to political news, which is higher mainly when there are elections and where the amount of content devoted to public affairs is more than audiences typically want as opposed to what journalists provide (Boczkowski and Mitchelstein 2013). The discrepancy between what journalists provide and what audiences want to read and watch (and hear) also comes across in research that compared agenda-setting in traditional news media with online news media. The study, by Neuman et al. (2014), asked: do social media (in this case, Twitter, blogs and discussion forums) differ in terms of agenda-setting compared with traditional media? What they found was that 'social media are more responsive to public order and social issues and less responsive to the abstractions of economics and foreign affairs' (2014, 7). What we can see here is a gap opening up between what audiences want and what digital news media provide for them.[9] In view of the displacement effect identified by Prior and by Westlund and Weibull (discussed earlier), and since people's total use of political media is not simply expanding with each new medium, it is clear that there has been a shift in content as well as in format or channel.

What, then, are the dangers and opportunities of digital media? The main danger is that elites react more to media signals than to non-mediated demands, becoming skewed to the potentially more misrepresentative inputs of digital media. The main opportunity is for the agenda to shift more closely to issues or groups that have been overlooked in traditional media, and this includes challengers or outsiders of all stripes (including populists, as we shall see in the next chapter).

The combination of the two could be – not polarization, but differentiation, whereby more diverse content and simply more content could enrich the public arena in some ways and impoverish it in others. The bias of political communication research and research on new technologies is to tell us that a more diverse and content-rich media environment should lead to more political participation and better-informed citizens. Yet the result could also be the reverse: more mediation could leave politics the same if the impetus to engagement and the level of interest in politics is the same or declines, or if media become more responsive to extreme political forces. Further, the extent and quality of mediation could leave (some) citizens less engaged and less informed, a constant worry in media research. And if the input into the agenda-setting process from the public is more diffuse, this could give more power to political elites, as could a more diffuse media input into the political process by media professionals. The position advanced here is thus that political elites are able to manage their communication more and target their messages more powerfully, and the same is true for media professionals. Enhancement also applies on the side of awareness and engagement among some citizens, as well as some underrepresented groups and their leaders – all of them limited by competition within a limited attention space or a limited space for visibility. Hence the benefits of new digital media in coordination and selection are balanced by the diffuseness of engagement and by the constraints of attention.

The crucial change in the political agenda promoted in the media is not that this agenda has become more fragmented or narrower with digital media. Instead, it has shifted somewhat and become more diversified and differentiated in format and content, even as the overall breadth of this agenda has stayed the same or increased only marginally because of the limited attention space on the one hand, but also the lack of major new social forces to broaden it on the other, though some of the forces that will be discussed in the next chapter – the populist right – may yet make for a new political direction. The shift has thus meant that the added element of public opinion and inputs must be catered for, a coupling that occurs because of a more accurate gauging of public opinion and inputs that can at the same time be skewed towards certain sources. Again, these patterns are part of a longer-term trend towards a greater responsiveness to ever more mediated inputs by the public. But we should be wary of equating this greater responsiveness with a more fundamental democratizing change due to digital media.

2.4 Media systems in China and India

India and China together account for well over a third of the world's online population. They are also often seen as two quite different models for the future role of the internet in developing societies. Research about the social implications of the internet in India is still embryonic, partly because internet penetration is still low. There is more research about mobile phones in the country, but far less about smartphones. In terms of China, many publications have looked at the internet and politics, but the vast bulk have concentrated on the internet and censorship, and to a lesser extent on online protest (Qiu and Bu 2013). These are important topics for China, but censorship and opposition to the regime also need to be seen in the wider context of how old and new media together contribute to liberalization or reinforce the regime's control. As already indicated, the main argument here will be that, in both countries, the most important factor with regard to digital media is that they represent some civil society forces more powerfully by circumventing traditional media, even if digital media are also used for greater control in China and they are heavily skewed towards elites in India.

Discussion of the internet in these two countries tends to differ from what has been discussed so far: it has often been tied to a developing world discourse about how information and communication technologies (ICTs) lead to economic development (ICT4D). For India, the emphasis has been on economic development and for China it has been on political opening or otherwise (Rangaswamy and Benny 2015). Yet there has also been a recent backlash against ICT4D. Anthropologically informed researchers have argued, for example, that the ICT4D research agenda is biased: why should scholarship for the developing world focus on economic and social development, when the main uses of old and new media, here as elsewhere, are for socializing and leisure, which surely deserve equal attention (Rangaswamy and Arora 2015)? At the same time, the regimes themselves envision a high-tech ICT-led future. The Chinese government, for example, has the so-called 'Internet Plus' policy to promote uptake of digital services, just as the Indian prime minister has embarked on a 'Digital India' programme. Both aim to 'leapfrog' more advanced parts of the world.

The arguments about economic development will be left to one side here since the main focus is on new media and politics (and in later chapters on everyday life and on the online economy mainly related to big data). Yet there is a larger question about convergence and divergence and development, and here the argument against modernization (convergence) has been made by post-colonial (India) and post-socialist (China) theorists. Against modernization or convergence, post-colonialists argue that modernizing elites who try to impose a modern Western rationality on India are being resisted by local indigenous forces. Similarly, post-socialists argue that the indigenous legacy of a communist developmental path will resist an entirely capitalist and democratic future. As we shall see, these arguments can be improved upon by identifying specific elements of convergence and of divergence. In any event, it is important to bear these discourses and debates in mind to put the politically relevant uses of media into a broader context.

We have already encountered some of the debates about the media or the internet and politics, but we can briefly revisit them in this context: as mentioned, these debates have been dominated by two approaches, one focused on democracy and the public sphere (Habermas 1982) and the other on how capitalism skews democracy towards powerful economic elites (Castells 2009). Yet the public sphere, as Habermas recognizes, does not exist in a vacuum, and one of his main arguments is that the public sphere has been progressively 'colonized' by the forces of capitalism. For India and China, this poses immediate problems: for China, especially, an *autonomous* 'public sphere' barely exists, and for India, this autonomy is limited by the disproportionate role of economic and political elites in the media. Similarly with capitalism and how it impinges on media: even if market forces have in recent decades increasingly shaped media in both countries, this has not overridden how media continue to be subject to distinctive political forces and media systems, not just in China, but also in India, with its legacy of a public-service broadcasting system.

Still, the yardstick for media and politics in both countries, as elsewhere, is whether they contribute to more responsiveness by the government – or the opposite, more elite control? This yardstick can be seen as a measure of modernization or convergence. And as mentioned, China's media system is commonly seen in terms of censorship and authoritarian control. But as a number of commentators have pointed out, this is too simple. A broader question is whether the party-state, via China's media, is responding more to input from society, or moving to constrain input and exercise more centralized control via media? The consensus among scholars is that the party shows little sign of relinquishing its power and maintains control of the media to this end (Brady 2008; Brady 2016). At the same time, the party-state is pushing media to become a tool for gauging public opinion in order to maintain social order. And recent work by Chen et al. (2016), for example, has highlighted the fact that the authoritarian state permits and even encourages government to become more responsive to citizens, at least on a local level. Moreover, the idea of responding to public grievances and guiding public opinion for the social good has a long history in China. As we shall see, digital media have also to some extent created an environment for social protest and expression, which have pushed the boundaries of control. So beyond censorship and propaganda, it is important to consider how the state is responding to the pressures coming from new media.

India's media system, on the other hand, has been shaped by strong collusion between economic and political elites. This means that the autonomy of Indian media, a key characteristic that distinguishes different media systems (Hallin and Mancini 2004), is weak. It is also thus because public-service media have not been independent of government influence, and because journalists have often been unduly influenced by owners of private-sector media. It has been argued that from the 1990s onwards, global neoliberalism has been the main force shaping the Indian media system in favour of the interests of capitalist economic elites (Chakravarty 2004). Yet this, again, is too simple: while market forces have certainly driven the expansion of media offerings in recent decades, the influence of politicians on media has been just as strong for news as the influence of economic interests. Further, for India, any discussion of media must also take into account the broader issue of the lack of reach of media due to a weak sociotechnical infrastructure (Doron and Jeffrey 2013). Nevertheless, the internet has been a powerful force among a small, mostly young and urban, part of the population. And, as we shall see, even 'low-tech' mobile phones can be used for political mobilization. Unlike in China, however, where digital media are the most unconstrained part of the media environment, in India smartphones have yet to reach the majority of the population, and online politics is shaped by how smartphone adoption fits into the broader – skewed – media landscape.

It will be useful, again, first, to sketch the background of the two media systems. Then we can focus specifically on where the internet makes a difference: in China, for circumventing how people obtain news outside of traditional media, and secondly for enabling certain groups to spread ideas outside of official channels. In the case of India, examples of circumventing traditional media include the ways in which mobile phones have made a difference in elections. This is not a like-for-like comparison, however: China does not have democratic elections, and in India there is not the same need to obtain news outside of state-controlled media. Nevertheless, in both cases, new media go beyond traditional media, and there are lessons to be learned from comparing the two.

Any account of the two current political and media systems must provide some background about their longer-term historical trajectories. This will not be possible in any detail, but some major features can be sketched. For India, it has been argued that there was an incipient public sphere even before the imposition of colonial rule (Bayly 2009). The empire and its colonial government then imposed a media infrastructure that was shaped by capitalism and by the needs of administering a large territory (Jeffrey 2002). After Independence (1947), the new government reacted against this foreign infrastructure by developing a national public-service media system that would strengthen the government's modernizing aims. By the 1980s however, partly due to the advent of satellite broadcasting, public media had to compete with the private sector, especially for television audiences, and this liberalization and deregulation has continued to the present day.

Two other features set India apart in terms of the history of media technology: one is the country's high newspaper readership – among the highest worldwide (Jeffrey 2000). Although, as elsewhere, television has become more important as a source of news than newspapers, the latter continue to play a relatively prominent role in India. In terms of both newspaper readership and television viewership, regional languages are growing faster than Hindi and English, though Hindi is the dominant language for political media and English for business media (Ninan 2007; Mehta 2015). The second distinctive feature is 'small' technology (Arnold 2013): it has been argued that India's social development relies more on technologies that are not based on extensive infrastructures, but rather on standalone technologies that do not depend on large-scale capital-intensive networks. The spinning wheel, bicycles and now mobile phones (at least if cellular phone networks are compared to cable networks) are good examples. The media landscape in India today is thus highly diverse, shaped by a legacy that, unlike the strong states in the West and in East Asia, produced only a weak ICT infrastructure. The current government, like earlier ones, is attempting to overcome this weakness and strengthen economic development by means of promoting ICTs. Yet apart from grandiose plans for smart cities (and the 'Digital India' programme, already mentioned), the most visible part of this strategy is the country's Universal Identification Number system (UID, also known as the Aadhaar system, discussed in chapter 6), which is mired in legal controversy and undergoing as yet piecemeal implementation.

A different perspective on India's media system is in terms of the responsiveness of the government to the increasingly mediated demands of civil society. Before broadcast or mass media, India's public arena was tightly controlled by its colonial rulers, but there was also a nascent sphere of media contestation. The era after independence brought the mobilization of media on behalf of nation-building, following a Nehruvian model of modernization by means of technological infrastructure development. In this case, the effort concentrated on developing what some would see as a paternalistic public broadcasting system during the era of Congress Party rule, which aimed to educate the population and revive classical Indian culture. Yet with the marketization and liberalization of the 1980s and 90s, Athique says, 'the old, bourgeois culture of the neo-colonial class, and its autocratic socialism, has been supplanted by a more emotive, populist and middlebrow culture' (2012, 146). The more commercial orientation of the media that has been promoted by recent governments also fits well with the political and economic elites' vision of a high-tech India competing in a global digital economy.

The upshot of this thumbnail sketch is that the interlude of the state's attempt to modernize via the media system has been eclipsed. Public broadcast media now have a far smaller reach than commercial media. With marketization, the television audience in India is highly fragmented, with no television station attracting more than a 20 per cent share of the national market. Many politicians own television stations to promote themselves, and there is much corrupt money in television ownership (Mehta 2015). Yet Doordarshan, the public broadcaster – the largest broadcaster in the world by number of employees, larger than China Central Television (CCTV) – now has only a tiny audience share (Mehta 2015). In any event, the cronyist relationship between political elites and newspaper and television proprietors skews media influence towards the mutual benefit between parties and powerful economic interests. This relationship is hard to pin down systematically, yet a number of accounts attest to the cosy and often corrupt relationship at the level of national politics (Mehta 2015). On the local level, too, politicians promote themselves via advertising in newspapers and television, while news media have become dependent on this advertising for revenue (Ninan 2007). Still, in India, TV has become the main source of news. And the independence of media from the state, despite being encoded in law, is still not properly enacted, so there is much state manipulation of the media sector and of telecommunications, and again, extensive corrupt practices, as evidenced by the scandals surrounding the auctions of telecommunications spectrum.

In China, too, there are unique trajectories of media technology: the public has historically sought redress from the state (Yongming 2006; Thornton 2007) and the state tried to extend its military-logistical reach, especially via ICT infrastructures. The colonialist impact was much weaker in this case than in India's, leaving the historical media tradition more intact. Yet before the communist regime took power in 1949, there was a brief period when a Westernizing drive meant an efflorescence of an open and private media sector in China, though the development of autonomous media was also severely curbed by the civil war and the Japanese invasion. One question therefore concerns the extent to which the current liberalization of media harks back to this 'modernist' period, or if it is shaped by the longer-term history of how emperors responded to people's demands, or by the newer strong state control of the Communist party-state. As we shall see, it is a mixture of all three.

Again, seen from the vantage point of responsiveness to civil society, before the advent of mass media in China in the twentieth century, there was an ethos whereby a benevolent emperor and a meritocratic stratum of mandarins should guide people's morals and govern their well-being. This tradition has continued under communism, with regimes mobilizing the population to improve the nation. The media system has been increasingly central to this guidance of the population, and the tradition has continued into the pro-market reform era. Current efforts to gauge public sentiment via social media can be seen as an extension of this process, as are uses of media to promote social stability and promote a high-tech economy. The flipside of this is the elimination of discontent and disorder. The regime sees the media as a threat, particularly in the light of the collapse of the Soviet Union and the Tiananmen Square protests. The question then is to what extent the regime's aims have come into tension with the recent commercialization of media and the widespread uses of social media.

As in India, television still sets the political agenda, but in this case, there is one dominant player: 'CCTV is still the main source of news and information for most mainland Chinese' (Zhu 2012, 7). This is partly because, by government edict, only CCTV can cover national-level news, but it is also partly because watching CCTV is a holdover in the more rural and remote regions and among an older population from past viewing patterns when there were no alternatives. Among an urban and younger population, on the other hand, CCTV is passé. But while the Chinese generally do not trust the state broadcaster, this does not necessarily mean that they are critical towards the regime: quite the reverse; much of the population supports the regime's maintenance of social stability and control over the media for this purpose.

The tension between critical media and supportive media also extends to journalists. As in other media systems with public broadcast media, media professionals have been imbued with a public-service ethos but also with the Anglo-American ideal of impartiality and objectivity (Zhao 2012) – the basis of an autonomous media system. But in this case, there is also an ethic of guiding the nation and providing its moral compass, which stems from a longer-term self-image that Chinese intellectuals have traditionally had (see Zhu 2012, 59, 102). The same applies to the party, which, as Zhu says, 'believes much more in "guidance *of* public opinion" rather than "supervision *by*" public opinion' (2012, 253). At the same time, journalists have begun to see themselves in a watchdog role within the limits of where the regime tolerates or promotes this role (Hassid 2016). But journalists at CCTV have come to feel conflicted: since CCTV now relies almost entirely on advertising income (more than 90 per cent) and it has ever more competitors, journalists feel under pressure to provide entertaining news that is popular with audiences, rather than in-depth serious investigative coverage or media content with an educational or morally guiding function (Zhu 2012). CCTV is thus squeezed between the regime's straitjacket, which has loosened somewhat over time, and commercial competition for audiences, which has intensified (Stockmann 2013).

2.5 Digital media and politics in China and India

Against this background, we can turn to the discussion of digital media. For China, the main point to begin with is that, despite common perceptions in the West that China's regime suppresses online activity, in fact, the use of digital media for political engagement is extensive and highly complex, even if it is ultimately kept within bounds. One way to make this point is to draw on the study of the online public sphere by Rauchfleisch and Schäfer (2015), who carried out an in-depth examination of the microblogging platform Sina Weibo. Sina Weibo used to be the dominant microblogging service in China, though it has recently been overtaken by WeChat. But what Rauchfleisch and Schäfer argue for Sina Weibo applies to other online media. The authors point out that, even for a single mode of online expression such as Sina Weibo, it is too simplistic to take an either/or view – that either there is a growing public sphere, or this public sphere is increasingly repressed. Instead, there are multiple public spheres on Weibo – seven, in their view – and it is useful to list them briefly to give a flavour of the variety they found by analysing Weibo content: 1. thematic discussion of issues, such as environmental issues, which is continuous; 2. event-focused discussion, as with natural disasters; 3. 'encoded', whereby certain techniques are used to evade censorship, such as the use of undetectable homonyms or images containing censored words; 4. discussions pertaining to local issues, such as contention over building regulations; 5. debates about world affairs; 6. content that has been censored online but is stored on mobile devices for sharing; 7. discussion about censorship, a 'meta' discussion.

It is easy to see that most of these topics could not be discussed in traditional broadcast media, or that they would in any event be subject to greater control. At the same time, as Rauchfleisch and Schäfer point out, the party-state can – through its influence with internet companies as well as direct control – steer people in their uses of different social media platforms. The migration of users away from Sina Weibo and towards WeChat, where there is far less possibility for public expression and sharing content on a large scale, is one example. It is not clear whether this migration took place because of the better functionalities of WeChat, or if users left Sina Weibo for other reasons such as restrictions on content sharing and perceptions of censorship. Howsoever, WeChat continues to be a forum for political discussion, even if certain topics are heavily censored (Ng 2015). One point needs adding: internet companies in China generally did not achieve their success in dominating the Chinese markets because of the state's economic protectionism or censorship policies. Pan (2016) argues that Chinese social media such as Baidu (the equivalent of Google), WeChat (Facebook or Twitter) and Alibaba's Taobao (Amazon or eBay) were simply better at knowing the Chinese markets and meeting its needs. However, they still face the problem that they cannot expand into foreign markets because they do not have the legal or political policies in place to do so, especially for data protection.

In terms of censorship, one useful approach has been to focus not on the state's efforts at repression but on how people curb themselves. Thus Stern and Hassid (2012) talk of 'control parables', stories that circulate about how people may have got into trouble for what they said, and which keep others from doing the same. They make the point that it is often the uncertainty about what is going on – that it is not known whether or which repressive measures were used – that keeps people in line; for example, for fear that they may lose their livelihoods as journalists. Along similar lines, Arsène (2011) uses the term 'self-censorship' to argue that criticism of the regime is not expressed in the first place because of the fear of repercussions. These arguments point to a general issue: that it is difficult to gauge how much criticism of the regime remains unexpressed because of uncertainties about consequences, or if critics are resigned to leaving things unsaid.

It is also worth noting how digital media have shifted this problem: for broadcast media, it is journalists who do the self-censoring, and it is well known that they do so (for example, the top CCTV presenters interviewed by Zhu 2012). In the online world, we can distinguish between opinion leaders (famous business people, cultural celebrities and the like, who are very popular on Chinese social media) and grassroots activists. For both groups, self-censorship is not (or is less) tied to losing their positions due to party control, but rather is a self-imposed censorship for fear of reprisals. And in China, as elsewhere, the Chinese microblogosphere is dominated by a few users who make the vast number of posts. Svensson has therefore argued that microblogging is mainly used for 'visibility and witnessing rather than mobilization and activism' (2014, 179). Further, even for putting certain issues in the spotlight, the attention span of microblogs is short, which is of course true for microblogging compared to other media generally. Finally, it is difficult to gauge how many are critical of the regime. Brady (2008) has argued that the state's propaganda has been successful, and that most Chinese favour political stability, which can be assumed to include agreeing with muting voices that would threaten it. Along similar lines, Leibold (2011) suggests that most Chinese are in general supportive of the state's control of the internet, particularly as there are so many scams and wild rumours online. But to say that Chinese publics have adapted to being muted online is not to say they are uninterested in politics: according to Stockmann (2015a), more than 40 per cent have contributed to political discussions, and this can be broken down further into users of bulletin board services (BBS), who tend to be nationalists, and users of social media, who tend to be more in favour of liberalization. Like Rauchfleisch and Schäfer (2015), she argues that there are a number of different online publics.

This brings us to what political discussion and political protest in China are about. A number of scholars have documented censorship (King et al. 2013) and the rising number of online protests in China. Yang says that 'although hundreds of Internet protests occur every year, the main issues focus on corruption, social injustices against vulnerable persons, and abuse of power by government officials' (2014, 111). He notes the similarity between authoritarian China and Russia, with protests aimed at government abuses and oversights, whereas in democracies, protest is aimed more at government policies. He also says that the Chinese regime has adapted to these protests by learning to 'manage' them more effectively. Again, online activism and how the state responds to it must be understood conjointly.

Online activism must also be put in the context of prevailing political views or ideologies and, as mentioned earlier, it is difficult to gauge these in China. But Pan and Xu (forthcoming) have recently made an attempt to do just that: to elicit the range of political views in China – its 'ideological spectrum'. They did this by making use of a large-scale survey that asked respondents a wide range of questions about politics. What they found is a split between younger, more urban, more well-off and well-educated 'liberals', which in the Chinese context means those in favour of more freedom and democracy (and which also includes more 'liberal' views on cultural issues such as homosexuality, but not a pro-market view), as against conservatives, who support the state's authoritarian socialism and a return to pre-reform policies, from the left.

This is a good moment to contrast the role of political ideology in the media in authoritarian China and in democratic societies generally. First, and most obviously, the valence of political ideology is reversed: Chinese leftists would be on the right in Western democracies, and its rightists would be on the left. But there is also a more fundamental difference: in China, this ideological spectrum can be seen as a measure of public political opinion, whereas the official and only legitimate ideology of the regime, including in the media, is that of the party, which sits 'above' right and left public orientations (although there are right/left factions within the party, but again, this is different from the situation in democratic multi-party societies). This point allows us to turn to the main contrast: in democracies, including India, political ideologies also arise from the public and they are articulated within parties and in the media; in addition, they compete for legitimacy and power.

In China on the other hand, as long as the party-state remains in power, the public's political orientations or ideological preferences influence the regime in the sense that it uses them to enhance the party-state and the nation. This harnessing of public opinion influences the direction of the state only indirectly, via the party. Public opinion may also strengthen or weaken competing factions within the party, and may soften the regime's control. But we should note the fundamental difference: in democracies, media, with an autonomous media system, are a transmission belt for ideologies, whereas in authoritarian regimes they are less autonomous and function as a thermostat that is used – but also kept within bounds – by the regime. At the same time, as the discussion of new media has suggested, the online public arena is where many go for news and political engagement to circumvent traditional media, which they know to be far more controlled by the state. And this applies particularly to certain parts of the population rather than others, which makes digital media far more important relatively (and relatively autonomous compared to traditional media) than in other media systems, because they serve and reflect parts of civil society better. Yet this online activity can be a double-edged sword: while much has been written about progressive forces pushing for more openness and dissent and protest against single-party rule (Yang 2009; 2014), the Chinese online public arena also contains a strong and visible extreme populist nationalism, as we shall see in the next chapter.

India, on the other hand, not only has a lively online public arena, as in China, but also an open one. But internet use, and also internet-based mobilization, is still mainly confined to a small, urban and younger minority. For example, one of the first incidents to gain widespread attention via social media, mainly on smartphones, was the Delhi gang rape that took place in December 2012. In response to this event, many activists and journalists went online, many on Twitter, and succeeded in drawing far more attention to the event than mainstream media would have done. However, this attention was confined to a small internet-savvy part of the population (Belair-Gagnon et al. 2014). In China, this way of drawing attention online to events such as crimes and disasters, underplayed by the government and traditional media, already has a much longer history, going back to the early to mid-2000s. India has a lively civil society, but new media are simply not used widely enough yet to make a large difference.

Nevertheless, even without widespread internet penetration, new technologies can be important for politics, and the best way to illustrate this is via the use of mobile phones in an Indian election. This was documented in detail by Doron and Jeffrey (2013, 143–64), in relation to the case of the election in 2007 of Mayawati as chief minister of Uttar Pradesh (UP), India's most populous state by far. At the time, mobile phones had just broken through to reach a sizable part of the population – 31 million of the 200 million people in UP. As Doron and Jeffrey point out, although mobile phone ownership was heavily skewed towards the middle class, it was also widespread among the Dalit (formerly known as 'untouchables') civil servants working in the government's Post Office and Communications departments. Mayawati's party, the Bahujan Samaj Party (BSP), was based on a Dalit political organization, and she herself came from a humble Dalit background. Dalits, 20 per cent of UP's population, had continued to be widely disenfranchised, despite laws against this; for example, by not being allowed in certain public spaces and through intimidation by landowners (including during elections). Doron and Jeffrey also note that the 'major newspapers and television channels', controlled by Hindu elites, were 'disdainful of the BSP and often hostile to Dalit-oriented policies' (2013, 154). Yet through government policies ('reservations'), Dalits also held a certain proportion of government offices, and so could afford mobile phones, and they were a core among BSP party activists.

The BSP's election victory, and Mayawati's subsequent appointment as Chief Minister, were regarded as a major breakthrough by a disprivileged caste, gaining them power in India, and Doron and Jeffrey argue that the use of mobile phones was a necessary even if not a sufficient factor in this victory. It was achieved through the creation of an alliance with the Brahmins (10 per cent of the population), with both groups persuaded that a BSP government would benefit them. The election was won by combining a top-down and a bottom-up strategy for mobilizing voters at the level of election booths: party activists were contacted via voice and text message at organizations comprising both Dalits and Brahmins around thousands of polling stations. They were mobilized to get (especially sympathetic women) voters registered and out to vote, preparing for visits by party leaders and disseminating their text messages, and making sure that they knew the correct symbol to push on the voting machine and ballot papers (in India, where illiteracy is high, each party has a symbol – in the case of the BSP, an elephant). Doron and Jeffrey draw analogies here with the election campaign that took President Obama to power in 2008, where a similar person-to-person ground-level campaign was fought. They note that this person-to-person strategy was especially important in UP, establishing trust between Dalits and Brahmins and persuading them that the BSP represented their common interest.

Another key element was the fact that mobile phones were used to report wrongdoing and intimidation to the Election Commission, including taking pictures of irregularities. Finally, at the time, the other parties lacked such mobile phone-based mobilization. As Doron and Jeffrey note, they have subsequently remedied this, so the advantage of the BSP's innovative mobile phone use has vanished (indeed, in the 2017 state election, the nationalist BJP of Prime Minister Modi, discussed in the next chapter, won overwhelmingly in UP). Still, on this occasion, they argue that mobile phones played a crucial role, saying that it constituted a 'disruption' in Indian politics that 'bypassed mainstream media' (2013,

163). We should note that mobile phones worked differently from other media and from the internet in this case, enabling two-way connections, with the expectation that relations between party officials and activists would be maintained. This involved one-to-one conversations rather than mass mailings, and made 'widespread frequent communication possible and involved people who would rather speak and listen than read and write' (2013, 154). In short, like the large populist rallies that characterize Indian politics, the use of this (small) technology fits well with mobilizing a part of the population using cheap and easy-to-use devices via the right modality.

As mentioned, online activism still reaches only a small part of the urban and educated population, mostly journalists and activists. This limited reach also applies to online politics generally, except when online media become a major platform for a much wider reach. They have recently begun to do so, but only by being amplified via traditional media, unlike in China – as we shall see. Still, what we can already see with regard to India are various forms of online or mobile phone-based media mobilization – during election campaigns, by political leaders and for issue-based social movement mobilization – that are rooted in longer-standing populist politics and civil society activism in India. Even if television and newspapers still dominate, far more so than in China due to the lack of reach of the internet or the lack of technological infrastructure, activists (and especially nationalists, as we will see in the next chapter) have a wider resonance among the population and as a movement. In both countries, then, it is important to take the wider media system and traditional media into account. However, parts of civil society gain disproportionately from new media insofar as these enable forces and information to be visible that are not represented in traditional media, and where these forces resonate among longer-term movements and ideologies 'from below'. Equally important is the way that elites use new media to shape the public agenda and mobilize the public; the Communist Party in China and the BSP's election are both examples of this.

To summarize: in the Chinese case, the regime and civil society are adapting to each other as use of the internet becomes more widespread and intensive. But there is a strain whereby the regime needs to contain dissent, and a potentially more serious strain whereby the regime's strategy of becoming an economic and high-tech superpower relies on a less constrained sphere of everyday internet use, utilizing online activity as a means of obtaining feedback, and expanding online markets that may need to go beyond borders. These tensions around how to enable Chinese citizens to participate more via digital media – but at the same time containing what they can do, also in relation to the world-at-large – are bound to intensify and raise questions about the regime's legitimacy. Recently, discussions of the climate of media policies in China have portrayed President Xi as adopting a tougher and more controlling stance. However, Brady has argued that he is merely perpetuating a longer-standing tradition, in operation since at least 1989, whereby periods of greater openness alternate with periods of greater control. The same applied to Xi's predecessors, Jiang and Hu. Xi, she says, 'is not trying to suppress public opinion or the "public-opinion oversight" role of the media, but rather is trying to keep it within acceptable boundaries that do not harm the party's core interests' (2016, 11).

India's smartphone use will go from 20 per cent to 80 per cent in the space of a few years (Donner 2015). Its economic development is not following the East Asian statist route and its markets are becoming more open to the world, which is a mixed blessing insofar as global internet companies dominate (unlike in China, where national companies dominate). However, India's IT sector also provides the strongest share of exports. Civil society in this case is largely unconstrained, but strong elites continue to skew Indian development towards the interests of businesses and parties. With a weak state and fragmented pluralism, a plethora of civil society groups will press against these dominant interests, and against corruption. But here, as in China, these civil society pressures include intolerant populist forces, and in India, these forces also benefit the ruling nationalist party and its leader, who can mobilize support from a wider base, bypassing traditional media.

Traditional media, newspapers and television, will continue to set the political agenda in both countries. But smartphone use has made the internet accessible to most in China, and will do so soon in India, which means that the debates will also move beyond economic development and access (Donner 2015). Online activism will increasingly influence politics, in India in a pluralist political and media environment competing for attention with traditional media but with a rapidly growing population of internet users. In China, it will be within an environment contained by an authoritarian party that will need to balance managing the pressures for greater responsiveness and maintaining stability with a deepening and extensive online sphere.

Both countries have lively politics emerging from online civil society. In China, the lid is kept on by the state, whereas in India, small burgeoning civil society forces are outweighed by elites. In both countries, major examples of online activism include protest and pressures for less corrupt and more responsive government. There are wider lessons here for the double-edged nature of the political implications of digital media. The internet is changing politics, but it extends inputs from civil society only within the confines of the workings of different media systems, and includes forces that demand more responsiveness from government in the direction of greater pluralism and accountability – but also, as we shall see, calls for a stronger, less tolerant state and a more exclusive nationalism. In any event, the role of online forces is a – perhaps *the* – central question for Chinese and Indian political development. That is because, unlike in established democracies, with their autonomous media systems and well-established competition for visibility among many inputs, in China and India the online realm will continue to provide the main alternative to entrenched political power and its hold over traditional media.

3
Digital media and the rise of right-wing populism

Studies of the internet and politics often focus on progressive politics – on the internet as a democratizing influence or on movements such as Occupy Wall Street in the United States. The other main area is the deviant internet of hackers and mischief-makers like trolls. What gets far less attention are retrogressive mainstream political forces such as right-wing populism, which, I will argue, have been the single most important political change in at least three of the countries examined here (in China, they are among the most important). To make the argument, this chapter compares four right-wing populist movements: Donald Trump in America, Narendra Modi in India, the Sweden Democrats and Chinese nationalists. Digital media have been a necessary precondition for the success of all four, but in quite different ways, depending on the media system, including digital media, in each country. Common to all four, however, is the fact that digital media have bypassed traditional media gatekeepers.

Trump's success in becoming the Republican candidate was achieved by dominating the agenda of mainstream media via his use of Twitter. In India, Modi used Twitter to mobilize his Hindutva supporters to become elected as prime minister; like Trump, he circumvented his own party. Sweden Democrats have online newspapers that create an alternative to the consensus in public broadcast media and among parties that lock them out. And in China, the government uneasily keeps in check extremists who promote the stronger assertion of a nationalist agenda using social media. In all four countries, populist politicians, parties and movements have used digital alternatives to get around the mainstream media, which populists and their leaders perceive as biased against them. In doing so, they have been able to promote a message online that is less visible in traditional media, partly because it would be more contested there, and sometimes because their message is unacceptable within mainstream media or is against media regulation. The strength of populism cannot be understood without a theory that takes into account how new technologies enable parties and movements to become counterpublics that reshape the political agenda in media.

To understand this force, we must define populism. It has been defined as a belief that 'juxtaposes a virtuous populace with a corrupt elite and views the former as the sole legitimate source of political power' (Bonikowski and Gidron 2016, 1593; see also the review in Gidron and Bonikowski 2013; Mudde and Kaltwasser 2013; Mudde 2016 for a recent account of European populisms). Populists, in Mueller's view (2016), claim that they are the '100 per cent' people. They are the only true and virtuous people whose views are underrepresented and they want to exclude 'others' from the right to full citizenship in the nation. Mueller also defines populists as anti-elite: they are against the media and the political 'establishment' in the case of right-wing populists and against wealthy economic elites in the case of left-wing populism (which is outside the scope here since it plays a much more minor role in the four countries examined). In addition to being the '100 per cent' people and anti-elitist, a third characteristic of populists is that they espouse the ideal that the government should more adequately represent 'the people', which is where media come in.

The 'exclusionary' characteristic of populism raises a question or paradox that can be dealt with immediately: namely, are, or can, populists, once they are in power, be democratic? Populist parties can form parts of or dominate governments, and there can be majorities in favour of a populist agenda without forming parts of government. If populists rule or govern, however, they cannot be more adequately represented since they would have become the '100 per cent' people and will have become the elite (unless there are two versions of populism in the same state). This paradox can be resolved by pointing out that the characteristics that make parties or movements populist will diminish when they come into power, although they can of course still pursue stronger populist agendas when they are in government. Mueller argues that populists are anti-pluralists and so anti-democratic, that their aim is always a moral one, and Bonikowski and Gidron (2016) say it is mainly a tool of 'political challengers'. But it is also possible to define them without this moral component, and to recognize that they can change their colours when they are no longer challengers. Their claims that their version of the 'people' needs more representation and that they are against established elites may lose force when they are in government. However, an 'idealistic' belief system or ideology is not unique to right- or left-wing populists. Populists change once they are in power, but there is nothing inherently contradictory or anti-democratic about espousing a stronger or more 'exclusionary' representation of 'the people' (though the exclusion of 'others' is anti-pluralist and in this sense populism is also illiberal).

A general account of the causes of populism is outside the purview here; the main aim is to understand what role is played by traditional and digital media. It is relevant to note at the outset, however, that, for the four cases under consideration, a purely economic explanation (Judis 2016) is insufficient. It is not just economically disadvantaged groups that turn to populism, and populism has not just been a response to economic crisis (which does not coincide with the timing or the economic well-being or otherwise in the four cases here). Any explanation of populism must focus squarely on politics: it is about excluding those who are not part of 'the people' from full citizenship. This applies to left-wing populism, too, but here the 'exclusion' is economic and the enemy are economic elites, whereas right-wing populism aims to restrict and strengthen especially social citizenship rights to co-nationals against 'others' such as immigrants. Over the course of the twentieth and twenty-first centuries, the main force for social change in the developed world has been the interplay of classes and nations over the extension of citizenship (Mann 2013), but in the twenty-first century, class and nation are becoming intertwined in populism. In the developed world, and perhaps beyond, limits are emerging to extending social and other citizenship rights (Schroeder 2013). And these limits produce support within civil society for those who want to restrict these rights to 'the true people' and harness their anti-elite political representatives to this agenda.

Furthermore, politics is not just domestic: external enemies are also supposedly threatening the nation, economically and geopolitically, and a populist agenda aims to overcome these threats and put the national interests of 'the people' first. Thus, religion, ethnicity and immigration play a role in all four cases. But it is not just negative ill-feeling or racism towards other groups within the country or externally that defines populism, as with right-wing extremist or anti-immigration parties focused on this single issue. Populists are also anti-elite, and want the 'virtuous people' to be more adequately represented in government beyond the issue of immigration alone.

Nevertheless, there are different varieties of right-wing populism. It is useful to distinguish between Sweden and the United States on the one hand, where populists have gained traction largely, though not exclusively, with anti-immigration policies, as against India and China, with religious/ethnic and nationalist/ethnic versions of 'the people' respectively, and which focus more strongly on the corruption of elites. Still, this difference is a matter of degree; a nationalist and anti-elite agenda, and the demand for more 'true' representation, is characteristic of all. It can be mentioned that an admixture of left-wing populism, which is aimed against 'rich' corrupt elites, is particularly prominent and difficult to separate in the Chinese case, though elements of animosity towards corrupt elites can be found in all four cases. And again, in all four, one external enemy is economic globalization, though Modi's populism (and some elite factions in China) also favours a more capitalist agenda in order to strengthen the nation. The threat of Islamic terrorism, too, plays a role in all four cases.

A crucial point to stress at the outset is that any explanation that takes into account only digital media on the one hand or populist forces on the other is insufficient. Both are necessary. Populist ideology cannot simply be seen as a media construction or the beliefs of leaders and parties that have been foisted upon 'the people'. Instead, the strength of populism rests on the social conditions that give rise to movements and parties which define 'the people' in exclusionary terms and rail against elites. At the same time, I will argue that the success of populists, their strength in the four cases examined, could not have been achieved without non-mainstream digital media. Put differently, populists have gained a disproportionate advantage with digital media compared to how they fare in traditional media, and compared to how established parties or political movements use media.

3.1 Trump's ascent via Twitter

In the 2016 presidential primaries, Donald Trump dominated the news headlines on the side of the race to become the nominee for the Republican Party, even though he was a party outsider and the party favoured insider candidates. His dominance was achieved largely because of social media, mainly Twitter (though he also used other social media such as YouTube and Facebook), where he tweeted controversial positions on a range of issues. These positions then featured prominently in television newscasts and newspaper headlines. Many of these headlines were critical of Trump's positions, which were far from the political mainstream and promoted a populist right-wing agenda, including, most controversially, an anti-immigrant stance. Yet the headlines ensured that his views received a disproportionate amount of attention. The relation between the number of tweets in which Trump and other candidates are mentioned and their coverage in mainstream media over the course of the primary campaign and beyond has been tracked at http://viz2016.com/ (Groeling et al. 2016). It shows a clear correlation: Trump is mentioned in tweets far more than any other candidate in both parties, often more than all the other candidates combined, and the volume of tweets closely tracks his outsize coverage in the dominant mainstream media (which, in the same tracking analysis, includes CNN, Fox News, MSNBC, ABC, CBS, NBC and local news). Polling data (such as http://www.realclearpolitics.com/epolls/2016/president/us/2016_republican_presidential_nomination-3823.html) confirms that Trump pulled ahead of other Republican candidates in synchrony with his dominance of the media attention space, despite the fact that his nomination as Republican candidate was opposed by the party up until the party's convention and beyond.[1]

Traditional news media were compelled to give a lot of time to Trump's views since, as we have seen, the American media system is characterized by horse-race politics and market competition for audience share. Tomasky (2016) quotes the television executive Les Moonves, who said during the primary election campaign that 'the Trump phenomenon "may not be good for America, but it's damn good for CBS"'. The 'free' extensive media coverage also meant that Trump had to spend far less on political advertising than his rivals. Furthermore, journalists covering the campaign, themselves extensive users of Twitter, eagerly picked up newsworthy items on Twitter. Hamby (2013) has argued that Twitter has changed presidential political campaigns, with journalists relying on Twitter as a major source, not just to follow candidates and campaign teams but also to follow each other. However, they are also under pressure from their editors to feature such 'breaking news' in their stories, especially attention-grabbing issues, to maximize audience share. Thus Trump was able to set the agenda by tweeting positions that were guaranteed a wide audience in mainstream media.

Hamby criticizes the dominance of Twitter, especially the way it contributes to the greater prominence of trivia or focuses on the process of campaigns rather than the substance. He notes that this is not a new criticism, but the trend is intensified by Twitter since messages are unfiltered – or, put the other way around, there is less editorial control – which allows minor incidents to gain widespread attention quickly. Here it can be noted that Trump's tweets also went against the grain of the tighter management of campaign messages on social media, which has been characteristic of other presidential campaigns (see Kreiss 2016).

He tweeted himself (and still does so!), and the controversial nature of many of his messages means they are a boon to news-starved journalists. Hamby describes how there is often a desperate search to find something newsworthy to report among journalists during the primary campaign, and Trump often provided tweets (and again, still does) that were considered newsworthy enough to be reproduced in full in the news.

Trump's position could not have been achieved without the support of a substantial proportion of the electorate. His base of support consisted of a part of the population that considers itself left out by the country's media elites and its established party elites.[2] And while there is an economic aspect to the demographic of this support, it is among the less educated, male, more rural, white population. Trump supporters are against established state elites and share a distrust of government, a deep-rooted tradition in American politics (Hall and Lindholm 2001). Their anti-immigrant, anti-refugee and anti-Muslim stances are more to do with citizenship rights and economic nationalism than purely economic disadvantage or uncertainty.

As we have seen, unlike elections elsewhere (such as in Sweden – Dimitrova and Strömbäck 2011), the focus during American elections in the media is on the horse race between candidates, who rely on personal media attention (as opposed to attention on parties and policies), within a media system where news is driven more strongly (and almost exclusively, unlike Sweden, with its public-service media) by market competition for audiences. The role of Twitter can be singled out here; it was a transmission belt to visibility in traditional media. It did not play a decisive role once Trump was the nominee of the Republican Party since, from that point onwards, the candidates of both parties were guaranteed a roughly equal share of media attention (and Trump could also gain attention by seeking media appearances). But Twitter did play a decisive role in his success in becoming the nominee for the Republican Party and, for a crucial period, he was able to circumvent media autonomy – or use digital media to amplify his message in traditional media.

This success cannot be explained by reference to Twitter alone; rather, again, the explanation relies on how Trump's political message – his unconventional remarks on Twitter – received a level of attention in traditional media that would have been impossible had he relied on press conferences or traditional broadcast coverage. In other words, by communicating via Twitter, Trump was able to bypass the conventional gate-keepers of journalists and mainstream TV and newspapers because they were compelled to report his views in a competitive environment that relies on audience share. Put differently, Trump did not directly speak to his audience via Twitter – too few Americans are on Twitter. But he could rely on traditional media to broadcast his new media messages. As Karpf (2016) argues: 'In a world with digital media, but less analytics, this election drama would have unfolded differently…journalists and their editors would have been less attuned to the immediate feedback of Trump's daily ratings effects, and this would have led them to spread their coverage more evenly (as they always have in the past). Trump's media dominance isn't just driven by our attention, it's driven by the media industry's new tools for measuring and responding to that attention.' As we will see in chapter 6, these analytics have become important beyond politics and elections and now also shape the competition for online audiences generally.

In any event, the role of the media and of Twitter was decisive inasmuch as other factors that typically play a role can be ruled out: the argument that the party and its elites 'decide' on the candidate (Cohen et al. 2016) did not apply on this occasion (though arguably, it applied to Hillary Clinton's nomination). Second, Trump had fewer resources; he spent far less than other candidates during the primary campaign (and he also spent less, and there was less overall spending, than in previous campaigns). Third, Trump did not have an effective data analytics-driven or ground campaign; in this respect, his campaign was less sophisticated than that of his competitors.

Populists have traditionally been adept at using the mass media of their day. But the reach of their media was limited, as with direct mail and magazines or latterly email (Kazin 1998, 259–60), unless populists could also obtain sufficient attention in the mainstream media. Other populists have had a critical attitude to the mainstream media, and Trump has also maintained a critical – even conspiratorial – attitude towards the establishment-dominated media throughout the election (and beyond) and accused the media of being 'rigged' against him. The extent to which this attitude drove his supporters to alternative media and social media has not been systematically examined (to my knowledge). But the key is that Trump was able to continue to have his message relayed from his tweets to the mainstream media, even though the mainstream media often covered him negatively (and covered his claims that the media were biased against him).

Trump stands in a long line of right- and left-wing populism in America, though as Kazin (1998) points out, populism has generally moved rightwards since the Second World War. Populism as an ideology has waxed and waned in the post-war period, though it has often been just as strong as left, right, moderate and libertarian ideologies

(Claggett et al. 2014). Trump's language was strongly populist; only Bernie Sanders rivalled him on the left and Ben Carson on the right for populist language, as Oliver and Rahn (2016) show. They also show that support for his views was strong among voters, and argue that such populist views have not been taken into account by parties, and by the Republican Party in particular, which they say constitutes a 'representation gap': 'Donald Trump's simple, Manichean rhetoric is quintessentially populist...the opportunity for a Donald Trump presidency is ultimately rooted in a failure of the Republican Party to incorporate a wide range of constituencies' (2016, 202). In other words, his populist appeal mattered too. In short, Twitter, translated into mainstream media, plus populism, explains Trump's success.

3.2 The Sweden Democrats' alternative media

The Sweden Democrats are a populist anti-immigration right-wing party that has risen to prominence in the past decade, though their popularity pre-dates the recent migrant crisis (the party was founded in 1988). Indeed, their roots lie partly in a neo-Nazi movement that has been on the fringes of Swedish politics since the 1960s or earlier, though as the Sweden Democrats have gained electoral support, they have had to distance themselves ever more from this association to appear respectable (Baas 2014). Another predecessor of the Sweden Democrats were the New Democrats, a right-wing challenger party sparked by an anti-statist tax revolt of the early 1990s, but whose support quickly petered out. Sweden Democrats, in contrast, have gained strength in the recent elections, particularly as immigration and refugees have become an increasingly salient issue. They are also Eurosceptic and see Islamic terrorism and Islamic values among immigrants as a threat. Yet they were ignored by other parties and by the mainstream media until they entered parliament in 2010 (Hellström et al. 2012; see also Strömbäck et al. 2016).

The populism of the Sweden Democrats is part of a broader family of right-wing populist parties and movements in the Nordic countries (Lindroth 2016). A comparison is often made with the Folkeparti (People's Party) in Denmark, which has formed a part of coalition governments. In Sweden, in contrast, the strategy of the other major parties has been to place a 'cordon sanitaire' around the Sweden Democrats, in this way keeping them out of government. The political effectiveness of this strategy can be put to one side here. But while outside of the mainstream, the Sweden Democrats have also attempted to claim to represent the left-wing tradition that has dominated Swedish politics, the ideal of a 'people's home' or 'folkhem'. This social-democratic ideal aims to create a welfare state for all Swedes. The populist agenda here can thus be described as welfare chauvinism, restricting the benefits of citizenship rights, and especially social citizenship, of the 'folkhem' to the 'true people', and in this sense can be described as right wing.

Sweden Democrats have been blocked from having influence in the government. The so-called 'December Agreement' after the 2014 election kept the Sweden Democrats from playing the kingmaker role, which their share of parliamentary representation could have afforded them since neither the left nor the right bloc of parties achieved a majority. This agreement has enabled the left coalition to rule with the support of a right-wing bloc of conservative and liberal ('borgerlig') parties. Subsequently, however, the parties from this conservative bloc have entertained the possibility of allying themselves with the Sweden Democrats, so that this agreement and the 'cordon sanitaire' could unravel. During the summer of 2016, the government also made immigration laws more restrictive, no longer allowing family reunification for refugees and immigrants (which had been one of the Sweden Democrats' demands). Whether partly adopting the Sweden Democrats' core agenda in this way, or making common ground with them, dampens their populist support, remains to be seen.

The electoral support of the Sweden Democrats has come mainly at the expense of the Conservative party (Moderaterna), which has traditionally favoured a pro-immigration stance for humanitarian and labour policy reasons. This has meant that the Sweden Democrats, claiming to protect Swedish values in contrast to such 'openness', could gain support among right-wing voters. They have also presented themselves as martyrs and paint the media as being biased against them (Schall 2016, 181), just as Trump has done in America. And, like Trump supporters, they are less educated, more rural and male. As they have also received mostly negative coverage in the mainstream media, a raft of alternative media have sprung up in support of the Sweden Democrats, self-defined as 'alternative' to the mainstream media.

These alternative media consist of online newspapers, but the Sweden Democrats have also made extensive use of social media. Larsson found, during the 2014 election, a 'tendency for ideologically marginalized parties to gain more traction in novel media spheres than in the coverage curated by established media actors' (2015, 12), which also benefited other smaller parties such as the Feminist Initiative and the Pirate Party. However, unlike these two parties, by 2014 the Sweden

Democrats were no longer marginal, and had gained the third-largest share of votes (they had already passed the 5 per cent threshold of votes to gain seats in Parliament in 2010, unlike the other two). Polls since the election have put them at around 20 per cent (for example, Sannerstedt 2016). And the public's distrust of mainstream media on immigration has been high; among Sweden Democrat supporters it stood at 93 per cent, whereas it was 60 per cent among the general population (Rydgren and van der Meiden 2016, 22).[3] At the same time, attitudes towards immigrants and refugees have generally become more positive among Swedes supporting other parties, whereas among Sweden Democrat supporters, they have become more negative (Demker and van der Meiden 2016).

In Sweden, the dominant media gatekeepers remain in place. Public broadcasting is still the dominant source of news among the population, though among the younger generation, as we have seen, social media have become more popular (Westlund and Weibull 2013). Since the 1980s, commercial broadcasters have also taken an increasing audience share, even as the Swedish government continues to support newspapers with subsidies to enhance a diverse press.[4] In short, the Swedish media system remains a distinct and mixed public/commercial system (Hallin and Manicini 2004). But whereas traditional media did not pay much heed to the Sweden Democrats until they entered parliament, now they receive more attention than some established parties, even if it is mainly negative (Rydgren and van der Meiden 2016). Audience figures for alternative media, on the other hand, are difficult to come by. The online newspaper Avpixlat, according to Rydgren and van der Meiden (2016, 22), gets 200,000–300,000 unique visitors per week. Holt (2016a) has used Google Analytics and registered the number of unique visitors to four sites in 30 days (Fria Tider 1,419,573, Nyheter Idag 416,214, Avpixlat 788,282 and Motgift 80,770; though he points to the limitations of what these figures indicate). Sweden Democrats, he says, rely more than other parties on 'alternative media'– not just online newspapers but also social media.

Holt (2016b) also analysed the content of a number of online newspapers that support the Sweden Democrats. These deliberately contrast themselves with the 'mainstream media' that allegedly distort the truth. What Holt found is that these 'alternative media' are in fact heavily dependent on the 'mainstream media' since they have few independent journalistic resources, and so take content from the mainstream media and give it an interpretation that fits with populist right-wing beliefs. Interestingly, in comparing the content of 'alternative' with 'mainstream media', he found that they are not more sensationalist, but focus more on domestic and international politics and so do not cover the breadth of topics (sports, economics and culture/lifestyle) covered by mainstream media. But the coverage of domestic and international politics is different in these online media, particularly in respect to immigration, which is linked to criminality and the abuse of welfare, and rails against the 'political correctness' of multiculturalism as well as the threat of Islam.

Apart from driving supporters to alternative media, it is not clear whether the largely negative coverage of the Sweden Democrats in the mainstream is helping or hurting them. Social media and online newspapers are useful channels for the Sweden Democrats to communicate to wider audiences since their political position is widely regarded as unacceptable in mainstream public discourse. Populists in Sweden have thus developed an alternative media presence in support of a party that is outside the political mainstream and whose views lie beyond the politics in traditional media. But unlike in the United States, they compete for attention in a multi-party system, so their success in gaining a share of power depends not only on alternative media but also on whether other parties can continue to outflank them by locking them out or adopting a strong-enough stance to keep them out of government.

3.3 Modi's religious nationalism on Twitter

Narendra Modi's use of Twitter in his 2014 election campaign to become prime minister has been compared to the Obama election campaign in terms of the sophistication of social media use, but Trump's campaign is a better comparison. Like Trump, Modi used Twitter to circumvent traditional media to engage directly with his populist base of supporters and to challenge the elite and the media. Modi's media campaign strategy, like Trump's, deliberately bypassed his own party (Price 2016, 94), and like Trump, he criticized and taunted politicians from his main competition, the Congress Party, and especially Rahul Gandhi, who was the main competitor to become prime minister in 2014. Modi's campaign on social media, again like Trump's (among his supporters), had to overcome the lack of an extensive base of social media users in India. So unlike Trump, Modi's campaign adapted high-tech tools to a variety of low-tech outlets. These included holograms, through which he reached 15 million people (Price 2016, 136) and TV screens that were set up in villages to carry his speeches and rallies. Large popular rallies are, of course, common in Indian political campaigns.

Modi and the BJP were not the only ones to benefit from social media. Ahmed et al. (2016) analysed a large random sample of tweets from all of the major parties during the national election, and they also came to the conclusion that the internet (and first-time voters, who are more likely to use mobile phones and the internet) played a crucial role in the BJP's success. Interestingly, the party that had the next greatest Twitter presence was a relatively new and small challenger party, Aam Aadmi (common man). This anti-corruption party rules in Delhi, where there are strong progressive civil society organizations, and like other non-traditional parties (recall the Feminist Initiative party in Sweden), they gained disproportionally from social media.

Modi's use of Twitter was part of a deliberate strategy to craft his image as a technology-savvy leader who is transforming India into a world-leading nation via information technology. Jaffrelot (2015a, 6) calls it 'high-tech populism'. This appeal was directed at a younger urban elite. Modi's Twitter and social media strategy was similar to that of other political leaders in focusing on self-promotion, updating his followers about events in which he participated or that put him in a good light, such as posting pictures with popular cricket and Bollywood stars (Pal et al. 2016). He has also followed high-tech icons on Twitter such as Bill Gates and Eric Schmidt, which gives him prestige, as well as following Indian spiritual leaders, which fits into broader social media uses in India (Miller et al. 2016). One difference from other leading politicians who use Twitter to communicate one way is that Modi has engaged with ordinary members of his BJP (Bharatiya Janata Party) Hindu nationalist party and of the RSS (the Rashtriya Swayamsevak Sangh Hindu nationalist volunteer organization) by following them. Pal et al. (2016) give examples of tweets by these followers in which they say that they are proud to be followed by Modi, and will do their utmost to further his cause and the cause of Hindu nationalism.

What these authors also show, again exhibiting a pattern typical of populist politicians, is that the more extreme Hindu nationalist themes of Modi's posts early in the election campaign, energizing his core, taper off in the run-up to the election, when he needed to be more restrained to appeal to a broader base outside of the nationalist right wing (the same goes for Donald Trump and for the Sweden Democrats). Towards the end of the campaign, Modi's tweets and most frequent retweets were those that attacked the 'established elites', the Congress Party and especially the Gandhi family – in particular 'an infantilizing reference to Rahul Gandhi', his main competitor to become prime minister in 2014 (Pal et al. 2016, 58). (This recalls Donald Trump's tweets taunting 'Little

Marco' Rubio, one of his rivals for the Republican nomination.) After he was elected, Modi's tweets became less political, in the 'style of a benign ruler' (Pal et al. 2016, 59), a point at which he had more than 10 million followers, and each of his messages was being retweeted and favourited at least 1,000 times.

Another parallel – and a common feature of populism – is that Modi's election campaign was partly a personality-centred campaign that went against his own party. He used Twitter to challenge the elite and the media, which of course could not happen in China. In India's highly competitive democracy, as Rajagopal points out, there has been a wider trend whereby election campaigns used to be coordinated by parties to mobilize people; now, he says, 'political campaigns came to resemble personality-centred marketing operations' (2016, 127). Modi presented himself as an outsider and claimed to be 'anti-establishment'. His social media team, focusing on Twitter and Facebook, operated outside of the party's media campaign team, and was run by the American advertising firm Ogilvy & Mather (Price 2016; Chakravarty and Roy 2015). But Facebook reached only 10 per cent of Indians in 2014 (according to Palshikar 2016), and 'the most visible and high impact campaign events were big public rallies that were mostly, and are still, held in "maidan", or the public grounds in most cities that are meant for holding large public events' (Neyazi et al. 2016, 412) – though half a million people also participated in Modi's Google Hangout session, according to Price (2016, 63).

Modi's campaign was able to circumvent the elite-dominated English-language media and found a ready audience in other vernacular language media. As Chakravarty and Roy (2015) point out, television stations were only too eager to devote attention to Modi since he boosted audience ratings. Yet even after he was elected, Modi used Twitter and other social media for direct contact with people: there is a 'near-total lack of contact, as Prime Minister, with traditional news media. Outside of prepared speeches at major events, what we see of Modi is almost all we see of him. And yet, Modi comes across as the most interactive prime minister the country has ever had,' say Pal et al. (2016, 60). It can be added that Modi's interaction with his supporters needs to be put into a broader context, that this self-staging also translates into mainstream media, though little is known about this in India (whereas the mutual dependence and independence in the Swedish and US cases is well known: in China, as we shall see, there is a tension between them).

Hindu online nationalism is more widespread than Modi and his party.[5] Udupa has documented a movement of Hindu nationalists online that promotes a 'dream of a resurgent "new India" purged of corruption and "Muslim menace" to recast Hindu nationalism as an entrepreneurial, ideological project of net-enabled youth' (2015, 433). They also have offline meetings that are then available on YouTube, with speeches by Hindu nationalist leaders. Unlike Modi's tweets, these tweets (often anonymous) and videos of meetings can be more extreme than communication by the party – even if they clearly support Modi and the BJP. Udupa also describes how these meetings, such as the 'Global Patriotic Tweeples Meet' in Mumbai, attract wider audiences, with attendees taking pride, for example, that the event's hashtag trended nationally for several days. Apart from meetings, conflicts flare up on Twitter when extreme Hindu nationalists and their Muslim extremist counterparts exchange insults. And, as in China, there are also attempts by online amateur historians and others to reinterpret history in line with India's great Hindu past (Udupa 2016; George 2016, 101–8).

Modi is not the only populist using new media in politics. As we have seen in the previous chapter, Mayawati had already used a more low-tech approach in her election campaign in 2007, and she can also be seen as a populist (Subramanian 2007, 89–90), since she sought to circumvent the hostile mainstream media and the political elite with her own, in this case mobile-phone supported, organization. And unlike China, India has a lively civil society, including protest and social movements that are carried by the media. But unlike China, online mobilization is still confined to a small, urban, affluent and younger minority. Active online political engagement outside of elections is mainly limited to activists and journalists. Yet, as in China, online politics centres on corruption or on high-profile events such as crimes – here related to communalism. Even if television and newspapers still dominate – far more so than in China due to the lack of reach of the internet – activists, including nationalists, can gain attention in mainstream media by agitating online. Thus, again, it is necessary to take the media system, including both traditional and new media, into account. But populists gain disproportionately from new media insofar as they can disseminate messages that are too aggressive or inflammatory for mainstream media, so they need to evade media autonomy with messages that have come to resonate widely among a large part of the population.

Modi pursued a high-tech strategy, including lots of spectacle, to gain visibility in a low-tech environment. His social media strategy was successful because he could gain widespread mainstream media attention in a highly competitive media landscape. His tweets and text messages to mobile phones were 'part of a conscious effort to use social media to force the newspapers, TV and radio to take notice of every speech and to cover them in a way that reflected the priorities of the campaign' (Price 2016, 103). Jaffrelot says 'Modi literally saturated the public space' (2015b, 157). Now that he is elected, he no longer needs social media, but having mobilized his Hindutva supporters, as George points out, 'it is difficult for him to restrain them, since their platform of religious nationalism got him elected' (2016, 108). Though he adds: 'The main restraint on the Hindutva agenda may be the country's sheer ungovernability – an obstacle that has thwarted Indian leaders' most progressive intentions, and may do the same to Modi's nationalism' (2016, 109).

3.4 Containing online nationalists in China

In China, right-wing populism has found widespread expression online. Leibold (2010) examined nationalist websites, and estimates those who post most to be in the thousands, while readership is likely to be in the millions. They advocate Han supremacism, asserting the superiority of the dominant Han ethnic group over minority ethnic groups and the superiority of Chinese culture in the world-at-large. But unlike in the other cases, the regime tries to keep a lid on them, even while encouraging populism when it suits the government. There are also right-wing populist sympathizers among factions within the regime, and among other professionals, such as academics and journalists. They champion different kinds of nationalist agendas, but find support among a broader population that gives vent online to the idea that China should pursue a strong and distinctively Chinese path of development.

In China, as we have seen in chapter 2, the political agenda is still set by officially controlled media, even if much of the population seeks alternative sources of political and cultural information in order to evade what is widely known to be official propaganda in public-service and mainstream commercial media. China's online populists, like other movements that are critical of the regime, therefore use social media to promote their ideas under the radar of censorship. A crucial feature that sets China apart from the other cases, however, is that the party – the political elite or 'the establishment' – cannot be criticized in such a way that its legitimacy is directly challenged. Still, populists complain that the mainstream media do not represent their views and are too liberal (Osnos 2016: 337–8), so they express their views online instead.

Although the regime is not democratic and so does not depend on popular support, this is too simple. As Perry (2015) has noted, the regime sees itself as a 'populist democracy' whereby it is the party's duty to embody the will of the people for the public good. Tang (2016) has argued that the Chinese regime can be described in terms of 'populist authoritarianism'. That is, it is a regime that has achieved stability based on the strong support it has from the population as well as its 'hyper-responsiveness' to public inputs – despite the absence of strong democratic institutions such as elections, independent political organizations and the rule of law. He calls the regime 'hyper-responsive' because, unlike in democracies, where, once elected, rule is guaranteed until the next election, the party-state must be constantly attuned to public opinion. Indeed, in Tang's view, the direct responsiveness of the leadership to the people's will is a continuation of the longer-term tradition in Chinese politics whereby the emperor's legitimacy or his removal rested directly on the public's approval.

While Tang calls it 'populist authoritarianism', Stockmann and Luo (2016) call it 'responsive authoritarianism'. The contrast of both is with 'elite authoritarianism', imposed from above without consent or without requiring popular support or legitimacy, which implies that the regime must maintain coercive rule or face collapse if it does not. This is not the place to adjudicate the debate on whether China's authoritarianism will collapse or survive (or adapt). Suffice it to say that the regime has strong support among the public, and this support, including pressure on the regime for improvements – and keeping these pressures within bounds – increasingly finds its strongest expression online. As Wu (2007) argues, there is a misconception that the assertive nationalism in China's online sphere is instigated by the regime. In fact, as Wu shows, nationalist fervour aimed at shaping domestic politics and foreign relations (especially anti-Western and anti-US sentiment) comes 'from below'; it is a 'grassroots' nationalism that the regime must control lest it get out of hand.

The legitimacy of the regime thus rests on maintaining stability at home and in foreign relations, and any elements that threaten this stability can be attacked as unpatriotic. At the same time, the regime's legitimacy rests on continued economic growth. If such growth were to come to an end, or if the benefits of citizenship were to be further curtailed – there has already been a widening gap in this regard – popular support for the regime could wane. At that point, integration of China in a global economy could be scapegoated, as it has been in other right- or left-wing populisms. Or the regime and populists might want to blame political enemies within, such as Islamic ethnic groups in the west of the country, or external geopolitical enemies (Islamic terrorists, or Hong Kong,

Taiwan and Japan), and assert Han or Chinese cultural supremacy more aggressively vis-à-vis Western democracies or vis-à-vis the United States.

But while populism has assumed the form of virulent nationalism, it has not so far been a threat to the regime. Leibold argues (2010; 2016) that online nationalists are likely to be kept in check by the regime since they share the aim of the territorial integrity of the People's Republic, even if they also criticize the Communist Party for not being aggressive enough towards non-Han ethnic groups within, or not promoting Han civilization and claims over disputed Chinese territories in the world-at-large. The government's policy has been to recognize the needs of ethnic minorities and it has tried to foster a multi-ethnic state. It has also been cautious about promoting public sentiment that is too aggressive towards its foreign policy antagonists. At the same time, Zhao (in Carlson et al. 2016) quotes a survey by Tang and Barr which shows that China has the strongest support for nationalism among 22 countries surveyed (the United States is next strongest, with Sweden among the lowest). He says that 'while the Chinese government made effective efforts to control nationalism...before 2008, it has become increasingly reluctant to constrain its expression and more willing to follow the nationalist calls in confrontation against Western powers and neighbours...this strident turn is in part because the government is increasingly responsive to public opinion', including a 'growing number of ways such as the social media to express...nationalist feelings'(Carlson et al. 2016, 440).

It is worth bearing in mind when thinking about right-wing populism and nationalism in China that the left/right split operates differently, as we have seen. In Pan and Xu's (forthcoming) analysis of the ideological spectrum in Chinese public opinion, rightists support going back to Mao-era communist politics, a conservative position if it is contrasted with modernist liberalizers who are in favour of embracing capitalism and Western values. That is why it is difficult to categorize Han supremacists or nationalists as right-wing in a Western sense. It is also difficult to identify a coherent populist right-wing agenda, as this may promote traditional Confucian values, communist (Mao-era) values, or embrace Western values and capitalism (for different orientations among intellectual and political elites, see Fewsmith 2001). In all cases, however, the aim is to strengthen a distinctive Chinese culture and a stronger nation. In the other three cases of democracies, not only are there public opinion surveys, but populists can be measured by their share of votes. In China, apart from measuring nationalist sentiment, an equivalent could be to examine, in a Kremlinological way, the strength of populist-leaning elite factions within the ruling regime.

In China, the ethnic divide also exists, but another fault line (as in India, and to a lesser extent in America and Sweden) is between 'the people' and the corrupt elites that are enriching themselves. Note however that there is a difference between left-wing populism in other places (Southern Europe, Latin America), where the wealthy who are enriched by capitalist globalization are the target (Mueller 2016), whereas elites in China are targeted if they are enriched by corruption via the state (though these may be differences in degree, not kind). And Western capitalism can also be criticized in China as being contrary to a Chinese economic model based on Confucian civilization or on Maoist anti-capitalism. As in India, too, history is thus also a major battleground for online nationalists. One prominent online historian discussed by Leibold, for example, 'views China's past through...a struggle between civilization and barbarism, with the Han state and its Confucian morality standing firmly on the side of peace, stability, and progress' (2016, 9). The 'moral decline' of China, on the other hand, is attributed to 'unsubstantiated conspiracy theories about how minority elites are teaming up with foreign forces to split China and undermine its national interest' (2016, 11). Gries, echoing this debate, argues that 'pride in the superiority of Confucian civilization is central to Chinese nationalism today' (2004, 8) and adds: 'the legitimacy of the current regime depends upon its ability to stay on top of popular nationalist demands' (2004, 136). Again, the party elite as such cannot be attacked here, but only those elites that have lost Chinese 'virtues' and become corrupted by the West or by economic corruption.

It can be noted that the regime sometimes has an interest in encouraging populism to get rid of corrupt party elites. Tai (2015) speaks of a 'vengeful populism' whereby party officials or wealthy elites who flaunt the law or who are seen with luxury items are hounded by the public on social media. The public can thus take part in 'grassroots surveillance'. But the government can also engage in top-down surveillance by using social media to gauge popular opinion (Stockmann 2015b), as we will see further in chapter 6. This allows the regime to respond to populist outbursts or populist sentiments that are deemed excessive. The government may also want to weaken factions in the party or in the media that are not nationalistic enough. But again, 'not nationalistic enough' can itself mean different things: too Western, but also not Western enough if Western modernizing strategies could strengthen the nation; too Confucian, if left-wing Maoist strategies are seen as the best way to strengthen the nation – and vice versa.

The same applies to geopolitics and ethnic politics, which could be isolationist or empire-seeking, assimilationist or advocating ethnic chauvinism. Populism can take different forms, as long as it does not challenge the party. It could also conceivably take a left-wing populist turn, if inequalities continue to grow, and then be aimed at the super-rich inside the party and among business elites. But left-wing populism can be defused with egalitarian policies. Right-wing populism, on the other hand, can be defused only by aligning what the 'virtuous people' regard as the 'true people' with government policy, which is a more elusive goal.

Nationalist populism is not new in China (Dikötter 1994). The 1988 multi-part television documentary 'River Elegy' attracted hitherto unprecedented audience levels and generated much debate. It was critical of nationalism, but also characterized by nostalgia for when media were oriented more by national interests and not just by commercialism (Zhu 2012, 120–7). Recently (2006), another popular documentary 'Rise of Nations' (Zhu 2012, 104–10) criticized Chinese policymakers for not learning enough from other great powers about how to strengthen China. Like other forms of political expression in China, populism or nationalism also waxes and wanes around events: flare-ups occur during periods when there are perceived threats by Japan or terrorist attacks carried out by ethnic minority groups. A major wave of nationalism erupted during the Beijing Olympics in 2008, when Western media were attacked for being anti-Chinese.

In China, populism is under control for the foreseeable future. It cannot destabilize the government unless the party-state has a broader crisis of legitimation and so needs more populist or other support. This point emerges by noting that in the other cases, anti-elite sentiment draws its support from civil society and aims to democratically replace established elites (recall the discussion about whether populists can be democratic). Populists in China support the state's authoritarianism, but the government also worries that they may support the nation more strongly than the party (Osnos 2016, 147). At the same time, the regime enjoys widespread – if not universal – support in China, and it needs to be mentioned that most Chinese are generally supportive of the state's control of the internet (Leibold 2011).

3.5 Prospects for mediated politics

All four cases of online populism can be seen through the same lens: the responsiveness of politicians and governments to their civil societies – which consist of citizens or publics and social movements. Populist demands, and responsiveness to them, take place almost entirely via media. How populism is articulated vis-à-vis the state and elites varies among the four cases, but a common feature is that populists are challengers or counterpublics: they blame established parties, their politicians and the media, and they do so most successfully using digital media, gaining a proportion of attention that they could not obtain via mainstream media. Populism is aimed at national governments and bounded within national media systems. The share of attention they obtain is gained in competition for limited attention to dominate the political agenda space. Thus, even if populists get negative attention in the mainstream media, this deprives political rivals and alternative political views of visibility.

All forms of populism are anti-elite; this is the main fault line – a virtuous people against an unresponsive elite. The content of populism differs, although strengthening the nation with the aim of more representation for its distinctive tradition of embodying 'the people' is common to all four cases. Another 'exclusionary' commonality is holding anti-Muslim views, fuelled by domestic terrorist or violent incidents and Islamic fundamentalism in the world-at-large. But American populists see a strengthening of a 'pure' people in a right-wing leader espousing a racist anti-immigration agenda, and Indian populists a religious/ethnic strengthening in a leader who will give more space to Hindu nationalist views. Sweden Democrats also have a primarily anti-immigrant agenda, and believe their party will restrict the people's home to 'pure' Swedes. Chinese populists seek a stronger assertion of their national culture, sometimes seen in ethnic terms but also in civilizational terms, at home and in the world.

Populism has been the single most important recent political change in India, Sweden and the United States, though it is currently not the main challenge in Chinese politics, flaring up episodically as it does. Rising inequality and the regime's authoritarian control are more important in China. But populist nationalism could become more important in China if conditions change, as with an economic downturn or foreign aggression. If the regime becomes threatened, the party and populist movement can blame external enemies (geopolitical enemies, or 'foreign' capitalism in the sense of both economic competition and a competing economic culture or system) and enemies within (ethnic groups, 'foreign' capitalists, corrupt elites). And as long as the state sets the political agenda via media, and the public's opinion is not reflected in mainstream media or opinion polls but can be manipulated and encouraged while also growing 'from below', it may yet come to be a major force. While Indian and Swedish populism do not have worldwide geopolitical repercussions, Chinese and American populism do. And American and Chinese populist fears about their geopolitical rivalry also mirror each other.

The prospects for online populism vary, with media systems being a crucial factor. In competitive commercial media environments (the United States, India), without strong public media (unlike Sweden) or state control (unlike China), online populism can directly appeal to the public without counterweights. The political systems also matter: populists in Sweden can potentially exploit being kingmakers in a multi-party system without a clear majority (unlike in other countries, such as Denmark). In the United States they are restricted in national politics to competing in a majoritarian American presidential race. China's populist-nationalists can also goad the party towards Han or civilizational supremacism, but the party may also need to adopt stronger nationalist policies to make up for a loss of other sources of legitimacy. Populist messages are often unsuitable for mainstream media, and so can only be expressed, or expressed more forcefully, online. In all four cases, neither new media technology nor the rise and strengthening of populism alone explain the change in the political landscape; combined, they do.

The similarities and differences can be summarized as follows:

- Populism is leader-centric in the United States and in India, party-centric in Sweden, and a diffuse social-intellectual movement around a common core in China.
- In China and in America, populism lacks strong organizations, whereas in India and Sweden, it has organized bases.
- In all four, social media have been used to circumvent the gatekeepers of traditional media, and to circumvent party and media 'establishments'.

Populism is gaining strength in many parts of the world (Mueller 2016). It is not caused by new media, but equally it would not be such a potent force without new media. Populist counterpublics thrive in the online public arena. In terms of media theory, digital media add to the mediatization of politics (Hjarvard 2008); however, in the sense of circumventing traditional gatekeepers, online populists also disintermediate (vis-à-vis traditional gatekeepers) while adding to the role of media with regard to how political actors respond to civil society. This change is unthinkable without digital media. One mechanism is that 'while the mass media adhere to professional norms and news values, social media serve as *direct linkage* to the people and allow the populists to circumvent the journalistic gatekeepers' (Engesser et al. 2016, emphasis in the original). But this mechanism needs to be put in the context of different media systems (Stanyer et al. 2016), and whether these systems enable or constrain this 'linkage' to become part of overall media attention space – or not. Populisms are gaining ground in the twenty-first century, and digital media help make it so.

4
The internet in everyday life I: sociability

Nowadays, much of our online time, apart from looking for information, is spent socializing.[1] In everyday (as opposed to workaday) life, this is no longer via email, but via sites such as Facebook and Twitter. 'Social media' has become the commonly accepted label for these technologies, which can be used here to refer to media for interpersonal (rather than institutional) active mutual engagement. This also sets them apart from passive or one-way use of entertainment media, and from the broader term 'digital media', which also includes searching for and using information that is one-directional. Miller et al. (2016) describe in rich detail how new media are used in different ways across the globe – they say 'the world shapes social media' (in other words, contexts shape their uses), and I shall draw on this work. But I will ask: are there also common patterns; in other words, do social media also shape our world, or our everyday lives?

Currently, social media are used most intensively among younger and, in India and China, affluent urban populations. It is difficult to know what to make of the difference between this and the usage among older, rural and poorer users. As in Sweden and America, these differences will fade over time, but as we shall see (we have already seen some examples), there continue to be divides, including in how people socialize via media. However, the argument here will be that the main effect of social media is to reinforce bonds by means of sharing content and fostering constant tetheredness to others and – as will be covered in the next chapter – to information. This online socializing now occupies much of people's free time, and it is distinct from economic online activity (shopping and the like) and from the use of online media for politics (which was covered in chapters 2 and 3) – even if there are also overlaps between all of these; for example, when entertaining content about politics is shared.

Social media for socializing are still changing, but a few are dominant across the globe. These include Facebook, Twitter, YouTube and their Chinese equivalents, but also others such as Pinterest and Instagram.[2] Surveys exist that tell us how many users of social media there are, including studies of particular aspects of social media or specific groups of users. But as yet, few studies have examined the uses of social media as they have become embedded in everyday life (the main exceptions will be discussed below). Fewer still have a global or comparative purview. Yet, as we shall see, for all the difference that, for example, the use of different social media companies in China make, there are some patterns that are quite similar across the globe, or at least among the four countries examined here.

4.1 Tethered togetherness

To understand online socializing, we need first to solve a puzzle that was mentioned in the introdution: that social media are neither broadcast nor interpersonal media. Instead, social media entail that people spend a good deal of time monitoring what others are doing. Here we can take Facebook as an example: from the side of the user's Facebook page, we have the – online – presentation of the self (a concept from the sociology of face-to-face interaction), and from the side of those they are displaying themselves to, we have 'audiences' (a concept from media research). One way to think about bridging this divide between the two research traditions and between face-to-face and mediated interaction is to make the two sides symmetrical: to consider the presentation of the self as a form of mediated communication, and to treat how audiences receive this self-presentation as a form of receiving a personal address rather than as a (broadcast) media message.

If we do this, we notice immediately that a user's Facebook page is a mediated front stage, a means of presenting the self in a communicative format (via text, image/video and voice); so for self-presentation, media work is needed. On the other side, the 'audience' interprets the mediated and staged self in terms of participating in an interaction that is like a face-to-face encounter rather than passively watching a performance: this is so unless the 'audience' has no interaction with the person posting – as when a Facebook post is aimed at an 'imagined audience' (Litt and Hargittai 2016), but the post is never read. In this case, however, there is in fact no effect of the medium except on the person posting. This means that we can treat social media users as media performers or actors on the 'sender' side and the audience or 'receivers' as being onstage and facing or listening to the performer or actor. Put differently, social media always involve interaction and social selves, never one-way communication.

Now, if we frame social media interaction in this way, we have different dramatic encounters taking place and linking people: people engaging in mediated, though asynchronous, encounters where they manage the impressions about themselves ('news' about oneself and how one sees the world) and responses by their audiences (posting a reply), and so there is bi-directional impression management in a ritual of social (here, sociable) interaction. Notice that there is no backstage, as in Goffman's work, since both the self that one 'gives off' (see Baym 2015, 105–19), and how the audience responds by affirming that they recognize the self that is given off, take place in public (though as we shall see, access can be stratified). This, again, puts the audience on stage and makes it active: posts typically take the form of affirming the other, or affirming that people agree with or recognize how the other person presents him or herself. In short, the audience becomes active, while the performer elicits this activity. Further, the performer cares about how the audience responds, monitoring the responses to his or her self-presentation.

A different way to put all this is that there is selectivity on both sides: in terms of how we present ourselves (this cannot be done in the same way as in traditional interpersonal communication, since we write, for example, to one person, or speak to them; nor as in mass communication where self-presenters play a pre-defined role, as with a news anchor or movie actor), and also in terms of the audience for this self-presentation (people monitor and respond in a more selective fashion; again, this is less possible in interpersonal communication and in mass communication). In other words, even when social media encounters expand, they are hemmed in by limited attention – on both sides. At the same time, anyone who uses social media is devoting more attention and more time to online as opposed to face-to-face sociability (not entirely, because of multi-tasking, but this, too, has limits). Online sociable interaction, which is becoming more frequent, can thus be treated as a mediated encounter, defined by a shared, though often asynchronous, focus of attention.

This way of thinking about social media combines Goffman (Meyrowitz 1985) and Durkheim (Ling 2012), whereby online sociability is pushing society – or at least our freely disposable time devoted to socializing – towards greater solidarity inasmuch as our mediated roles (self-presentations and how these self-presentations are perceived) are becoming more complex and differentiated. Indeed, the increasing multiple interdependencies between people in various differentiated roles form the defining feature of Durkheim's 'organic solidarity' (even if he discussed this in relation to the realm of work, rather than sociability, as here). These encounters are also becoming routine or everyday rituals, tethering us more to each other, which can be seen as a Weberian cage. It is, though, a 'rubber' rather than an 'iron' cage since socializing online is part of our freely disposable or leisure time, and creates emotional solidarity rather than impersonal or 'cold' constraints (Schroeder and Ling 2014). 'Caging', or 'tethering', is nevertheless apt since these mediated relations are inescapable – they are the norm – even if, again, it is a rather pleasant cage. The space of the encounter is a 'third place' (Oldenburg 1989), neither work nor home, but it is also less public than third places (such as Oldenburg's hairdressers, parks or pubs) since social media are confined to small groups of more sustained relationships. In short, social media uses constitute tethered togetherness.

4.2 The spread of social media

Against this background, we can briefly examine mediated sociability from a comparative and historical perspective. Sociability via media is, of course, not new. In the early days of the telephone, in the late nineteenth and early twentieth century, it was thought that this new technology would be used for very important political and business communications by only a few significant people. Instead, as Fischer (1992) has documented, and contrary to these expectations, the telephone first became widespread when ordinary people wanted to keep each other company over distances. Even phones only extended existing forms of mediated sociability: they added to and complemented letter writing as a means of mediated sociability (Licoppe and Smoreda 2006). Jumping forward, the main difference with regard to social media is not so much the new devices or technology, but that they extend this sociability still further. They add multimodality to one-to-one voice and text – and now, also images and moving images, plus asynchronous anywhere connectedness, not just to a single person in a single location. Social media have proliferated since the early days of social network sites and they have become a routine or taken-for-granted part of everyday life (Ling 2012). In contrast to stationary phones and PC-based email, with smartphones, our sociability is 'always on' (Baron 2008): people often report that they check their devices first thing when they wake up and last thing before going to bed and that they would feel lost without their smartphones, their constant companions during the day.

Nowadays, Facebook dominates globally, but it was not the first, or the dominant, social network site to start with. In Sweden, Lunarstorm, with the same functionality as Facebook, was popular among the majority of young Swedes in the late 1990s, even before Facebook was launched, though Facebook has now eclipsed all other sites in Sweden. In India, Orkut was the dominant social network site before it was displaced by Facebook. And in China, Facebook has been banned, although there are still tens of thousands of users in mainland China. In any event, China has a variety of equivalents, including an early site, Renren, that was quite similar to Facebook in being centred on university students. But among the four countries here, China is now the only country where Facebook is not the main social network site. In China, WeChat has become the most popular site, but China is also unique inasmuch as there has been much competition between several different sites, and especially QQ and Sina Weibo. Even in China, however, the main function of social media is online sociability. Miller et al. (2016) detail that there is a rich variety in terms of what people post. But for young – and in India and China, affluent – people, social media have become the dominant means of mediated togetherness, by time spent and number of 'contacting episodes'.

Facebook is the main social media site in Sweden, America and India. According to Statista, in 2014 (http://www.statista.com) Sweden had more than 5 million active Facebook users (in a population of just under 10 million), the United States just over 150 million (in a population of almost 320 million) and India almost 110 million (in a population of more than 1.25 billion). According to Pew (Duggan et al. 2015), 70 per cent of online Americans use the site, 45 per cent several times a day. In Sweden, the same proportion of online Swedes (70 per cent) use the site, and almost half use it daily (Findahl and Davidsson 2015, 40), with Swedes using social media for almost an hour per day (2015, 48). There are no figures on frequency of Facebook usage for India (that I am aware of). In China, WeChat is the most popular social media site, with more than 650 million monthly active users, 90 per cent of whom use it every day, 50 per cent of whom use it for more than one hour, and 61 per cent of whom open it more than 10 times a day (Tencent 2016). While these numbers are interesting, what is more important is their significance in terms of the way they change daily life.

Everywhere social media are proliferating and becoming more differentiated: from the original function of connecting 'friends' (university classmates), these sites now connect more and less outward-facing groups (for example, some use them within the family, some for presenting the family to the world at large) and for different socializing purposes (WhatsApp for messaging, Pinterest and Instagram for sharing hobbies and photos, and YouTube for sharing video). Beyond social media, there are other tools for sociability, such as Skype for video communication. And apart from sociability (which lies beyond the scope here), there is even greater differentiation: there are social media for work, such as LinkedIn; journalists forming separate cliques with their own followings on Twitter; or celebrities becoming marketers and advertisers on Twitter and YouTube, and many more.

Greater differentiation leads to denser, more frequent and more multiplex or multimodal sociability, where multimodality also includes sharing content. It can be added that from the perspective of the social media companies, proliferation is a problem, since these companies want their products to be as multipurpose as possible so that users spend time on their network exclusively (or several, if they are controlled by the same company; for instance, Google+ and YouTube). Here, too, there is a competition for limited attention. Some platforms are more successful in this than others; for example, QQ and WeChat combine many functionalities.

Networks do their best to lock users in so that all of their relationships stay on the same network, but China has seen a migration of people from one set of networks to others. This may seem to contradict the fact that networks have many functions, but in fact, in China people use several social media in a complementary way, and it is not yet clear whether some will fall by the wayside. In any event, despite competition for attention (or lock-in to one network), unlike in politics, this is not a zero-sum game: people can use several networks and spend more time. The limit here is the amount of time people spend socializing.

The number of social media is growing, and content is therefore ever more differentiated, but this is compatible with the trend whereby a few top social media sites dominate: differentiation and concentration are not mutually exclusive. But in all four countries, digital technologies are increasingly market-oriented. China is something of an outlier in this respect, with its different nationally specific social media companies. These are more strongly subject to influence by the state in terms of political and social control (see chapter 2), though here, as elsewhere, they emerged in competitive market conditions (Pan 2016). Differentiation also applies to content, but people don't 'select' open-endedly: they pay attention to limited types of content. And while devices are also proliferating, different functionalities can be combined on devices such as smartphones: device convergence or de-differentiation is compatible with differentiation and divergence in types of content and modalities and uses.

In short, there is simply more mediated sociability. Yet there is also a major divide: Napoli and Obar (2015) say that a 'mobile underclass' is being created. In India and China (of the countries discussed here), social media are commonly the first experience of the internet, via smartphones. And smartphones also continue to be the most common way to access the internet in the two countries, rather than computers. Yet what Napoli and Obar show is that smartphone access to the internet is generally inferior to computer-based access: the disadvantages include the fact that fewer sites with lesser functionality are available, that screen size and a smaller keyboard entail shorter and less 'immersive' sessions, that downloads are slower and that users often stay within the 'walled gardens' of apps.

Napoli and Obar discuss this divide in the abstract (based on a review of studies); Donner (2015) discusses it from the point of view of extensive study 'on the ground', including in India and China. He notes that, even with extensive mobile access, in these and other countries, where for large parts of the population, data plans represent a major expenditure, there is a 'metered mindset' whereby people use social media only sparingly.[3] At the same time, he cautions against the idea that the more restricted uses in the developing world should be seen as inferior: many non-instrumental uses of the mobile internet can be seen as equally important as those used for economic activity and the like. Nevertheless, in Sweden and America, most people have access to the internet and social media sites via computers, too, and mobile access is added to other ICT uses (including tablets) rather than restricted to mobiles. This divide will continue to play a role even if it also shrinks over time (Schroeder 2015). Suffice it to say here that the denser and more intensive sociability via social media remains hemmed in in India and China, a sociotechnical divide quite apart from lower internet penetration rates.

4.3 Sociability and social divides

Sociability is about belonging to groups: family, friends and acquaintances. For the sites that Miller et al. examined across several countries, their subjects 'generally assumed that people seek to show the best or idealised versions of themselves to their peers, at least on public platforms' (2016, 156). Belonging is thus also about aspirations, and so groups try to set themselves apart. Aside from the sociotechnical divide between mobile-only social media users and those who use various devices, what kinds of social divides or forms of stratification are there in social media uses?

One group that has been studied in detail is the professionals who work in Silicon Valley at high-tech companies, including of course social media companies. In her book *Status Update* (2013), Marwick shows how this group pays an extraordinary amount of attention to its online self-presentation in order to enhance its status within the relevant social circles and beyond. Marwick argues that this is a requirement of the new neoliberal mode of capitalism, where an entrepreneurial self needs to be fashioned. Put differently, capitalism is shaping how this elite group sets itself apart in terms of the 'idealized version' of its appearance.

But it is not clear that this kind of self-presentation is unique to neoliberal capitalism. Take, for example, the farmers studied by Oreglia (2013) in China who seek social status by gaining points in the online game Farmville, which also chimes with their occupation. Status seeking, as Miller et al. (2016) show, or conforming to the norms of one's social groups, is common across social media around the world. On social media, people affirm belonging or status online, which in the case of Silicon Valley professionals happens to be the 'hip' culture of the high-tech world. But status seeking is on display everywhere on social media, for example, in the luxury clothes and celebrities found on the Facebook pages of poor urban Indian youth (Rangaswamy et al. 2013), or the fantasies of consumption, including sports cars and luxury weddings and interiors, posted on QQ among urban and rural Chinese (Miller et al. 2016, 168–9). Status seeking, rather than being a sign of selfish materialism, can be seen as a sign of 'belonging', not just in consumerist capitalist societies but also in Asia (Trentmann 2016, 399).

It might be thought that in Sweden, a society known for its egalitarianism, such status seeking and stratification would be less common. Nevertheless, Sweden also has a wealthy stratum just like other societies, and it is revealing how social media reflect these divisions. To give just one example: Holmqvist has given a detailed account of Sweden's most elite suburb, Djursholm, on the outskirts of Stockholm. Djursholm is known throughout Sweden as the home of its business, political and cultural elite. Holmqvist (2015, 41 ff.) discusses a blog from 2011–12 that was maintained by a homemaker under the name of Housewife@ Villa Drott with 828 posts. The blog is a diary of an opulent lifestyle of a very well-to-do household, with the self-described housewife narrating and sharing photos of the consumption of healthy foods, her exercise and weight regime, exotic holidays and the splendours of her environment. The blog reads as if it belongs in a lifestyle magazine about the rich and famous.

This blog (www.djursholmsmsfru.se, as it then was) provoked a strong reaction on other blogs, with one blogger (https://www.flash-back.org/t1647478) accusing 'housewife' of 'living in a bubble'. Others weighed in to defend or criticize the appropriateness of celebrating wealth in such a public forum. Holmqvist argues that this is a case of Durkheimian boundary maintenance around an exclusive lifestyle, but it could equally be seen simply as an expression of online consumerism. This example also shows that stratification and social cohesion are not necessarily at odds, at least online: Sweden's egalitarianism is affirmed by this Durkheimian boundary maintenance, just as the aspirations of Silicon Valley professionals affirm the American hierarchical status order wherein these elites set themselves apart.

Everywhere, according to Miller et al. (2016), people need to arrange their social relations online, putting people into different groups on different social media platforms and organizing various kinds of relationships with them. While this is a leisure activity, it can also be burdensome, as Nippert-Eng (2010) has documented: she says that people learn how to 'manage demands' (2010, 179; see also Burchell 2015), which includes giving priority access to oneself for different people or groups via various channels (and ignoring or blocking undesired and 'spam' contacts altogether). This 'management' creates a hierarchy or stratified order of access, as with offline relations. And it takes substantial effort to maintain different front and back stages, though with social media, the only back stage is when sites are kept private for certain groups. Maintaining this order of access has become so routine that it is often invisible to the participants themselves, even if it is evident to the social scientist.

Other social divides include gender and age. Here it can suffice to mention that in India and China, according to Miller et al. (2016: 117–18), social media use is highly gendered, with families upholding ideals of femininity and virtue. The same applies to the gendered use of mobile phones, though Doron and Jeffrey (2013) found that restrictions on mobile media by women and girls were balanced by the way that their uses also undermined traditional gender roles. For young people in India and China (as in America and Sweden in the early days of social media), social media use affords status among urban youth (for India, see Kumar 2014), as does the number of friends. And these urban youths post pictures of sport idols and cinema stars with whom they would like to be associated, just as older people might post pictures of family and children and grandchildren. To sociologists of culture, it is no surprise that status is differentiated by age and gender, offline and online.

In India and China, there is still a major divide between urban and rural. In the urban factory town setting studied by Wang (2016), where rural migrants made up two-thirds of the population, there was a strong segregation, both online and offline, between migrants and the original population of the town, which used to be mainly engaged in agriculture before the rapid growth of factories and the arrival of migrants. Yet this kind of 'snobbery' is not confined to the 'locals': migrants from rural China also delete their former friends and ties from home, since they want to distance themselves from their origins and aspire to the 'better' new 'modern' lives of their destinations.

Similarly with the migrant women in China studied by Oreglia: 'The Internet was,' she says, 'in many ways, the safest place to explore their new-found urban identity – away from the reproaches of their families who were suspicious of the freedom these women had found in the city, but also away from the criticism and the instructions to "improve themselves" that they constantly received from urban residents' (2013, 111). In India, too, mobile phone use is slowly allowing younger people to shift away from customary divides in rural households (Doron and Jeffrey 2013: esp. 183). Across all these divides, we can see boundaries being maintained around the groups with which one socializes, while social media also reinforce the cohesion within these status groups.

4.4 Visual co-presence

Most social media users post pictures and many also post videos, though far less is known about this more recent phenomenon (but see Miller and Sinanan 2017). Duggan (2013) found that over half of American internet users had posted photos and over a quarter had posted videos they had taken themselves. But the phenomenon is widespread around the world: Miller et al. report that 'in many of our field sites, posting on social media is overwhelmingly visual'(2016, 155). One reason why posting photos has become so popular, apart from the fact that mobile phones have cameras and this makes taking pictures easy, is that photos enable people with lower levels of literacy to express themselves more easily and powerfully (Miller et al. 2016, 170). The same applies, of course, to mobile voice communication in India, for example, which enables those with lower literacy to communicate (Doron and Jeffrey 2013). It can be added that leaving voice messages has been a very popular function on WeChat, so it is not only visual communication that overcomes low literacy (or the effort of typing).

What kind of visual material do people post? Hu et al. (2014) examined the content of photos among personal (rather than institutional) users of Instagram and found that almost half were either 'selfies' or photos of 'friends', with roughly half in each of these two categories. The other six categories, in descending order of popularity, were 'activities' (outdoor and indoor, such as landmarks and concerts), 'captioned' photos (i.e., memes with text), 'gadget', 'food', 'fashion' and 'pet'. Users could be grouped by which of these types they posted most frequently, but in terms of the number of followers that this gained them, none of the groups stood out. It can be added that Miller et al. argue that selfies are far from narcissistic: in the English field site, for example, young people post five times as many of themselves in groups than alone (2016, 156). On Instagram, in contrast, photos posted are 'usually' of individuals (Miller 2016, 82), so different social media also vary by the type of content posted. Along similar lines, they also differ in terms of whether they are shared within groups, as among the young people in England that Miller studied and who avidly used Twitter, or if, as with Instagram, the content is more directed at the world-at-large or outward facing (Miller 2016, 84).

Instead of narcissism, then, visual self-presentation, unless it is for entertainment or commercial gain, is part of sociability. The survey carried out by Malik et al. found that photo sharing on Facebook was carried out mainly with 'an intention to gain popularity and attention' or for 'seeking affection' (2016, 134). People frequently post photos of social occasions, which include both special events but also mundane everyday life. They seek to share these occasions, not just cementing their bonds through these photos, but also generating a sense of being together online. Licoppe (2004) spoke some time ago of 'connected' presence, as applied to mobile phones and phatic communication, but this notion can just as well be applied to posting and sharing photos. For photo sharing, Ito and Okabe (2005) therefore speak of 'intimate visual copresence', which points towards visual togetherness.[4]

The same applies to YouTube and other means of video-mediated communication. Lange (2007), for example, describes how some of those who post YouTube videos use this channel as they would a social media site, posting for only a small circle of friends and family and engaging in bi-directional exchanges (as opposed to celebrity posters who broadcast in one direction, though they may also engage with their fans via comments). Postigo (2014), examining video-game commenters, notes that commenters mainly engage sociably with those who subscribe to their channels, and need to avoid excessive commercialism so as not to alienate them. Cunningham et al. (2016) similarly talk about YouTube and other social media as being 'connected viewing', where having a site that brings commercial gain may not necessarily be in tension with socializing with one's audience or fans. Or again, although Skype is often seen as an instrumental mode of communication, Kirk et al. (2010), studying video-mediated communication in the home, found that it was mainly motivated by a desire for 'closeness'. And the same applies to messaging apps like WhatsApp, which are similarly mainly used for everyday togetherness or solidarity, and less so for instrumental reasons such as arranging to meet up and the like (see O'Hara et al. 2014).

To be sure, with regard to posting images and video, there is a need to be careful about what is made public. Lange (2007) discovered, for example, that people posting for their social circles conceived of ways to tag on YouTube such that only those for whom the videos were intended would be likely to find them. Since the focus here is on sociability rather than on policy issues, we can leave to one side the extensive literature about the suitability of posting certain photos on Facebook and other social media sites. But we can see that for being together online, photos and video provide an easier and often richer way of conveying sociability and reinforcing social bonds. For visual social media, also, the main function is reinforcing cohesiveness, even if here, too, there are divides. And while displaying photos on social media used to be regarded as tech-savvy and, in China and India, as 'modern', it too is rapidly becoming domesticated and commonplace, including the appropriate norms.

4.5 Alone or together?

The increasing use of social media has prompted debates about whether being online is fragmenting society and isolating people. What is telling is that when this concern is aired, it always seems to apply to others, not to those who write about the topic. Yet it is understandable that this should be a concern, since the decline of sociability or of social cohesion has also been a perennial worry in terms of offline life, especially in America (Putnam 2001). Many studies have found, however, that there has been no such decline in sociability (Hall and Lindholm 2001; Fischer 2011; 2014). Fischer (2014), for example, argues that there has been no overall increase in social isolation in America: he illustrates the point by noting that although people may have fewer family dinners, instead they eat out – together – more. And he argues that surveys show people report less loneliness overall and that people who use the internet 'increase the volume of their meaningful social contacts' (2014, 24). The internet is a social technology, whereas books and TV could be seen as more asocial, though they can be highly social too if we think of reading groups and 'water cooler' conversations about TV programmes – or sharing YouTube links. As Miller et al. (2016) argue, the idea that socializing online takes away from offline socializing is misleading: there is much more to talk about offline if one can talk about online content, something also true of television.

There are also moral panics about whether social media are causing a decline of face-to-face togetherness, as with Turkle's *Alone Together* (2012). She argues that we learn less about ourselves and each other as we interact more and more with and through technology. However, this can partly be explained by the bias that human beings (and researchers) have for seeing face-to-face interaction as the gold standard for social interaction. This is misleading, as Walther (1996) showed some time ago: he argued that we can in fact learn more about each other in a mediated environment with fewer social cues, though it takes longer – as, for example, when we get to know a stranger online via text. This can take time, but mutual self-disclosure in words can be more revealing since it is devoid of, for example, the social cues of appearance.

The question then is whether Walther's finding from experimental social psychology also applies to mediated togetherness in everyday life. Clearly, online sociability is different from face-to-face encounters: we can choose what we pay attention to, though not entirely, since, for example, there are expectations about paying attention to each other even in asynchronous mediated interaction, and also in groups as opposed to pairwise online and offline interaction. Sociability requires reciprocity, unlike mass mediated communication. In social media, unless mutual attention is paid, there is no bond or shared emotional mood, which is a prerequisite of both off- and online sociability. This is also why, as mentioned earlier, the notion of an audience, if understood 'passively', is misleading for social media: unless there is active engagement, unlike with solitary or one-way engagement with mass media, there can be no sociability. An audience makes sense for social media when the aim is to address the 'public', as with online celebrity or civic engagement or marketing; in other words, for purposes other than reinforcing personal bonds. Social media for sociability, in contrast, are aimed at an intimate sphere in which personal relations are affirmed.

To understand sociability in this way, we can consider how, even when mass media content is consumed together – say, on a couch – it is the common mood and shared attention that are the sociable elements, not the content itself. Consider further how, if social media are used for self-promotion or for the promotion of products, this detracts from their sociableness: social media must be regarded as authentic, as personal, in order to count as part of socializing. Finally, we can think about the post on social media that receives no comment or feedback; without receiving attention or a reply, the person posting may feel lonely or left out. The mutuality of sociability thus explains a difference between social media and face-to-face encounters: the former are more diffuse since they are episodic; the latter sustain the emotion or intimacy as long as there is physical co-presence and a common focus of attention. But episodic mediated interaction also sustains ties, and larger groups can equally sustain a shared mood, as with face-to-face interaction, though there are limits online in this regard just as there are with offline interaction – for example, in large crowds. Nevertheless, online, these ties and moods are also dispersed across time, whereas offline, they are bounded by space.

The limits in both cases are the boundaries of the groups with whom we have close ties. A number of studies (Dunbar 2012) have demonstrated that being online does not increase the size of the small group, consisting of a handful or two, of people with whom we have intimate relations, nor the larger groups with whom we socialize (up to 150) or the even larger number of up to some 2,000 that we know by name. Apart from the number of people with whom we interact socially, the geographic reach of online sociability should also not be exaggerated: Ling et al. (2014) have shown, for example, that our regular and most frequent contact via mobile phones, both text and voice, is with a small number of people. They analysed mobile call records from the dominant mobile operator in Norway over a three-month period and found that most connections are with a small group close by: 'the mobile phone...is used in the maintenance of everyday routines with a relatively limited number of people in a relatively limited physical sphere of action...the stronger is our tie...the closer they are likely to be geographically' (2014, 288). Social media may no doubt expand sociability geographically beyond the text and voice of the mobile phone, but like mobile phone interactions, they mainly add to the frequency and density of online interactions.

With frequent and multiple interactions, there are also limits, aside from the size of the sociable group, in terms of the time spent on these interactions. Lomborg (2015) notes, for example, that with smartphones, people are constantly checking and devoting only partial attention to content, and managing these interactions takes continuous effort. Along the same lines, Burchell (2015, 48), studying daily smartphone habits, says there is 'an expanded realm for communication . . . without focus on any single interaction'. Monitoring others via social media, or 'listening', as Crawford (2009) puts it, has become a routine part of everyday life, and it is simultaneously and paradoxically a way of taking time out from everyday life – in other words, making time for sociability – if by everyday we mean work or other practical tasks in which one is engaged.

There is yet another limit: although social media posts can be posted to anyone, social network site users imagine that they have more and less circumscribed types of audiences. In a study by Litt and Hargittai (2016), in over half the posts participants said they were addressing an 'abstract' audience of anyone. However, just under half the posts had a target audience in mind, and most of these were addressed to 'personal ties'. Importantly, when they were addressing an 'abstract' audience, 'they at times were focused more on the act of self-presentation and their rationales for sharing the content, rather than on the receiving audience' (2016, 7). When they had a more targeted audience in mind, on the other hand, 'they tended to have more audience goals, and were focused on the end-receiving audience' (2016, 7). Put differently, social media users expect more from their closer groups.

Over time, the expectations of social network sites about reciprocity have become settled. Brandtzæg (2012), in one of the few longitudinal studies of social network sites, found that those who use social networks for socializing increase over time, as opposed to those who use them for debating, lurking and sporadic use. It is true that some social media sites focus more on self-presentation than on socializing: so, for example, Naaman et al. (2010) analysed and categorized the posts of a sample of personal Twitter users (as opposed to organizations), and found that the largest message category was 'Me Now' (45 per cent) – that is, giving an indication of what the user is doing now. Other categories such as 'information sharing' (22 per cent) were less common, and so Naaman et al. could also divide the users by the proportion of messages posted into the more common 'Meformers' and the less common 'Informers'. Yet giving an account of one's state can also be a way of reaching out or, again, fostering 'connected' presence (Licoppe 2004). And it may simply be that Facebook is more social compared to Twitter, or that different social media have different kinds of sociability depending on the group that uses them – since Miller (2016) found Twitter uses among English teenagers more intensely social than their Facebook uses.

The moral panic or worry about a decline in togetherness is partly explained by attitudes to new technologies, which often hark back to a golden age of small-scale togetherness (no cars, no large and supposedly impersonal cities, no television and the like). Of course, for young people, learning how to present oneself to a larger public may bring with it many difficulties and anxieties, as boyd (2014, 199–214) has documented for American teens. Yet for teens this was also the case before the internet. And online togetherness is often experienced as helpful (Rainie and Wellman 2012) and rewarding and pleasurable too, just as face-to-face interaction can also bring a mixture of experiences. Further, interacting with technology should not be confused with how attention is being colonized by marketing or other forms of information overload (which, in fact, people do not, on the whole, experience as overload; see Hargittai et al. 2012). Instead, it can be argued that social media enhance togetherness since, unlike traditional mass media, they are not consumed passively. And if they displace traditional media, they are just as likely to take away from one-directional and solitary uses of media. Much writing about social media and the internet has focused on deviant behaviour, such as bullying and issues requiring policy interventions, especially privacy. Again, while this research focuses on important issues, it should not reflect on or deflect from the vast bulk of social uses. Durkheim saw society in terms of an increase in ever more differentiated solidarity, which can now be extended to mediated solidarity. The fact that 'deviance', in the Durkheimian sense, accompanies this process, should not be surprising.

4.6 Globalizing sociability

Do the uses of social media evince any common or global patterns? Among the countries examined here, China is unique in having social media that are separate from the rest of the world. However, it is not the social media platforms that are important, but what people do with them, and aside from the issue of state control, this means Chinese users are not so different from others. Further, it is important not to exaggerate the significance of the isolation of China in terms of sociability: in the urban and rural Chinese settings studied by Miller et al. (2016), few people care about the 'Great Firewall', unlike in the West where this topic dominates discussion of the Chinese internet. One reason why Western discussion takes this form is that less is known about Chinese social media, since few outside of China have social media accounts on Chinese platforms, just as few Chinese have Western social media accounts, though they have often heard about them. The fact that the Chinese do not have access to the largest websites worldwide is important for activists and professionals, but mainly it is a matter of curiosity for the ordinary people studied by Miller et al., who know about the large American internet companies and regard their commercial success with envy, but who are also proud of their own 'national champions' among internet companies. In any event, the main difference between online sociability in India and China as against Sweden and America is that social media use in India and China is more mobile-centric. And, as Ling has argued (2012), being available on mobile phones has become the norm everywhere.

The growing uses of social media do not erase cultural differences. Miller et al. (2016) highlight how the uses of social media represent different social norms in different cultures: men posing with beer and women with wine in Britain, or the different types of inspirational messages that are often tied to different religious and cosmological traditions in India and China. What is equally remarkable, however, again, is how much homogeneity there is in this diversity: social media present an idealized self and an idealized or desired lifestyle everywhere. Urban youth in India and China, for example, perhaps at the other end of the extreme from the American tech entrepreneurs and Sweden's powerful elite discussed above, express their aspirations on social media just as much as others do, although these aspirations may take a different form.

Everyday sociability takes many forms on social media, yet it is structured in similar ways by the affordances of social media. The interface layout, for example, shapes how people present themselves in their profiles, and it structures the chronology of updates and how others engage with the site. And despite the diversity of interfaces and content, there is a similarity of both form and types of content: for example, there is much diversity in how often people post, but the amount of time spent on social media, as we have seen, has grown everywhere. Similarly, shared moods, connected presence and the expression of aspiration can be found everywhere. Sociability via social media has become a daily ritual, and while ritual has so far been mainly used in the study of mobile phones (Ling 2012) and of mass communication (Rothenbuhler 1998), it applies equally to everyday habits of managing online togetherness. The many interactions or mediated encounters differ from face-to-face interactions mainly in the sense that they are episodic (when to engage in them can, to some extent, be chosen). Hence online interactions are also more diffuse, even though the frequent affirmation of ties, or the attention devoted to them, is also limited to an intimate sphere. Sociability via social media complements sociability via traditional technologies, and displaces other mass and interpersonal media uses, rather than displacing face-to-face sociability. The frequency, density and modality of connected presence is expanding, tethering us more to each other in ritualized exchanges.

Hence, as with other information and communication technologies (Rantanen 2004), social media are becoming globalized but they are also being domesticated in diverse ways. At the same time, more frequent exchanges are common everywhere and these interactions are becoming part of everyday life. Companies such as Facebook dominate across the globe (and Tencent is dominant in China), which is part of the reason why ideas about globalization focus on production and consumption at the macro level (Tomlinson 1999). And globalization is also correctly regarded as driven by the domination of a few global media companies, including social media: in India and in Sweden, only two of the top ten websites are Indian and Swedish respectively (http://www.alexa.com/topsites/countries), while the rest are American or global – for instance, Wikipedia (again, China is the exception). Yet sociability is driven by user content, not commercial or institutional content. At the micro level of everyday sociability, social media everywhere, or at least in the countries discussed here, have reinforced a more complex and differentiated sociable solidarity, and led to online togetherness becoming more visual, more frequent and more dense – an ever more homogeneously diverse way of life.

This change in the way of life has been caused by technology; technology has shaped cultural change. This idea is in keeping with the 'realism' that has been argued for in chapter 1, that technoscience transforms the social – including cultural, here socializing – environment. Socializing is also a good place to adopt cultural relativism; the idea that different ways of life – or at least (mediated) sociability – cannot be judged by supra-local norms (Gellner 1992). There is an exception insofar as some disadvantaged members of society, whether by dint of fewer sources or discrimination, depend more on social support via socializing than others. In this case, as with information seeking (as we shall see in the next chapter), media – or here social media – shape our capabilities (Sen 2009). Yet apart from this, again cultural relativism is appropriate for understanding mediated sociability. And more tethered connections, apart from shaping culture, are also one factor shaping how we are connected to the economy (as when our social relationships are used for marketing) and political changes (as with sharing news). But this connection is an 'orthogonal' one – orthogonal in the sense that political and economic changes and their increasingly mediated nature and our increasingly mediated sociability do not shape each other directly – political changes, for example, do not affect sociability, and vice versa. One of the questions for the next chapter will concern whether the same applies to information seeking.

5
The internet in everyday life II: seeking information

Increasing tetheredness has been enabled by a large technological system – an infrastructure – that grew out of landline telephony and morphed into email and mobile phones. In the previous chapter, this was updated to include social media. These developments in communication are well known and their social implications much discussed. Far less attention has been paid, however, to the change in information seeking. This is, in some respects, a more momentous change, since, before the Web, there was no ready equivalent to an encompassing information infrastructure. At the same time, as we shall see, seeking information online has become an activity that ranks roughly equal in importance– in everyday life, or in terms of time spent, for example – as sociability online. This chapter will begin by examining the infrastructure on which information seeking relies. Then it will turn to how we search for information and how search engines can be seen as gatekeepers. But what information do we search for? Here we must turn to the Web, taking both a top-down perspective of how attention is distributed around the world, as well as a bottom-up perspective of people's information-seeking practices – and also some examples of what they seek, such as information on Wikipedia.

5.1 A new information infrastructure

The strength of the domestication framework is that it grounds our understanding of new technologies in the context of everyday uses; its weakness is that it leaves out the larger technological and social forces that shape these changing uses.[1] However, there is a well-established concept that, with some modifications, explains these larger forces: 'large technological systems'. This concept was developed by the historian of technology Thomas Hughes, who used it to chart the development of technologies such as electricity, transport and communication that grew into vast systems or infrastructures (Hughes 1987). In their early phases, Hughes noted, these systems were still quite malleable and could take various directions. With maturity, the technological and social components increasingly intertwined, congealing and developing a momentum of their own (Hughes 1994). This also means that their force becomes inescapable and their uses become so routine as to be invisible.

The internet and Web are clearly a 'large technological system' that builds on previous systems – not just telephony, but also cable television, satellites and more. But this large technological system is also an 'infrastructure'– except that 'infrastructure' is often used for systems with universal or public-service provision. Yet the internet and Web are partly public and partly commercial. Other media in the pre-internet era such as radio, television and telephony also often straddled both, as did other large technological systems or infrastructures, for instance, transportation systems. The internet has extended media infrastructures, and nowadays Google, Facebook and others rely on 'common carrier' networks even if they are also private companies.

The internet and Web, enabling information seeking (just as they enable sociability), can therefore be seen as a large technological system or as part of a media infrastructure that includes print, broadcast and telephony. There has been a deepening and broadening of this infrastructure, leading some to speak of an information 'revolution' brought about the radical increase in the amount of information available (Hilbert and López 2011) or of an information flood (Gleick 2011). But even though the supply of information has increased dramatically, people do not perceive there to be an information overload in their everyday lives, and there are limits to the amount of online information that is routinely used, even if vastly more is provided (Hargittai et al. 2012; Neuman et al. 2012).

Seeking information is only part of what people do online. And only a small proportion of online information use is of interest to social science – search engine optimization and online advertising and shopping may be interesting for marketing and business scholars, but they are of limited significance to media scholars or those concerned with social change. Nevertheless, there has clearly been a change, perhaps not on the scale of the print revolution (Eisenstein 2005), but a change that can be appreciated when we think of the extent to which people use the Web on an everyday basis, and now also on mobile devices. People have become tethered to information, just as they have become more tethered to each other with email and social media.

Yet both information-seeking behaviour and the infrastructure that enables it are still changing. For example, there are now 'apps' that provide access to information – these are downloaded and in this sense are not part of the open Web. At the same time it can be anticipated that having information at our fingertips is 'taken for granted' (Ling 2012), as smartphones and other devices become commonplace, and as the online information infrastructure becomes more enveloping. Put differently, people are becoming dependent on the Web as an infrastructure in a similar way to how we rely on electricity and roads today. This makes it imperative to understand how the Web extends the media infrastructure without exaggerating its effects.

5.2 Seeking information

Searching for and accessing information online has become one of two main everyday online activities – sociability or communicating is the other. Communicating (email) used to be the main function of the internet before the arrival of the Web, but now communicating and information seeking are roughly equal in terms of what people do online (Purcell et al. 2012). As already mentioned, much has been written about communication and also about the economic and regulatory aspects of search engines, but we know little about information uses in everyday life. This is partly due to the fact that the vast bulk of studies on search engine uses and information seeking have been conducted by information scientists, who typically examine quite specific or narrow tasks. Jansen and Rieh admit that 'information retrieval researchers have paid little attention to the social aspects of information use' (2010, 1530).[2] Nevertheless, there are several studies that will allow us to piece together the larger picture of search engine uses and information practices in everyday life.

A useful way to think about information seeking is to note how routine this activity has become; in other words, this activity has become domesticated.[3] Domestication is a useful way to understand search engine uses since, as it turns out, these uses are to a large extent dominated by consumption. But much search engine use aside from consumption relates to practical, everyday concerns, and so also fits the domestication framework. What is missing in the domestication framework, as mentioned, is an appreciation of larger issues such as the gatekeeping function exercised by the dominant search engines or how the

Web is dominated by a few major websites or information sources. Before we turn to uses of the Web, we can therefore begin by examining the uses of search engines.

5.3 Search engine uses

Search engine use has become the second most common single activity on the internet – or at least we know this is the case for the United States. A survey by the Pew Internet and American Life Project found that 'search is only rivalled by email both in the overall percent of internet users who engage in the activity and the percent of internet users doing it on a given day'(Purcell et al. 2012, 5). This figure has steadily climbed since the early 2000s, so that by 2012, 59 per cent of adults using the internet used a search engine on a typical day (2012, 3). Google's share of American search engine users and the gap between it and the next most popular search engine also grew dramatically (Google has 83 per cent and the next is Yahoo! with 6 per cent: 2012, 9).[4]

We may also want to know, however, among other things, to what extent people using the Web go to a search engine or whether they go to a specific page. Here the Oxford Internet Survey (OxIS) for Britain (Dutton and Blank 2011) can help, since it asked internet users: 'In general, when you look for information on the internet, do you go to specific pages, use a search engine, such as Google or Yahoo!, or do you do both about the same?', to which 61 per cent say 'mainly search engine', 15 per cent say 'start with a specific page' and 23 per cent say 'both about the same' (2011, 22). When asked: 'How frequently do you use the internet for the following purposes', 'travel plans' is at the top of the list, but 'information about local events', and 'news' and 'health information' were also listed by more than 70 per cent of internet users (2011, 23). At the same time, OxIS asks a separate question about leisure uses of the internet – so not about information seeking per se – where 'listen to music', 'download music' and 'play games' all reach more than 50 per cent of those doing this frequently. However, as Waller (2011a) points out (and we shall return to this shortly), these OxIS questions could be interpreted differently from the point of view of the classification of various types of searches: why should 'listen to music' come under 'leisure', and yet 'sports information' (58 per cent), for example, comes under 'information' seeking in OxIS? Surely pigeonholing those looking for sports information as information seekers whereas music listeners, for example, are put into the category of leisure users, is problematic?

In any event, the key point here is that the internet has become a major source of information and leisure for British users. Unfortunately, the larger World Internet Project, which covers 16 countries, and of which OxIS is a part,[5] asks only about 'access to online information sites' and 'searching for products online' and not about 'search engine uses'. Yet if we also know that these users turn to the internet first when looking for 'professional and personal information' (rather than, say, using the telephone, going to visit in person, or using a directory or book: Dutton and Blank 2011, 22), and we further know that Google is by far the leading search engine in Britain,[6] then we also know that Google has become a major gatekeeper to information.

Apart from asking people how they search when they use the internet, what do their actual search queries tell us? Waller has had access to 'transaction logs to provide an analysis of the type and topic of search queries entered into the search engine Google (Australia) in April 2009', where it needs to be added that 'Google's market share is almost 90% in Australia' according to the company Experian Hitwise (Waller 2011a, 761). She also had data from the marketing company Experian about which of 11 lifestyle groups – broadly comparable to socioeconomic stratification groups – searched for which search terms.[7] She analysed almost 1 per cent of all search terms for a month, extracting a sample of 60,000 search terms, which accounted for 28.7 per cent of all search queries (a query typically consists of two or three terms). She then used 78 codes and amalgamated these into 15 broad subject groupings, such as 'high culture' and 'popular culture', 'Ecommerce', 'weather/time/public transport' and the like.

Her findings include that 'queries about popular culture and Ecommerce account for almost half of all search engine queries' and 'somewhat surprisingly, the distribution of topics of search query did not vary significantly across different Lifestyle groups for the broad subjects of popular culture, Ecommerce, cultural practice and adult' (2011a, 767). This is indeed surprising since others have found divides between more and less advantaged or expert and skilled users (for example, Robinson 2013), and we would thus expect different users to search for different things. We might also expect different lifestyle groups, or groups with a different socioeconomic status, to search for different things. Yet it seems that, in Australia at least, users from different socioeconomic groups have similar queries.

Another question (mentioned already) that Waller illuminates is whether people are 'searching' for something, or if they use Google as a means to get to websites they already know ('navigational search').[8] She says that 'only half (52%) of all queries were informational...For almost half of the queries (48%), the searcher appeared to have a specific website in mind' (2011a, 769). This means that informational searches have to be separated from searches where people know where they want to go: put differently, only half the uses of search engines are truly used to 'search' for content. Yet even for this 52 per cent of informational searches, she argues that leisure searches still account for one-third of these (2011a, 773). Since she finds such a high proportion of leisure searches, she says that 'to a searcher undertaking a leisure search, the question "Did you find what you were looking for?" is irrelevant' (2011a, 772). This points, again, to the fact that the information science approaches mentioned earlier, which focus on how effectively or successfully people find results, provide only a limited perspective.

Waller's overall conclusion is that the 'search engine is not only an interface to information or as a shortcut to websites, it is equally a site of leisure' (2011a, 761). Further, like other studies (for example, Hindman 2008), she finds that people looking for information 'on particular contemporary issues accounted for less than 1% of all search queries. Queries about government, including programs, and policies, accounted for less than 2% of all Web search queries'(2011a, 769). In short, search engines are mainly a technology for consumption, and less a technology for seeking knowledge and information. It can be added that it is of course difficult to separate leisure and consumption from other activities that do not fall into this category: a simple way to do this – this is my approach (Schroeder 2007), not Waller's – is to distinguish leisure and consumption, on one side, from work (including domestic work) or work-related activities, on the other. This distinction also coincides with the domestic or household sphere addressed by the domestication approach to new technologies, as opposed to the public world of commerce and politics.

Another question we can ask is: do people search for different types of content depending on where and when these searches take place? Segev and Ahituv (2010) analysed the most 'Popular Searches in Google and Yahoo!', that is, between 150 and 200 popular search queries, in 21 countries, over a two-year period in 2004–5. They looked at the differences between countries and whether users searched for political and economic materials, the variety of materials searched for, and how specific or general the searches were.[9] Their findings about the differences between countries are interesting, but in this case I want to highlight a different finding of theirs, which is how the most popular search queries can be classified. To do this, the authors made use of the Open Directory Project (http://www.dmoz.org/, now available only in the form of a no longer maintained mirror site), which was a volunteer effort to categorize the content of the Web. Using this directory in their analysis of 4,474 queries, Segev and Ahituv put 1,950 queries into the category of art – within this category, the five largest subcategories are music (839), performing arts (265), celebrities (187), movies (174) and animation (165); sports (473), which contains two dozen or so different types of sports; recreation (418), with the largest subcategories being travel (247) and autos/cars (49); and society, with the largest subcategories being holidays (181), chats and forums (69) and religion and spirituality (38). News (346), reference (197), shopping (180), business (173), games (167) and computers (86) make up the bulk of the additional search queries, with the remaining 4 categories totalling 59. What is striking here is that, as in Waller's analysis, which uses different categories, well over half of all the most popular search queries are devoted to leisure (if we include only 'art', 'sports' and 'recreation') in contrast with what we might understand as searching for information (if we put together, say, 'news' and 'reference', which make up less than 10 per cent and 5 per cent respectively). It can be added that although the authors show that there are national differences (for example, in specific versus general searches), these differences do not go against the broad patterns among the most popular searches that have been summarized.

Some further comments on this study are in order. It is clear that some of the categorizations of search queries are rather arbitrary (as we already saw in relation to OxIS): for example, there were 124 search queries in the subcategory of 'weather' under the main category of 'news' (346): but is weather news, or is it a search most closely related to the subcategory of 'holidays' under 'society', or perhaps to the subcategory of 'travel' under 'recreation'? This way of reshuffling categories could be subject to protracted discussion. However, again, the broad patterns of what people are searching for are clear, and by far the most popular searches are for entertainment (Segev and Ahituv 2010, 20). Within the Open Directory Project's classification, this preponderance of entertainment is catalogued under 'art', but a number of other descriptors, such as 'popular culture' or 'leisure' (which Waller might use), would work equally well.[10]

What these studies provide are some national, cross-national and cross-'class' results for the most common content that people search for, and for how these queries can be categorized or classified. These studies are from several countries (though focused on the Global North and using different methodologies: further research is clearly needed) and they provide us with at least a rough picture of search engine use: that search is widespread, that it consists only partly (perhaps half) of information *seeking* (while half of search engine use is accessing content one already knows), and that most of search engine use is for leisure or consumption.

5.4 Search engines as gatekeepers

Against this background, we can return to the question: do search engines act as gatekeepers? Search engines are clearly part of the infrastructure used to access information online. But there is one characteristic of infrastructure that does not quite fit search engines: other large technological systems typically have a sizeable 'hardware' component, and this is a major reason why they become so intertwined and congealed with social forces: power cables, roads and communications transmission all require a vast development of equipment and so major socio-organizational effort (including regulatory effort) to embed this hardware. Search engines too require considerable hardware: power stations, cables and an organization of tens of thousands of employees (Levy 2011) to provide search and other services. But compared to the internet and other larger technological systems, the technological and social components required for information seeking are relatively small: the main technological component of search engines is software, which is continually refined in the case of search engines. And software engineers are by far the largest share of Google's workforce (see Levy 2011).

However, search engines require one other constituent element that is unlike other large technological systems: billions of users' searches. Unlike with other systems (leaving aside the advertising part of search engines for the moment), these do not require great organizational effort, and they also do not need to be serviced in the sense of organizing user payment systems or support. Further, the regulatory aspects of search engines have been light so far in comparison with other large technological systems, and mainly relate to censorship, for example. The core of this large technological system is the operation of an – albeit by now quite complex – algorithm, combined with the massive scale of use that is made of this algorithm – a term to be discussed in more detail below.[11]

To be sure, as with any large technological system, technological and social forces are becoming more intertwined. As Hughes (1987; 1994) shows, these entanglements grow over time, and it can be expected that as Google and other search engines become more embedded within the infrastructure of the internet/Web, these entanglements will continue. For example, Google continues to expand, as with YouTube, and it has made forays into entertainment, shopping and other consumer areas. It has also moved into realms that are partly the preserve of public infrastructures – for example, with Google Books (again, raising relatively major regulatory issues compared to Google's core business). In the area of search itself (again, bracketing the advertising industry part of search), there are growing concerns over privacy, for example with the 'filter bubble' effect (Pariser 2011), whereby search engines are able to target users. These and other issues are bound to become increasingly regulated and bogged down in other social forces. This is the standard path for large technological systems or infrastructures – we can think here again of transport and electricity. Still, it is the technology of search (making use of relatively small-scale hardware), and the algorithm, working on a massive scale, that determines which content is accessed on the Web.

5.5 Does Google shape what we know?

Are search engines, then, and Google in particular, gatekeepers? 'Gatekeeping' as a term comes from a tradition in the study of media and political communication concerned with who decides what news is being watched, read or listened to. It has recently begun to be applied to the internet/Web (Barzilai-Nahon 2008). Yet there is a key difference between search engines and other media in respect to gatekeeping: on the one hand, the *whole* of the large technological infrastructure of the Web is available to users (again, putting aside for the moment issues of who lacks access, and China plus some other countries with censorship), in contrast with other media or infrastructures that are often national or have a limited reach. At the same time, gatekeeping in relation to search engines does not pertain to content: Google provides no content itself (or only a tiny amount), but it provides access (again, with exceptions such as censorship) to the whole of the Web's content.[12] Thus, instead of gatekeeping, it is more appropriate to speak, in the case of the search engine component of this infrastructure, of a monopoly of attention – in this sense shaping everyday life. Google has a dominant 'audience share' of attention, in comparison to all other gatekeepers; put differently, it determines online visibility or prominence.

In this (non-economic) sense, Google is monopolistic in shaping what we know. Caveats will be introduced shortly, but this is one part of how technology has come to shape everyday life. However, it is only half the story because it can immediately be added that Google is only the neutral algorithm that is shaped by what we, the users, want to find – again, unlike in the case of other media gatekeepers. As Granka puts it, 'aggregate analyses of Web traffic and Web behavior' as done by search engines 'only reveal the tastes of mass publics…we are not expecting search engines to change innate public opinion' (2010, 370). Or, more pithily, 'aggregate traffic merely reflects mass tastes' (2010, 371). Google and other search engines do not shape our attention, they only channel it. Put differently, whereas other media and information sources provide the content of our attention, Google focuses it.

Yet there is one modification we must make to Granka's statement: yes, insofar as users' attention is shifting to content on the Web, is being used routinely and as the main way to access information. We know the Web – or at least get to it – through Google. Hence this could be described as an autocracy – one ruler – though the ruler here is an automaton, a machine (or an algorithm), and a democracy – we, the people, or the users, determine its outcomes: an auto-demo-cracy.[13] This way of thinking about how search engines shape what we know can be contrasted with Introna and Nissenbaum's (2000) influential argument that search engines are biased and thus the politics of search engines matters. At the core of Introna and Nissenbaum's argument are two ideas: the first is that there is no transparency about Google's or other search engine algorithms. This is true, so one caveat is that neither I nor anyone apart from Google's engineers know just how autocratically-democratically its search engine works: for all I know, when I type in a query, there is a person at the other end – perhaps Sergey Brin, one of the co-founders of Google – who sends or serves me an individualized results page that he thinks suits me or that he wants to direct at me. This is highly unlikely, but it cannot be ruled out and points to the inscrutability of search engine algorithms. Brin and Page (1998) based their original idea for a search engine on the notion of hyperlinks as citations; that is, the more links (citations) a page gets, the more others must want to read it, or PageRank. This is still the underlying (algorithmic) basis of search, and this mechanism is neutral (it is an algorithm) as well as relying on having a large enough number of users – even if not a monopoly – to do this well. As Granka notes (2010, 367), the algorithm has become more complex than a single 'citation count' algorithm: in fact, to assess the 'authoritativeness' of a website, Google uses many rules, also to avoid spamming. Yet the underlying idea of PageRank still governs search. The problem, again, is that there is no way of knowing how this mechanism really works; it is a 'black box'.

Introna and Nissenbaum's second key argument is that search should not be left to market mechanisms since the Web is a public space or a 'public good'. They say that market competition between search engines will not necessarily reflect or provide the access needed – for example, to less visible sites that are overlooked by search engines – to sustain an open and diverse public space. In this sense, Google is biased against being a 'public good'. But again, it is hard to see what search engines are biasing us towards, except our own preferences, plus Google's 'content-less' aim of maximizing its audience or market share. As has just been argued, search engines are also a case of extreme democracy, the opposite of political bias, since each search or click counts as one 'vote' as to what others should read, see or hear on the Web (Google even suggests what we should 'vote' for, with its autocomplete function, which predicts and finishes our incomplete search terms). This may be a completely non-transparent regime, an autocracy, but it depends entirely on 'support' from its mass-democratic audience. If Google stopped having sufficient users, it would decline, since its results would become ever poorer as it could no longer update results in light of the changing content of the Web. Google's 'monopoly' thus relies on its users, except that, again, no one, with the possible exception of engineers within Google or other large search engine companies, knows what market or attention share, or what number of continuous users (what democratic constituency), is needed to keep a search engine working in an adequate way or in a way that is superior to its rivals.

Another caveat to the shaping power of search engines is needed: it could be argued that people have many ways to access Web pages without search engines, such as via bookmarks, links they are sent and the like. However, as we have seen, this is not how most people 'find' information most of the time: they use search engines as an easy means of accessing Web pages they already know, that is, the 'navigational' uses (in Waller's study, again, this constituted almost half of all uses: 2011a, 774). While alternatives exist, in practice, these common uses of search in accessing the Web dominate and thus shape everyday life in a pervasive way. In other words, there is a link between how these widespread uses reinforce the power of the technology – and vice versa. Or, to put it the other way round, it would nowadays be difficult to see how the Web could be accessed without search engines much of the time, which is how this large technological system and its key algorithmic component have become deeply embedded in everyday life.

It is true, of course, that Google has become a large commercial behemoth, which needs to generate large-scale revenues to sustain itself.[14] Yet this revenue-seeking does not bias the 'organic' (non-advertising) results as opposed to the 'sponsored' (advertising) results.[15] Hence, for advertising, there is a 'bias' towards a market mechanism, with those who have paid the highest price being placed at the top. Aside from this, search results are based on an algorithm and the ways in which it has been refined over the years. It can be noted that this is also why this large technological system has so far not encountered much entanglement with other social forces: roads and cars require a lot of regulation because they affect many other parts of society; search engine results are not affected by such entanglements. However, the exceptions – such as censorship of results and the like – are telling, and these exceptions have curtailed or shaped Google's dominant position.

The absence of an extensive hardware infrastructure can be seen in that the system of power plants and fibre-optic cables, for example, though complex and requiring considerable resources, is largely separated from users and results. Unlike other infrastructures, whose infrastructures are much more extensive, visible and physically demanding – if we think of road transport, for example – search engine infrastructures are largely 'invisible'. (Road infrastructures are too, but they have become so over the course of a century, and still often become visible, as when they break down.) Again, all that users see of this infrastructure, and use, is a simple rectangular box on their screen into which they put their query, plus the search engine results pages. The remainder of the 'system', the internet/Web, provides the bulk of the infrastructure, also not very visible to most users. The power of the technology rests to a large extent on its use by millions of users every day, and they are therefore as much a part of Google's dominance as the algorithm itself: I cannot think of any other large technological system where the users and uses of the technology reinforce its dominant position to a similar extent.

Note that I am not concerned here with term 'monopoly' in the economic sense (see Pollock 2010) or the market side of search engines, and thus with sponsored results (advertising). In fact, from the consumer side, the product is free, whereas monopolistic market behaviour can typically extract high costs. Monopoly could be used here to designate the dominant effect of technology uses in people's or consumers' everyday lives: in this sense, globally, and in the countries examined here (always excluding China), Google has a dominant share of searches performed – where dominant means, say, more than two-thirds. (In fact, Pollock points out, in economic regulation against monopolistic behaviour the cut-off that is often used is 50 per cent.) This figure of more than two-thirds market share applies globally (91.66 per cent),[16] and it applies in the United States (85.88 per cent), Australia (94.2 per cent) and the UK (88.99 per cent), the main countries discussed earlier, as well as Sweden (93.69 per cent) and India (96.65 per cent).[17] The exceptions are China, where Baidu (more than 90 per cent) dominates search engine use, and Russia, where Yandex dominates, and a few others: note, however, that these shares do not go against Google's globally dominant position in terms of attention.[18]

It is also worth noting that consumers or audiences are not the only search engine 'users'; equally there are all those who want to become visible, even if they are not advertisers: for example, academics. If we subtract advertisers (and thus sponsored results), these others include all those who would like to have an audience for the information they provide, such as bloggers, non-commercial news media, non-governmental organizations and many more. Ideally, the demand of consumers for information should be met by the supply of these information providers. However, in this competition for attention, these information providers, like search engine users, do not have much of a choice: how visible they are, or how much their web pages are accessed, depends to a large extent on search engines, especially the dominant one, and how attention is channelled by users.

The thrust of the argument can be appreciated by pitting it against two widespread ideas about Google. The first is the statement by Eric Schmidt, the executive chairman of Google during antitrust hearings in the US Senate, that 'it's also possible not to use Google search...the competition is just one click away'.[19] This statement is true in principle, but in practice, as we have seen, it is misleading, or at least sociologically naive: Google derives its power partly from the number of users, and partly from how its algorithm has been refined within a large technological infrastructure. More than that, it is not clear how fleeting Google's monopoly is – in the way argued by Schumpeter that technological advantage is inevitably fleeting, to be undone by 'creative destruction': it is conceivable that Google will maintain its advantage for some time, just as other large technological systems have done and continue to do.

The second misleading idea is that Google maintains its power through its political or social position. To be sure, there are instances of such entanglements: caving in to Chinese government censorship before the decision to abandon mainland China, or in relation to techniques to prevent 'gaming' visibility rankings, or lobbying the US and European governments in relation to communications and data policy, and more. These are no doubt important and, for reasons mentioned earlier, will become more so. Yet the statement is misleading because the bulk of how the technology works is indeed neutral: the results that are displayed are the product of an impersonal mechanism calculating the most relevant results, a combination of autocracy and democracy on a dominant – monopolistic – scale.[20] If Google no longer provided the results that people were seeking, then its powerfulness would presumably decline, despite the strength of its political or economic position.

A brief contrast can be made with Facebook, which also has a monopoly of attention based on users flocking to this free – aside from advertising – service. Facebook's overwhelmingly dominant position, however, is based on the well-known network effect whereby users are locked into their contact network – they are unable to switch to another network in which their contacts are not members, as with telephony in the early days, or with other social networks. Google's monopoly, in contrast, is based on the first mover advantage whereby the vast majority have used and continue to use its service without being 'locked-in' (Arthur 1989) by other users as their contacts.

It is important not to exaggerate the significance of monopoly and auto-demo-cracy: again, Google does not, for the most part, control content. It is a gatekeeper in controlling visibility and does so largely in a neutral way. Its power lies in the fact that a large part of our everyday lives is dominated and thus shaped by using the technology of one company. Google's slogan 'don't be evil'[21] seems apt here, as the *potential* for harmful control is highly concentrated in this case in a unique way. Yet any such perceived and known harm would also harm the company: indeed, the increasing awareness by users that Google knows a lot about people's habits, even where these do not pose a threat to individual users, is having adverse consequences for its reputation. Another famous Google slogan is equally apposite: 'Google's mission is to organize the world's information and make it universally accessible and useful.'[22] Again, the 'mission' is about organizing, not producing content, though this statement, like 'don't be evil', has the ring of an omniscient autocrat.

Again, this power should not be blown out of proportion: it is as if the electricity grid (another large technological system) was provided mainly by one company, though the electricity itself was provided by others. Indeed, this has been the case, and is still so, in a number of countries. Yet a dominant share of users use one grid. Or again, it is as if one company controlled the infrastructure of a medium such as the newspapers or television, with separate companies controlling the content, cases for which, again, there are examples. In both cases, as with Google, the dominant position inherent in Google's own slogans would be problematic only if Google used its position to deliberately extract advantage from a social science (not including economics) perspective, as here. Whether market dominance harms competition from the point of view of economics is a different matter (which I am not competent to discuss and not interested in here): the gatekeeping monopoly I am documenting is one of form, not content. Some scholars have hypostatized the effects of search engines and Google in particular, as their very titles suggest: *The Googlization of Everything* (Vaidhyanathan 2011) and *Search Engine Society* (Halavais 2008). But not everything is being googled, and nor do we live in a society pervaded by search: the uses of search engines must be put in their – limited, but significant – social contexts.

5.6 The Web of information

If search engines provide access to the Web, the Web itself is the source of information.[23] The Web has now been with us for more than a quarter-century and it has, like the internet of which it is a part, become a major part of everyday life. Yet like other digital media, it does not fit existing theories of mass or interpersonal media – for example, with user-generated content, which is a sizeable part of the content of the Web. So we can begin with a brief discussion of disciplinary approaches before we turn to examples of some everyday information practices, including Wikipedia, one of the most well-known and important sources of online information. And it is also important to examine the shape of the Web. We have already discussed what people search for around the world, but how global or otherwise is the Web's audience?

Like search engine uses, research about the Web has taken place largely in information science. But information science, again, focuses on narrow tasks or on specialized groups (such as library users) rather than on how people seek information in everyday life. Information seeking has so far been poorly theorized in the social sciences (Sonnenwald 2016; Jansen and Rieh 2010) and there has been scant research on the role of information seeking in everyday life (Hektor 2001; Rieh 2004; Savolainen 2008; Aspray and Hayes 2011). Search engine companies and marketing companies, of course, have a lot of knowledge about 'user behaviour' in information seeking, though little of this knowledge finds its way into academia.

Information can be defined as codified accounts that can answer questions such as 'who', 'what', 'where' and 'why'; or, as a cognitive input that makes a difference to the person's relation to the physical and social environment (a 'cybernetic' definition, see Gleick 2011). This sets information apart from the more complex 'knowledge', which can be seen as the more analytical processing or organization of information on one side (Stehr 1994)[24] and from the simpler or raw 'data' (to be discussed in chapter 6) on the other. Information can also be distinguished from communication: information is one-way (seeker to source), communication two-way (a sender to many receivers with mass communication, sender and receiver engaging in mutual exchange in the case of interpersonal communication). This makes it possible to distinguish the Web from other sources; the Web is primarily a one-way online source of information. A complication here is that the Web allows sharing via the sending of links, for example (for sharing news, see Kümpel et al. 2015). Still, these links are first sought – and then shared or communicated.

Accessing information is increasingly taking place online. But a distinction can be made between serious and non-serious information, a distinction that can be found (though it is not developed) in Savolainen's work (2008). Serious information relates to human needs, the practical means to develop one's capabilities (Sen 2009), as opposed to wants, which are not required for capabilities but rather for leisure or consumption. Wants and needs can perhaps be distinguished only in political philosophy, but Savolainen makes a distinction that is based on social practices, whereby serious information is restricted to 'not solely frivolous…purposes… [but] to monitor everyday events and to solve everyday problems'(2008, 51). And in this chapter, we can limit ourselves to information uses apart from work – in other words, outside of formal economic purposes, and also apart from news and political information, which have been dealt with in chapters 2 and 3.

Seeking online information is still changing, but it has also become so commonplace as to be invisible: we can think here of how often we, or anyone with internet access, 'googles' something every day. We can also think of the variety of questions that are 'googled': persons, places, schedules, brands, services, scientific and technological novelties, diseases, popular culture references and much more. Or again, think of how often we ask: 'what did we do before Google?' This question highlights the novelty of seeking information online. Accessing information on the Web is a departure not only from traditional mass and interpersonal media but also from offline media, which were constrained by their physical availability. And, as Savolainen (2008) points out, information practices have become increasingly central to making sense of the world; solving everyday problems depends on these practices. Information is both something required for short-term projects as well as a life-long endeavour in the sense of learning about the world.

One approach to understanding information seeking is to conceive of individuals selecting content from abundant or limitless sources online. But this approach overlooks the fact that there are new gatekeepers such as search engines or social media feeds or other constraints on the visibility or accessibility of web pages. And people do not select from all information; there are constraints to what they seek and find, dictated, among other things, by their digital literacy. And content competes for attention: for example, even if Wikipedia is often among the top results when using a search engine, there are many other online and offline sources that could be used instead (with and without the use of search engines). Online information sources are also examples of content being pushed towards users in a targeted way, as when search results prioritize finding Wikipedia articles – to continue with this example – because the search algorithm has been tailored towards particular users (Pariser 2011). Finally, these new online sources add to and complement others, but media systems also shape them: in mainland China, the Chinese-language version of Wikipedia has been blocked for certain periods, and a different online encyclopaedia, Baidu Baike – containing content controlled by the company Baidu, which is in turn influenced by the government – is dominant (Liao 2009). However, it is true that, apart from these new gatekeepers and competition for attention or visibility, online sources extend existing ones, often making them openly accessible, and so increase what can be 'selected'.

A number of methods have been used to understand information behaviours, including interviews (Savolainen 2008, Rieh 2004) and focus groups (Hargittai et al. 2012). Focus groups are useful because they can elicit responses of which people may not even be aware in their own behaviours (information seeking is often of this nature, since people do not consider it a separate activity, even though researchers do). For example, what Hargittai et al. (2012) found in their study of information seeking is that Americans did not think of themselves as overburdened by the flood of diverse types of information; in other words, there was no self-report of 'information overload'. What people found objectionable was the low quality and repetitive nature of this information – scandals, endless crime reports and tabloid-type news. Tellingly, however, they nevertheless consumed this information in abundance.

A different approach is quantitative, and we have already encountered the study of search engine use in Australia (Waller 2011a), which found that the vast bulk of content sought relates to consumer activity and popular culture. In the light of the distinction between serious and non-serious information that has just been made, it can be mentioned that less than 2 per cent of search queries in Waller's study related to 'serious information' such as civic, health and political information. Yet this small percentage still amounts to millions of searches per day in a country with a relatively small population.

A different study, again by Waller (2013), provides a 'bottom-up' perspective, since a top-down or quantitative perspective misses how information is actually used. To be sure, online information is available and it may be reliable, but can people actually use it? Waller (2013) gives the example of an immigrant woman in urban Australia seeking information that she needed to obtain from the Red Cross. Because of her situation, she was unable to access any of the information she needed online. Instead, she had to make several arduous trips to find the relevant Red Cross office in person, and then wait in queues to be seen. Finding this information took her several days, something a young person with the requisite educational, linguistic and digital skills would have found online in minutes! This is admittedly an extreme example, but it behoves researchers who have access to devices, online resources and skills, and with the ability to ask others in their networks – the most extreme 'information haves' – to think about people who have access to neither the devices or the skills, nor to others who could help them, the 'information-have-less' or 'information-have-nots' (see Qiu 2009). It is also worth bringing to mind how access to appropriate – or again, serious – information is increasingly becoming a vital resource in all walks of life; information, again, can be seen as a question of justice, essential to developing one's 'capabilities' (Sen 2009).

The advantage of a bottom-up user perspective is that it can challenge conventional wisdom. One further example can suffice: it is often said that China's censorship is highly effective and that it is particularly aimed at preventing 'harm' by strictly and effectively censoring (among other things) pornographic materials. This may be true for some materials, but as Hockx (2015) has shown in his study of 'internet literature', it is also highly misleading. First, by way of context, he notes that around 40 per cent of Chinese access online literature (a specific literary genre rather than simply reading books on Kindle-type devices, and nowadays often on mobile apps) – a uniquely high proportion worldwide. This surprising result is itself worth pursuing from a comparative perspective: is seeking out a Web-specific form of literature uniquely popular to China, or can similar phenomena be found around the globe? Second, Hockx documents the popularity of erotic fiction, bordering on being pornographic, particularly among women. While the government partly censors this material and online publishers are working to contain this phenomenon within limits, it is clear that censorship here, as in politics, is widely circumvented, and that online literature represents a source of online material that transgresses or pushes the boundaries of what is acceptable (as we saw with news in chapter 2). These widespread ways of seeking material online are not much discussed in top-down analyses of government internet policies, or indeed in the study of literary and cultural tastes. Yet understanding commonplace ways of accessing online materials such as these is highly revealing – in this case about Chinese cultural tastes.

From a bottom-up perspective, it is also important to consider the device that people use to access information. For many in high-income countries, and certainly for the majority in lower-income countries such as China and India, smartphones are already the main means of engaging with the internet and the Web (Donner 2015). This momentous shift has already been mentioned and opens up new 'digital divides'(Napoli and Obar 2015): for example, it may not matter a great deal whether people contact each other via apps on smartphones since they also have other means to do so. But for information, if people use smartphones, which are becoming constant companions and the means of mastering ever greater parts of our lives, and if non-digital sources of information disappear – then how people access information via smartphones, and what they access, will become an ever more central question. Yet, as Napoli and Obar point out, the experience of the Web on smartphones can be quite different from the experience of the Web on a PC.

Another example of these differences or divides is the use of the voice interface to search on smartphones (Siri, the assistant on the Apple iPhone is the most well-known example): in what way do the results of voice searches differ from text searches? Only one technical paper (Guy 2016) on this question exists to date, and it finds that search queries are indeed quite different: they are longer (unexpectedly so) and more like spoken language (expected). But this is becoming an increasingly common mode of access: in the United States, more than 50 per cent of younger people already use voice search on a daily basis (Guy 2016). It will be more important for those who mainly or exclusively use smartphones, and will be used ever more widely by those who simply find it more convenient in certain situations to search via voice. If the results for search via voice differ in important ways from those obtained via text-based search, then it can be anticipated that new information divides will open up.

It is not just search engine results that have changed; the way in which information is passed to 'audiences' or 'consumers' has also changed profoundly. That is because there is increasing competition for attention in a limited space or in a 'marketplace of attention' (Webster 2014). One reason, already mentioned in passing, is that information is increasingly shared via social media. Bright (2016a), for example, found that what is most shared from the BBC news website does not correspond to what is most read in terms of the stories on the main page. This kind of measurement also allows examination of how people search for particular topics. For example, Anderegg and Goldsmith (2014) show how interest in climate change has waxed and waned over time and how different search terms have been used ('climate change', 'global warming' or 'global warming hoax').

5.7 Is the Web global?

Apart from a bottom-up view, we can also look at the Web top-down. Here a key question is: how global is this new information infrastructure? To start with, there are some evident boundaries. The best example is China, which is often said to be cut off from the global web. Yet this is misleading in some respects: even in this restrictive environment, savvy internet users who wish to get access to information from within and outside the country can for the most part do so, except where online information has been removed altogether (Taneja and Wu 2014). A different way to gauge the global web is to ask: how many companies dominate online attention? It turns out that, despite the global dominance of Google and Facebook in online advertising, media concentration among old and new media is in fact surprisingly varied across the globe (see Noam 2016). Google, Facebook and Amazon are among the top ten in most countries, but even in China there are dominant websites that closely emulate these three: Baidu the search engine, Tencent with its social network site WeChat, and Alibaba a major retailer.

Web visibility can be measured by several methods: examining top websites globally and nationally, use of keywords in search queries (Google Trends) or, as mentioned, trending keywords for particular topics (Anderegg and Goldsmith 2014). In addition, more specialized tools can be used, for example, for Wikipedia article readership (https://en.wikipedia.org/wiki/Wikipedia:Pageview_statistics). A common method to gauge web visibility in the past has been to use hyperlink analysis to see how interlinked the Web is as a structure. This method, however, has been found to be a poor indicator of online visibility and Web audiences (Barnett and Park 2014; Taneja 2016; Wu and Ackland 2014).

That is because hyperlinks are often an indication of the aims of the web-masters who created the links, as well as serving a number of other functions – rather than of audience interest. Other methods include shared website use for the most frequently visited websites, globally or nationally, using Alexa.com (http://www.alexa.com/) rankings (Barnett and Park 2014; Taneja and Webster 2016).

A different method to measure global (and national) visibility is to measure online attention. This method (using data from comScore) was used by Taneja and Webster (2016). Based on 2 million panellists from more than 170 countries, it is measured once per month, and includes the top 1,000 Web domains and subdomains that together account for 99 per cent of Web user visits.[25] Among the findings are that 'similarity of languages and a common geographical focus of any two websites offer the best explanations of audience overlap between sites' and (as just mentioned) 'the number of hyperlinks between websites explains very little audience overlap' (Taneja and Webster 2016, 175). These findings are based on the idea of 'audience duplication', whereby the likelihood of a user visiting one site if he or she visits another site is higher than chance. These data are then aggregated to establish patterns of audience attention, which can then be correlated with other factors.[26]

This method can be used to examine clusters of visibility and how clusters of the most popular websites change over time. Wu and Taneja (2016) showed, for example, that these clusters have changed quickly within the space of the past six years: whereas in 2009, a global/US audience cluster was most central on the Web and at the same time the largest, in 2011 it was overtaken by a Chinese cluster (even if this was not the most central cluster), and there was no longer a global/US cluster, but rather in second place was a US/English cluster followed by a global cluster. By 2013, the same two clusters occupied the top two spots by size, but the global cluster (of websites that are not language specific, such as Mozilla and Facebook) had slipped to eighth place (India was ninth and Germany tenth), followed by a number of other clusters including sites in Japan and Russia, but also Spanish-language sites and those in Brazil and France.

What we see here is the evolution of attention on the Web as it becomes more oriented towards the Global South (Spanish-language sites and sites in Brazil and also India). We also see, with time, that websites with a 'global' status have become fewer in number among the world's top 1,000 sites, and we see language playing an increasing role. State policies promoting information access (such as broadband access) are one factor here and shared language is another. Whatever the most important factors may turn out to be, the Web is not becoming a single whole, but rather a series of clusters: linguistic plus those that develop due to the policies of states and sites promoting shared interests such as economic development strategies. So from the top down, too, in terms of how it is accessed online, information falls into certain patterns; it is not just selected from a vast sea of limitless possibilities.

5.8 Wikipedia

Yet another approach is to look at a concrete example of a single information source. Wikipedia is a good example since it is the only non-commercial website in the top ten around the world (http://www.alexa.com/topsites/). Much has been written about the content of Wikipedia and how it is edited (Schroeder and Taylor 2015) and a review counted almost 3,000 academic papers about Wikipedia by 2013 (Bar-Ilan and Aharony 2014). Yet almost nothing is known about what content is read (even though there are computational tools and data sources for finding out; for instance, https://en.wikipedia.org/wiki/Wikipedia:Pageview_statistics). Wikipedia is used across the world and exists in many languages (https://meta.wikimedia.org/wiki/List_of_Wikipedias). Global differences in accessing Wikipedia content by language and in different countries could be highly revealing. Equally revealing would be to compare Wikipedia with its rival in China, Baidu Baike, which, as mentioned, is more popular than the Chinese-language version of Wikipedia in China because the government has championed it and curbed Wikipedia (Liao 2009). Wikipedia is used very widely, but it also falls into the patterns for media systems that have been discussed here; namely, that Chinese media are largely separate.

Wikipedia, like other openly available online information sources, extends the range of sources of information available: it is more accessible and more comprehensive than other, similar sources, such as offline encyclopaedias. It has also become a widely used resource on a range of topics for many internet users. Yet there are also new gatekeepers: Waller finds that in Australia, 93 per cent of clicks on Wikipedia come via Google, and Google is the dominant search engine in Australia, with more than 90 per cent share (2011b) of search engine uses.[27] Interestingly, she found that the entries which people seek are quite diverse: of the 600,000 search queries that took users to Wikipedia, at least 400,000 appear only once. We also know what kinds of information these users were seeking: 38 per cent sought popular culture topics (only 2 per cent sought high-culture topics) and second most popular (15 per cent) were articles relating to cultural practices (sports, religion, holidays and the like). Science and health topics garnered 7 per cent each. As in her study of Google, Waller finds that Wikipedia's 'appeal appears to be fairly even across different segments of the Australian population. However, as in the United States, it seems that those in Australia with more income are more likely to use Wikipedia and older people and people with lower income are less likely to use it' (2011b, 15). In other words, this new information source also creates new divides, aside from those created by Australians who do not have access to the internet or the skills to use it if they do.

There is an interesting exception to how little we know about Wikipedia readership, also compared to other sources: entries about medicine. According to Heilman and West (2015), there are more than 155,000 such entries, more than 29,000 of them in English. How often are they read? In 2013, the English medical content received 2.28 billion (non-mobile) page views, just under half that of medical content in all languages on Wikipedia. 'Medical content accounted for 0.64% (0.029/4.5 million) of all articles on English Wikipedia, yet these received 2.49% (2277/91,252 million) of all English Wikipedia page views'(Heilman and West 2015, 7). This makes medical content on Wikipedia the single largest source of online health information in English, followed by the websites of the National Institutes of Health (NIH), WebMD and the Mayo Clinic. It can be mentioned that over half the editors of medical content pages (another source of gatekeeping) were health-care professionals. And mobile views of English Wikipedia were over 30 per cent in 2014. This kind of audience or readership information tells us a lot about where people find medical information, subject only to knowing more about how this fits with or is complemented by their use of traditional media and offline sources.

But while Wikipedia provides a source that is widely regarded as reliable for serious matters such as health, most of the content that is sought on Wikipedia via the dominant search engine Google, again, concerns popular culture and the like (Waller 2011a), which arguably falls into the category of leisure rather than 'serious' information. But once more, this is also true of search engine uses generally, which are mainly used for leisure and consumer-related information seeking around the world (Segev and Ahituv 2010). Thus online information seeking, in this case using Wikipedia as a resource, is mainly for topics that are not crucial. Still, it is easy to see that some categories of information (such as for health, science and civic topics) can play an important role in people's lives, even if they are far less common. Finally, again, Wikipedia is the only non-commercial site in the top ten across most of the world, but the top ten make up a vast proportion of the uses of the Web as a whole.

5.9 Information seeking and gatekeeping

Over the course of the coming decades, the Web will continue to be only one source of information among many, but it is arguably becoming the single most important one. We have seen that it is important to identify the internet as an infrastructure, a large technological system that is continually being extended but which also shapes, via gatekeepers such as search engines, how information is accessed. It is also important not to exaggerate the implications of this new infrastructure, as an information revolution or similar. Nevertheless, especially in view of how serious information has been singled out from the bulk of everyday information practices, there are policy implications, above all about access and the diversity, accuracy and openness of information online. More concretely, is the information diverse enough, or do pages that are manipulated to achieve a high page rank, for example, but that are of low quality, dominate the results? Are the sources reliable when it comes to, for example, political or health-related information? Are results in different languages and the results obtained by people with different levels of digital skills and education (Hargittai and Hsieh 2013) of equal quality? It may be that skills and coverage of different topics in different languages become more important than, say, questions of access to or censorship of online information – though all these questions will continue to shape the role of the Web. And as we see again and again, smartphones are becoming the dominant means of accessing the internet. We shall come back to these issues in the concluding chapter.

This chapter has discussed a variety of perspectives on information seeking and the Web. An overall framework of understanding Web uses includes the infrastructure of the Web (and how it is part of the broader infrastructures of information), how people search for information, how information online is accessed, via search engines, as well as the content of the Web and its clusteredness and how this relates to the ways in which attention is dispersed or concentrated among audiences or information seekers in everyday life. This also includes what content is most visible and receives attention, including in comparison to other offline and traditional sources. Within this, it is possible to focus on particular sources such as Wikipedia (or access to political information, as in chapters 2 and 3). These elements have been presented only briefly, but in a way that fits with the focus on everyday uses while also taking into account the larger forces shaping information.

This is how the technological shaping of everyday life works from a social science perspective; a new infrastructure or large technological system is now in place, and people routinely rely on it. And there are a small proportion of searches that are socially important insofar as they can be regarded as essential to social and individual well-being. This could be interpreted as a normative perspective, but it is also simply a fact that serious information is a significant part of everyday life.[28] This includes information ranging from health to diverse cultural heritage, to accurate scientific information and the like. (Again, selecting these as 'essential', or distinguishing between serious and non-serious information, is contested and there is a grey zone, but there are also clearly materials that fall into one or the other category.) While these areas constitute a small proportion of the content that is searched for, in these cases it is important that technology works in a way that enhances certain social (and ethical) values – ensuring the accessibility, diversity and reliability of search results and materials found. Here we can also come back to the role of users in shaping search engines, their 'mass tastes' (to repeat Granka's words). In this sense, search engines are 'democratic', but in democratic theory, there is also the well-known problem that majoritarian popular support does not necessarily safeguard minorities. Whether this should be Google's task or the task of other search engines or content providers could be debated. But there is no mechanism within Google or other commercial search engines to safeguard the requirements of serious information needs. Put differently, the market logic of information gatekeeping and provision is orthogonal to – and does not address – the requirements of information in a diverse society that needs reliable and open information. This is a problem arising from the relation between markets and the cultural order, and one that we will have to return to in the conclusion.

6
Big data: shaping knowledge, shaping everyday life

Knowledge about society has recently taken a new direction, with groundbreaking studies of digital media. Examples include analyses of Twitter, Wikipedia, Facebook, Google and smartphone use. These studies have been made possible by the availability of unprecedented amounts of data – although they are often limited by the fact that the data originates from private-sector companies. Another limitation is that they are not well integrated with accounts of other media or existing social research. As we have seen in previous chapters, new media do not fall into the two main traditions in the study of communication – mass versus interpersonal communication. For example, if Facebook users share news among a group of friends, this is different from exchanging news between two people but also different from broadcast news. Or again, if Twitter hashtags are created for particular events, they create an audience around the event rather than being part of one-to-one or broadcast communication. Search engines that tailor results to particular users or groups (the 'filter bubble' effect, Pariser 2011) are yet another example. And one more quite different example is Wikipedia, which, despite being one of the most popular websites, does not easily fall into existing categories of sources of information, such as those produced by academic researchers or accredited media professionals. Wikipedia is a prominent source of big data research, and one that, unlike many commercial sources, is openly available to researchers.

When we examine examples of big data research, then, it will be important to see if it is possible to go beyond the mass versus interpersonal models. Regardless of whether this is possible, big data research has enabled powerful advances in knowledge about the role of media in society, reshaping social science towards more quantitative approaches. One common argument against this view is that there is nothing new with big data; data has always been used in various ways and big data is simply an extension of this trend. This chapter departs from that view: big data has initiated a new direction in the kind of knowledge available – but with different implications for research and for practical applications in society-at-large. The two are related, but they have quite different consequences: advancing cumulative knowledge in the one case, and enabling more control over audiences or consumers – or in some cases citizens – in the other. This chapter will therefore cover two topics: how research, and particularly media research, has advanced with big data; and how the application of big data knowledge is shaping media uses and has wider social implications. But the first task, especially in light of the 'nothing new' argument, is to address the thorny question of defining big data.

6.1 Defining big data

Techniques of quantification in the social sciences and in 'marketing' in a broad sense (including logistics) have a long history, and in that sense there is indeed nothing new with big data. Beniger (1986), for example, has documented the rise of scientific methods and psychological techniques for the control of consumer markets going back at least to the middle of the twentieth century. And for social science, Porter (2008) has traced how the relationship between academic and commercial research has waxed and waned in terms of their closeness, also in terms of data gathering. So is 'big data' anything new? 'Big data' can be defined as research that represents a step change in the scale and scope of knowledge about a given phenomenon.[1] Note that this definition does not rely on 'size' per se, but on size in relation to the given object or phenomenon being investigated – where the object may have so many data points that, previously, collecting and analysing data on a sufficiently large scale was difficult, impractical or impossible. Hence the definition concerns how big data research advances beyond previous research about particular types of objects (we will come back to this shortly).

But what is 'data'? In terms of science – or reliable and objective – knowledge, data has three characteristics: First, data belongs (in the ontological, not legal sense) to the object or phenomenon under investigation; it is material collected about the research object. Second, data exists prior to analysis. As Hacking puts it, the view that 'all data are of their nature interpreted' is misleading: 'data are made, but as a good first approximation, the making and taking come before interpreting' (1992, 48). He adds, 'it is true that we reject or discard putative data because they do not fit an interpretation, but that does not prove that all data are interpreted' (1992, 48). He also distinguishes data from other related parts of the scientific process, such as the calibration of instruments for data measurement. And third, data is the most divisible or atomized useful unit of analysis.

Apart from pinpointing how digital big data is novel, this definition of data has implications for how advances in social science can be gauged. It presumes a realist and pragmatist epistemology (Hacking 1983) because the definition requires that there is an object 'out there' (realism) about which more useful or powerful knowledge has been gained (pragmatism). Hacking defines science as the 'adventure of the interlocking of representing and intervening' (1983, 146); again, this is a pragmatist and realist account of the relation between scientific knowledge and the physical or natural worlds. I have developed Hacking's ideas (in chapter 1, and in Schroeder 2007, 9) by arguing that technology is 'the adventure of the interlocking of refining and manipulating' the world by means of physical instruments or tools.

With these definitions in place, it can be recognized that more powerful tools (for example, computational power) have become available in relation to large-scale and readily manipulable sources of data, thus linking the increased availability of data sources to the advances in technology or the tools that can manipulate them. Here, as elsewhere, quantification or mathematization, aside from the data source, is a key prerequisite for the growth of scientific knowledge, with the tools ('algorithms') proliferating and the instruments to implement them (computers) becoming more powerful. Another aspect of how technology was defined (again, in chapter 1) is that new technologies often move out of the laboratory and become part of everyday life in the form of consumer devices or their uses. This of course is just what has happened with social media, search engines and other digital media: new technologies have moved from the 'lab' into consumer devices or digital services.

These are philosophical ideas about what scientific knowledge and technologies do, or how they provide knowledge about and change the world. The key here is that these ideas provide an insight into the implications of data-driven knowledge: a 'realist' conception regards data as becoming available from a source out in the world and on a scale that is different from what was previously available about similar objects. Here we can think, as concrete examples, of the data we have about social interactions on Twitter, Facebook or Wikipedia, in the case where all data (or large samples) from these media are available, and how this compares with available data about landline telephone records, or about television watching, or about physical letters and their content, and senders and receivers.

This view of science and data has several consequences for the nature of social science knowledge and the uses to which different types of knowledge are put. More powerful 'representing' entails a greater grasp of the phenomenon, and 'intervening' takes place typically in relation to trying to make changes in the natural – or here, in the social – world. For big data media research, the 'world' of the phenomenon being intervened in comprises digital infrastructures (a term discussed in the previous chapter) such as social media and search engines that have access to people's digital data. But academic researchers typically neither have an interest in – nor the possibility to intervene in (or with) these digital technologies – except, for example, when they can control the environment from which digital data is gathered (as with, say, an experiment). Yet this kind of intervention is precisely what Facebook and other companies (and sometimes governments) that have access to these data and these technological systems are interested in.

The power of big data research, at least in an academic context, thus derives from its scientificity. But there is a difference between advancing knowledge and changing or controlling the physical or social environment. For example, in an experiment the 'laboratory population' can be subjected to different conditions; to apply the findings in the context of a social network site or search engine requires a different kind of effort, including accessing these digital media. And it can be noted immediately that experimental studies about digital media (the Facebook 'emotional contagion' study will be discussed shortly) are often not scientific in one crucial respect: the data are not openly available for replication – a crucial condition for science. The manipulation of phenomena is thus a more practical, applied exercise, a more powerful way to control specific parts of the physical or social world for certain purposes (a widely used example is changing the colour on Google's search engine start page to see if this enhances the 'user experience').

Again, it will be evident from these considerations that quite different possibilities attach to academic and commercial research. Academic social scientists are engaged in research in order to produce generalizable knowledge about human behaviour, not (for the most part, or in the first instance) to intervene in it. Within the private sector or in other applied settings such as public policy, on the other hand, researchers and those who use this knowledge (such as marketers and advertisers) do want to intervene in human behaviour. Thus the uses of big data for specific applications, influencing the behaviours of people, are not neutral – even if the knowledge generated for these purposes is neutral or scientific. Knowledge using digital data applies to human beings treated as abstract material governed by certain statistical regularities, while knowledge generated for use in technological systems to influence behaviours is much more bound to the context of particular times, places, populations and purposes.

Hence also the lesser powerfulness of the knowledge (in the sense of 'representing') of commercial or applied as opposed to scientific knowledge: the data are proprietary (whereas scientific data must be open), populations are not representative (scientific knowledge must be generalizable) and the aim is knowledge that should increase 'sales' or the like (the aim of scientific knowledge is to more powerfully represent the world, and of technology to refine control over the environment). Again, private-sector knowledge is therefore typically not cumulative. But, as with all technologies, and in line with the definition given earlier, it can enhance 'refining and manipulating', as with any technology based on scientific knowledge. There is thus a divide between the uses of big data in academic or scientific analyses as against the uses of big data in commercial, government and other applied settings. In academic research and science, big data is used to generate abstract knowledge, without prescriptiveness about how to use this knowledge to change behaviour. In applied settings, the reverse is true: social science knowledge is generated so that it can be harnessed to change behaviour.

This point can be related directly to the definition of data that has been used here: in settings where data is not obtained from 'raw' sources (the physical world), it is nevertheless treated 'as if' it were raw (in relation to human behaviour). Consider Twitter data: when tweets are analysed, this is typically done by counting word frequencies or messages sent between accounts 'as if' these were units without context. That is, Twitter accounts are treated as if they belong to one person or organization (though that is not necessarily the case – think of bots) and interactions between units are treated as equal (which, again, may not be true – think of users with multiple accounts). Or again, the frequency of words is treated as indicating a certain sentiment or intent without regard to the fact that words may be used in different ways – for example, ironically.[2] As such, Twitter data is treated as if it consists of abstract units and can be handled scientifically. And if the problems of this approach (for instance, a user with multiple accounts) are thought to be insignificant, then considering the data-driven approach to be scientific is warranted.

6.2 Advancing academic knowledge about digital media

We have already encountered big data research in previous chapters, including, in chapter 5, findings about search engine uses, searches on Wikipedia and the clusteredness of attention on the Web. There are many more (Ekbia et al. 2015), so it will suffice to give two more examples, relating to Facebook and mobile phone uses.[3] Then we can turn to the broader question of how this new knowledge fits into social science, and the wider implications of this knowledge.

One question about Facebook is whether 'friends' who share content also share political views or political ideologies. Bakshy et al. (2015) investigated this question for more than 10 million American Facebook users, and found that Facebook friends are ideologically quite diverse, which is partly because their ties reflect offline networks such as family, school and work – in contrast with Twitter users who share common interests or topics but not necessarily offline ties, and who are therefore more ideologically polarized (Conover et at. 2011). Hence how different social media are used in different contexts, combining their political uses and uses for socializing, could be one way to think about how new media are both personal but also scale beyond personal messages.

The same goes for another study of Facebook (Settle et al. 2016) that analysed the content of Facebook messages, and in particular 'status updates', which most (73 per cent, according to Hampton et al. 2011) Facebook users make at least once a week. It can also be added here that, at an earlier point in time at least, 60 per cent of Americans use Facebook and 66 per cent use it for civic or political activity (Rainie et al. 2012). Settle and colleagues were able to separate out content that was political in nature in relation to the US presidential election in 2008 and the healthcare reform debate in 2009. They could show that political messages closely track major events (in the case of the election, these included the party conventions, the election itself and the inauguration; and in the case of the healthcare debate, there was a shift in the discussion from using the term 'healthcare reform' to 'Obamacare'). Given the large number of Americans and others who exchange political messages on Facebook, this is an interesting way to track shifts in attention. It is also intriguing to see the fit with the argument made here that there is a limited attention space for political agenda-setting. At the same time, Facebook is only one of several social networking sites, even if it is the dominant one in the United States and across most of the world, so these findings need to be part of a broader analysis. And of course the data for this study, as for the Bakshy et al. study (and for the Ling et al. study below), is accessible only to researchers working with these companies.

From here, we can turn to the example of mobile phones. There have of course been many studies about how often people connect with others and across what kinds of distances via telephones (Fischer 1992) and mobile phones (Licoppe 2004). Yet as we saw in chapter 3, the most frequent regular contact via mobile phones, both text and voice, is nevertheless with a small number of people (Ling et al. 2014). Analysing mobile call records in Norway for a three-month period from the dominant mobile operator in the country, Ling et al. found that most connections are with a small group of people who are close by. So, like Fischer for the landline telephone, they could disconfirm the often mooted idea of 'the death of distance' or of a 'global village'. They could also distinguish between rural populations, where 'the largest proportion of calls is to those who are less than 1 km away', and urban ones, where 'the preponderance of calls goes to people who are more than 1, but less than 24, km distant' (2014, 288). This is a counterintuitive finding, since it might be expected that rural people's calls would be to more distant people and vice versa. However, if we think of the distances that urban people typically drive, also to get to work, and the ages of urban and rural populations, the findings make sense (and may have implications for transport, and mobile phone operator charging policies, among other things).

How mobile phones, as smartphones, are being used to access the internet, is nevertheless still not well understood, despite the availability of vast amounts of data. Perhaps the difference between them is becoming blurred, though Napoli and Obar (2015), as already discussed (in chapters 4 and 5), argue that mobile phone users represent an 'underclass' because of the much more limited functionality of mobile internet as opposed to access via desktop or laptop computers. They make this argument on the basis of a review of studies which shows that desktop or laptop computers are more useful for content creation and complex tasks, whereas smartphones are more useful for passive and constrained activities. Nevertheless, this argument goes against commonplace views since young people in high-income countries in particular use smartphones to do a wide variety of things.

Yet it is important to remember, as Donner (2015) points out, that these affluent and highly skilled smartphone users are a small minority worldwide. Moreover, affluent users almost invariably also have internet access via laptops and other devices such as tablets, as well as having high-bandwidth connections at a (relatively) low cost. So even if their smartphone uses are constrained, they can combine this with doing more demanding tasks on other devices. Users in low-income countries in South Asia and Africa, in contrast, have a 'metered mindset', with scarce bandwidth, which is (relatively) expensive and thus used frugally. These users 'dip and sip', rather than 'surfing and browsing', as Donner puts it, and they are also likely to have far more limited skills and restricted uses of their smartphones.

This new digital divide may close over time, but the difference between the vast majority of smartphone-only users and a minority of users with multiple devices is also likely to remain a deep fault line for many decades to come. And the contexts of use are important, if we think about how online payment and other services are much more common-place in China than in our other three country cases. In India and China, smartphones are the dominant way to access the internet. Put differently, the vast majority of internet users globally will for the most part access the internet via a mobile device, and may never (or rarely, apart from work) have access to a laptop or desktop computer. These widespread uses need to be put in the political and everyday socializing contexts discussed in previous chapters. Much data will be available from these uses, but this will not obviate the need for theoretically grounded knowledge of these contexts.[4]

6.3 The uses and limits of big data in the social sciences

Big data approaches take social science (and other areas of knowledge) in a more quantitative and statistical – and thus more scientific – direction. This has been a great boon to social science, but it is also important to spell out some limitations. Again, quantitative social science is nothing new (Porter 2008), and nor are efforts to introduce digital tools and data into research (Meyer and Schroeder 2015). What is new in big data research are the data sources, which provide access to readily manipulable (computable) data. Data in the social sciences in the past has been hard to come by, mainly via face-to-face interviews or mail and telephone surveys, and digital data is often fraught with difficulties in the case of proprietary and/or sensitive data. Still, the availability of data is a pre-condition for the growth of social scientific knowledge: data provides an independent means to check or verify (or falsify) results; it is the raw material that allows researchers to build on each other's work. Having more of these materials, about an aspect of our social lives that is itself rapidly growing, means that this area of research continues to thrive.

This is so especially because the software tools to handle this data have also recently proliferated (see Bright 2016b). The caveats are that the data needs to be such that it meets the criteria of science – being open to validation and replication.

At the same time, big data research is still largely in a phase of high task uncertainty and low mutual dependence (Whitley 2000): that is, researchers are exploring many new avenues, often without a sense of how this research may contribute to cumulation (Rule 1997). Put differently, and if we take a bird's eye view of social science knowledge, the current bottleneck occurs because there is a proliferation of high-powered empirical studies generated with big data, but these studies concentrate on certain easily researchable phenomena that have abundant or readily analysable data. The implication is that there is a need for dialogue across various disciplines so that insights from this research can be brought into more synthetic understandings of the social world. Yet these insights that are based on new data sources are also limited for other reasons: one, already mentioned, is that many studies are not generalizable (or they cannot be built upon) because the data comes from proprietary social media or commercial mobile phone networks. This means that the findings cannot be replicated since the data is not accessible to other researchers – or it is not known how the data was generated in the first place. However, Wikipedia is one counterexample where the data is completely open and replicable, and there are others (see, for example, the datasets on Dataverse (http://dataverse.org/)). Academic social science will thrive with the proliferation of these and other non-proprietary data sources (see Borgman 2015; Meyer and Schroeder 2015).

A second limitation of big data is that findings in applied or commercial settings are often of limited significance because they are aimed at short-term practical goals, as when social media data are analysed for marketing purposes. This means that the findings are unlikely to apply beyond a particular marketing campaign or a specific population being targeted or precise products being sold (and the question of whether the findings are scientific is unlikely to arise in any case). Third, studies may be limited because the source of digital data covers only a part of the world's population, even if it is a large part, for reasons of language or censorship or because a particular digital medium is only one of several popular ones. And it is only the context of the range of media being used that reveals their significance: media must be placed in the context of the (sub)system of which they are part. A fourth reason has already been mentioned, which is that many digital data sources are being investigated in different directions without a sense of how the findings fit into the larger picture of communication or social research; in other words, there is a lack of theories of digital media. The first two are practical problems, and the third pertains to the scope of the study. Yet the fourth, which is a question of making an effort in the direction of theorizing, synthesizing and integrating findings, can be overcome, and indeed this book makes an effort to do so.

Big data studies also require new theories because digital media uses are changing rapidly. They are displacing traditional analogue media that are steadily declining. Digital media make for a shift away from interpersonal communication (one-to-one) and mass (one-to-many) and towards interaction at levels between the two – as when content is shared on Twitter or Facebook, or search engine results are tailored to a particular group. We have also seen (in chapter 5) that media theories leave out seeking and accessing information. New digital media thus add an additional layer – traditional media cannot be ignored – to how the world is becoming mediated, and take another step in the ongoing process whereby technologies tether us more closely to information and to each other.

We can add another limitation in terms of how this knowledge is applied: even though social science is making great strides due to the availability of big data, this research mainly has an impact in certain areas of policy. This is because, as already mentioned, academic social science is only weakly coupled to transforming society or to social engineering. Watts (2017) thinks that this limitation should be overcome by means of frequent experiments in social problem solving, so that knowledge can quickly prove its worth and more forward. Interestingly, as we shall see below, this is most likely to happen in China, where there is a tradition of such social experimentation, and where the social conditions – authoritarianism – exist to carry them out. As for commercial applications, the vast bulk of big data knowledge in the media sector is related to advertising and marketing, just as the vast bulk in politics relates to developing more powerful messages addressed to the electorate (or, in China, to the public generally). Thus knowledge can be seen here as part of an ongoing rationalization – scientization – of how consumers and the public are being measured and quantified, for good or ill.

Put differently, there is a broader societal context to big data research, which is that academic research is only a small part of the research effort. Big data research is much more widespread in the commercial sector and to a lesser extent in government and other organizations, where it is used for practical purposes – social engineering, if you like. The main effect, in America, Europe and elsewhere, is that consumer marketing is becoming more effective. Another main area of application is public opinion measurement. However, again, the context is important: in China, for example, this type of research can be used not just to get feedback from the population, but also for systematic surveillance purposes (of course, China is not alone in this, but the preconditions for more powerful uses such as this are perhaps unique to China, at least on a large scale). At the same time, it is important not to overlook the fact that commercial applications are also paramount in China (Stockmann 2013; Pan 2016).[5]

These kinds of non-academic – social engineering – uses of big data research are still expanding and continue to bring benefits (marketing, governance) and dangers (surveillance, manipulation). Moreover, the context of more media management of the public – especially during elections, as we saw in chapter 3 – could be seen as advantageous for political elites (those trying to get elected, or to govern outside of times of elections) and a mixed blessing for voters and citizens. In the meantime, it is worth remembering that, even if the benefits of new digital data sources continue for academic scientific knowledge, and even with the growing role of social media and other digital media, the findings will be limited by the extent to which digital data sheds light on user behaviour: the data pertains only to certain behaviours. And while findings about digital media are growing, they also need to fit into the broader knowledge about people's media uses and patterns of social interaction. In this respect, the problem that new digital media often do not fit the established paradigms of mass versus interpersonal communication can be seen as a limitation but also as an opportunity to develop new theories about the social implications of information and communication.

There is a different way to highlight these limitations of applied knowledge based on big data: even if, for example, there are powerful big data techniques for establishing whether Facebook relationships can influence how people vote (Bond et al. 2012), that is a far cry from being able to influence how people actually vote. Or again, if we can show that Facebook friends share certain cultural tastes (Lewis et al. 2008), that isn't the same as getting people to make a purchase based on these similar tastes. Put differently, there tends to be a very narrow aim in the case of applied big data knowledge, whereas in academic big data research, the aim is to obtain the broadest or most generalizable knowledge. Conversely, applied knowledge must be 'actionable' – and this requires effort but also imposes limitations.

These points can be seen from a more abstract perspective in relation to the social implications of science. The process of generating more powerful knowledge invariably produces depersonalization, or a more deterministic approach to the world: inasmuch as the world is explained objectively, this leaves no scope within knowledge for individuality beyond impersonal laws or regularities. In chapter 1, this was described as 'caging'. In relation to law, as Mayer-Schoenberger and Cukier (2013) have pointed out, big data can help to undermine the idea of personal responsibility, and one of the cornerstones of the modern worldview is the idea of free will. But the issue they point to is much wider than law, since big data research also challenges our notions of individuality and self-determination outside of the legal context: if the aim of a study of Facebook is to be able to predict my personality or predict what I will do, this may not be legally ground-breaking, but it does undermine my sense of individuality on a personal level.

Similarly, the very idea of technological or technoscientific determinism – that my behaviour may not only be predicted but *manipulated* by a particular technology – goes against fundamental self-understandings and ideas about how society operates in accordance with individual and collective decision-making. Moreover, it can be mentioned that although deterministic knowledge about human behaviour may seem threatening for certain societal purposes, such powerful knowledge will also inevitably be needed – if we think, for example, about changing people's energy consumption habits in the face of the challenge of climate change. Further, it is worth recalling that it is not in the interest of firms to violate the privacy of people's data: firms collect personal data in order to influence our purchasing behaviour and the like, and data is thus a resource to be protected rather than shared – except where there is a prospect of gain from sharing. Similarly, democratic states want to protect populations from threats and obtain more powerful knowledge for policymaking and in some cases to 'nudge' the behaviour of populations – not necessarily diminish their freedoms (except where 'security' is at stake).

Hence identifying new data sources also highlights new opportunities and dangers deriving from these sources. It also points to the limits of big data approaches: there are only as many such sources as people who use the objects that provide them (such as social media or other objects that leave digital traces). Hypothetically, once the usefulness of analysing these sources is exhausted – if say, all possible social scientifically interesting relationships on Facebook or Twitter have been researched – then there will be diminishing returns for social scientific knowledge – but not for commercial or other non-academic uses of big data (though similarly here, the practical uses of knowledge are limited to users of particular social media).

So far I have mainly discussed the implications of big data for advances in scientific knowledge. When we turn to how this knowledge is applied, far less is known, and the effects are also much more diffuse. Here too there are limits, and without regulatory oversight and enforcement of transparency, these will remain less clear. Further, there are obvious benefits to using big data to target consumers. Facebook gains a competitive advantage in knowing my social circle, or Google in knowing my location and the search queries that reveal my interests. Companies use this knowledge and may want to manipulate people towards certain behaviour – if this leads to increased profits. But Facebook and Google have no interest in being propagandistic or being publishers of news, for example: like other companies, the less regulation, the better – and being a news medium may require more effort in terms of regulatory compliance.

Data-driven research in the commercial world (and, to a lesser extent, in government and in the non-profit sector) is typically carried out with narrow aims: if certain correlations, say, in purchasing behaviours are found, then these correlations can be used to encourage further purchases; or if certain crime hotspots are identified, law-enforcement resources can be reallocated to counteract them (Eagle and Greene 2014). But while data can be used to target specific individuals (to come back to the earlier discussion of 'determinism'), it may not be possible to change the behaviour of individuals, even if it is possible to 'nudge' populations. However, in many cases, it may be sufficient that these correlations work – at least in a profitable or useful proportion of instances – for this knowledge to pay off.

The ethical and legal aspects of big data research have been much in focus in contemporary debates because they require urgent regulatory and policy responses. What is overlooked with this focus (as with much technoscientific advance) is the longer-term 'creep' in terms of the effects of more powerful knowledge, derived in this case from big data sources, on society. A growing body of knowledge based on digital data is bound to have important social implications, but it does so *qua* knowledge, at a level that is mostly imperceptible because it is slow and diffuse. For individuals and policymakers, it is important to respond to immediate and recognizable issues in relation to data protection, even as the wider social consequences of the growth of knowledge are rather less tangible and less clearly identifiable.

The 'creeping' advance of scientific knowledge can also be seen in terms of how user behaviour is affected in toto, and how people are therefore shaped by this knowledge.[6] This type of knowledge inexorably moves towards a new type of omniscience – omniscience in the sense that everything that can be known via digital traces should be known, and will lead to a comprehensive understanding of human behaviour from individual actions to interactions at the global level (for example, Eagle and Greene 2014) about an increasingly important part of everyday life – life online. It would be easy on the basis of these reflections to draw rather apocalyptic conclusions, which are typical in the media and in some academic responses (Grimmelman 2014 contains examples), especially in view of the rather wide-ranging influence that has been discussed. However, it is also important to put these effects into perspective: the effects of this type of research are confined to uses for commercial advantage, for political indoctrination in authoritarian regimes and for nudging in democratic ones, and for advancing academic social science – and the limits to these that have just been discussed. Instead of exaggerating dangers, it is more accurate to point to 'creep', which is diffuse, pervasive and also a largely invisible process.

Counteracting 'creep', similarly, requires drawing lines in the sand: where should manipulation of user behaviour be regulated so as to be transparent or subject to explicit (and meaningful) consent?[7] When are users dependent on a service to the extent that it is an essential part of the social infrastructure and requires regulation? When does academic social science work in support of commercial applications that are ethically unacceptable? These questions will (hopefully) increasingly come into focus, and they provide a different basis for potential regulation – or for opening up data to benefit the public good – than narrower questions of research ethics or law and privacy in individual cases. And these questions can be usefully illustrated with the Facebook 'emotional contagion' study, to which we can now turn.

6.4 Facebook's 'Brave New Worlds'

Debates about big data often focus on the state and the Orwellian world of surveillance by means of mobile phone-tapping or internet surveillance. These debates were prompted by the revelations of Edward Snowden and Julian Assange (WikiLeaks) in the early 2010s about surveillance by intelligence agencies, and they have continued since. But instead of Orwell's novel *Nineteen Eighty-Four* and state surveillance, a more relevant vision is Huxley's *Brave New World*, where companies and governments are able to shape people's minds, and do so in such a way that users, knowingly or unknowingly (and it may not be easy to tell the difference), come to accept and embrace this. Facebook, in justifying the 'emotional contagion' experiment, argued that its main purpose was to improve users' experiences – and who wouldn't like to have their experience on Facebook improved? Or, to use a different example, who could object to being 'nudged' online by government to feel better about paying taxes?

Here we can take Facebook's 'emotional contagion' study (Kramer et al. 2014) as an example as it provoked extensive debate, though the argument applies equally to Google and other digital media that generate lots of data. The researchers experimented by dividing Facebook users, overall almost 700,000 of them, into two groups: one group of users had more positive words introduced into their newsfeeds, the other group was exposed to more negative words. The researchers then measured whether these users subsequently, in the light of the two 'treatments', themselves posted more positive or negative words. They found that indeed they did, confirming 'social contagion'. For our purposes, the main point is that the study showed experimentally that, unbeknown to Facebook users, their moods ('emotional contagion') could be manipulated. It should be noted immediately that 'manipulate' is used here in a neutral sense, in line with the definition of technology provided earlier – equivalent to saying 'to change what people do' or changing the physical or social environment, which can of course be negative or positive. The ethical and legal issues of the study can be left to one side here, except to note that some argued that the criticisms of the study and negative publicity it generated could lead to this and similar experiments going 'underground' (Meyer 2014); that is, not being carried out in the public gaze of science because of the bad press and hence also the negative view of Facebook that resulted. And indeed, in line with the argument about commercial research here, one of the social implications of this type of research is that the extent to which it has gone underground will likely not be known in full. Again, this is why it is important to distinguish between open scientific research and applied knowledge. But the social consequences of applied research are that it creeps forward and increasingly affects everyday life, even if there are also reasons – like the controversy provoked by the Facebook study – to stay hidden.

Apart from this 'hiddenness', there is also little research about how users are responding to uses of their data. Eslami et al. (2015; 2016) asked Facebook users about how Facebook uses data to shape the information they see. They were largely ignorant or mistaken about this. And it is not clear how they could be better informed, or if Facebook could or should do more to enable this. The same goes for other digital media – Facebook is simply singled out here as a prominent example: digital media users do not know how their data is being used to shape the news, advertising and messages from others they receive. Still, they adapt to this state of affairs, as do consumers generally in relation to how their data is being used by media companies (Turow 2017; see also Rule 2007). But it is worth remembering that they don't like the surreptitious manipulation of their thoughts and feelings, regarding it not as a trade-off for obtaining free services (as the companies, and economists, do), but as offensive. At the same time, as Turow (2017) found in surveys of Americans, people are accepting or resign themselves to this control over their lives.

The public and consumers are adapting to the uses of big data and how it is shaping commercial attention and political opinion, even as these continue to generate controversy when they become known. Again, despite its growing power, there are limits to big data, based on the amount of attention that digital media attract, and the extent to which this attention can be harnessed to influence consumers and citizens. Still, as a number of studies (O'Neil 2016; Pasquale 2015) have pointed out, commercial (and to some extent political campaign) uses of big data are problematic when there is little or no transparency or accountability. Examples of this are when behaviours are shaped contrary to individual rights, or when regulation has not kept up with socially harmful uses (as when knowledge about individuals or populations is used to target them unwittingly and misleads them about economic benefits).

I have focused here on big data and digital media, but big data is used for more than shaping attention: it also shapes credit scores, provides psychological profiles for employers, gauges educational achievement, targets shoppers and more. These are beyond the scope of a book about media, where the main focus is on news and citizens, information seeking, consuming entertainment and sociability. But people rely ever more on online market transactions in goods and services, and as online economic activity penetrates ever more into everyday life, the uses of digital media also create markets for data. These markets for data, in turn, rather than providing 'content' as such, can be seen as higher-level (or pyramided) markets, markets not for attention but for shaping attention. Such markets are based on information seeking and socializing behaviours, and provide an advantage not only to media companies but also to companies such as Amazon, Uber and LinkedIn, which are not media companies as such but companies that rely on data. Here, too, new divides are being created, and companies with access to data are gaining markets at the expense of other companies, and with these markets also gaining greater control over consumers.

6.5 Targeting publics, and the uses and limits of big data in everyday life

Competition for attention depends increasingly on analytics or metrics in a 'high-choice' online media environment. But do analytics shape the news that is read or viewed? There is as yet limited research on the consequences of this shift, and one problem is that people do not exclusively use online sources for news (and nor does news originate in online media only). Another complication is the shift to mobile news consumption about which, again, little is known. Still, it is clear that news organizations increasingly use analytics to gauge audience interest, and this quantification of interest shapes the news that becomes visible (Cherubini and Nielsen 2016; Petrie 2015). One way to approach how audiences are shaped by analytics is to compare different media systems. The United States and China are the extremes here, since the news is predominantly susceptible to market and state forces respectively (Bolsover 2017). Where market forces reign, metrics are used to gauge what readers and viewers are interested in. Where the state controls media, as in China, metrics are used to monitor public opinion – even if the logic of maximizing attention for commercial reasons also applies in China. But metrics are not just the preserve of the private sector or of the state; they are also used by public-service media, as in Sweden. And they are also used by the BBC, a global online news organization, to measure its audiences around the world, including in India. In all cases, metrics rely on what people click on and what is shared and liked, plus other data. Metrics and big data uses are thus becoming routine and pervasive, but they are also shaped by the context of different media systems and differences in media uses. And these also include the extent to which smartphones are used. Finally, big data analytics are also increasingly deployed for political campaigning (Kreiss 2016). Political campaigns are subject to more stringent regulation than commercial marketing, but they also partly overlap with organizations that do analytics in the private sector.

At this point it will be useful to digress briefly (the topic fits more with chapters 2 and 3, on politics) to look at how big data analytics can be used for political mobilization, which has recently been detailed by Karpf (2015; 2016). The internet has often been viewed as a tool to give new political actors a voice (as we have seen in the case of right-wing populists), but Karpf points out that it can also be a tool that allows political campaigns to listen – to gauge what citizens want and harness their engagement. The argument can be taken a step further: Karpf examines what he calls 'analytic activism', mainly from the point of view of activist or advocacy organizations that use analytics to target supporters and engage them. This includes A/B testing or conducting experiments to find out what works most effectively. This enables activist organizations in new ways, giving them more fine-grained information about what publics (voters, supporters, constituents) are interested in.

Yet in line with the argument presented here, and from the perspective of those who are being targeted, this use of knowledge could equally be deployed for manipulation, and in this respect it is similar to the commercial targeting, tailoring and manipulation that has been discussed here for consumers or audiences. Here, too, big data enables a closer yoking or harnessing of public inputs to how they are used by political actors and political regimes. Karpf recognizes this similarity, and points to a continuum whereby some uses of analytics (such as in election campaigns, or marketing that results in discriminatory practices for insurance, for example) are more harmful and thus require more regulation and means to ensure transparency than others (advocacy/activism, consumer advertising) – with some in between. But Karpf is mainly thinking about progressive activist causes – what if analytics are used to promote racism or intolerance, as with right-wing populists?

A different approach is to recognize that big data analytics produce more powerful knowledge, and that this knowledge must be regulated or curbed wherever it has harmful (market-distorting, or non-transparent propagandistic) effects. Where there is no harm or risk of harm, it can be left untrammelled. In this way, the effects of analytics could be taken into account from the point of view of consumers and citizens. The proposals that Karpf puts forward in this respect – including transparency and/or the means to ensure that analytics don't misrepresent populations – are useful. Yet as Karpf (and others) have noted, transparency is not always possible (because the data are proprietary, or because revealing the algorithms would allow the 'gaming' of, say, search engine results – though in this case transparency could be in the hands of a trusted third party: see Mayer-Schoenberger and Cukier 2013). And sometimes transparency is undesirable (as with political negotiations where compromise is necessary and cards needs to be kept close to one's chest or, again, if transparency would allow 'gaming' or the skewing of inputs). Another problem identified by Karpf is that analytics point to the public's preferences only as they are revealed in the data – without providing an understanding of any deeper concerns or wishes (Karpf describes these as 'revealed preferences' versus 'metapreferences'). Put differently, it may be problematic if activist organizations (or campaigns) are led by discrete data rather than a more holistic picture of what voters or supporters want.[8]

To return to the main themes of this chapter: big data is mainly used by media companies that analyse user behaviour. In contrast to Karpf's 'listening', I have used the terms 'tailoring', 'targeting' and 'manipulating'; all three can be seen as forms of 'shaping'. 'Tailoring' messages customizes them; 'targeting' aims them; and 'manipulating' entails enhancing engagement by shifting attention – sometimes in ways that keep users unaware. This allows attention to be funnelled towards advertising and marketing content – and thence purchasing. The idea, therefore, that people exercise greater choice in online environments than with mass media is misleading: both are shaped by targeting populations, and online mechanisms are more powerful in this respect.[9] Another difference here is that whereas media content used to be conveyed via separate devices – telephone, television, radio and newspapers – digital media can be tracked across devices and so shape attention more powerfully. Devices may be proliferating, but a (partly converging) media infrastructure shapes people's attention. Analytics also aggregate user behaviour across different media; for example, with Google able to track advertising across the websites people click on if they use Gmail or Google+ (*New York Times* 2014). And targeting relies to a large extent on information seeking (chapter 5), which, at least on the scale that it has assumed since the mass use of the Web in the late 1990s, is a new social practice. This new social practice has enabled search engines, and Google above all, to create a new market: a market not for information, but for knowledge about the information that users seek.

Technological shaping in relation to big data and digital media means that knowledge becomes more powerful or effective. In social science, this entails that scientific or quantitative approaches are becoming more prominent and often aim at prediction (a deterministic perspective). In the economy, big data knowledge helps (among other things) to shape attention because it can aggregate audiences or consumers even as these are being disembedded and reconfigured by moving online. The advantage of new online infrastructures is therefore a concentration of knowledge that is gained by the creation of markets of attention or consumption, which are aggregated from a range of sources. So, for audiences, there is a higher-level market that aggregates media sources (as with price comparison sites). There are two processes at work: one is how consumers are analysed scientifically or by computational (technological) means, as part of an ongoing process of rationalization. The other is how markets are becoming more disembedded as economic transactions (or purchasing interests, for example) are aggregated when they shift online. The two go hand-in-hand inasmuch as the parts of the economy that are most disembedded already (services, finance) are most amenable to shifting online, and the transactions that are most disembedded (which take place more online) are most amenable to computational analysis.

Control of more powerful knowledge thus leads to a new asymmetry whereby companies that gather lots of digital data about users have an advantage. But market competition rests on users being able to compare prices in a fair, like-for-like, way. With targeted and tailored prices, however, it is often difficult or impossible to do so since prices are offered in a non-transparent way (Turow 2017). If online markets do not operate transparently, they need to be regulated to do so. And while a few digital media companies dominate audience attention, and so exercise more centralized control, the shift online also enables new forms of cultural production that bypass traditional media outlets, such as stars with large YouTube followings.

These implications of knowledge are also, again, shaped by media systems. As in other respects, China is unique among our cases in terms of the control it has over its media. It is true that companies in China are mainly interested in increasing the amount of activity on their own services in order to maximize profits. Stockmann and Luo (2015) interviewed managers and developers of Sina Weibo, Tencent's WeChat and Baidu Tieba, the three social media most widely used in facilitating online political discussion. These social media are influenced by the government, but the companies are mainly interested in increasing political activity in order to maximize user engagement. What is different here is that, like other Chinese news media, they also see their role as 'guiding' public opinion. China has an advantage, with a market dominated by its own digital media, so that knowledge about its population can be used to monitor and influence public opinion, also in collusion with the government.[10] The disadvantage is that this use of big data knowledge does not extend beyond its borders. Google, Twitter and Facebook, in contrast, have global markets and the ability to reach global audiences, with the disadvantage (for policymakers) that they influence only audiences and consumers rather than citizens or publics.

This brings us back to the contrast made earlier: Orwell thought that people are increasingly misled by propaganda and submit to it. Huxley, in contrast, held the view that we are all being diverted by pleasures and become used to this. The Facebook example, among others, suggests that Huxley had a point. As Thomson puts it: 'We are all of us being profiled all the time as part of the techno-commercial system by which our corporate structures (private and governmental) attempt to keep charge of us and keep us in order as predictable elements in the market…That may seem alarming, but we go along with the system happily enough…We understand that our information and our whims on the internet are being used to place us and serve us "what we want". And shouldn't we be content if we have what we want – even if those desires are increasingly codified?' (2016, 264, 265). These implications apply globally, but it is somewhat different with big data for policymaking.

6.6 Big data and policy in different media systems

Policymaking in relation to the internet and Web, as we have already seen, must be viewed in the national contexts of media systems (chapters 2 and 3), so we can examine big data briefly in relation to our four cases. In China, the government is actively developing a big data strategy, now aimed more at 'social management' rather than 'e-government'. Zeng (2016) argues that there is a danger that these big data efforts could backfire, allowing elite factions to attack each other by using data to accuse enemies of corruption and the like (elite factionalism has been seen as a key cause of the collapse of authoritarian rule). But it is more likely that the main effects of big data are threefold: first, enabling the government to 'beta-test' policies in certain areas to see if they should be more widely adopted, so effectively undertaking policy experiments. The second is via digital individual archives or records ('dang-an'), which are kept on citizens, monitoring their good and bad behaviour, and developing a 'social credit' system that rewards them accordingly. The third is gauging public opinion on social media to be able to respond to it. The conditions for all three are obviously unique to China, particularly since Chinese social media collude with the government, and digital media are contained within geographical and politically acceptable boundaries.

India's 'Aadhaar', or unique personal identifier system, in contrast, is still in its early stages, though it is the largest biometric system of its kind in the world.[11] Yet in a country where infrastructure is weak, a single system that links individual records and ties a large part of the population to the state and to banking and payments for the first time has a large potential impact. Having said that, India's lively civil society has pushed back against the Aadhaar system, pointing to potential privacy concerns and commercial abuses. Proponents, on the other hand, argue that the system will enable the elimination of corruption – for example, in delivering benefits to welfare recipients that are otherwise often 'diverted' by middlemen. These considerations must be put in context, with smartphones being by far the most common way that people use digital media, mostly for entertainment and socializing, as elsewhere. Doron and Jeffrey say that 'the cell phone drew India's people into relations with the record-keeping capitalist state more comprehensively than any previous mechanism or technology' (2013, 224). And online payment via smartphones, alongside the government's efforts to introduce a more rationalized and effective way of capturing sales tax, are therefore the most likely foreseeable effects of big data.

In the United States, the Obama administration published reports aimed at promoting policy uses of big data and also safeguarding against risks.[12] The United States also has a legal requirement whereby data paid for at the expense of the taxpayer must be made openly usable. At the same time, there is a strong tradition of mistrust of government in America, exacerbated by recent scandals surrounding government surveillance. Perhaps more importantly, American digital media companies, though protective of their users' data vis-à-vis the state, rely on user data to target consumers, which (as mentioned) consumers do not like, but they feel powerless to do anything about it (Turow 2017). Nevertheless, these companies also dominate online media worldwide, amid mixed signals of pushback against uses of their users' data. American research is also at the leading edge of the research frontier in many areas of big data, but the application of this knowledge for governance will be hemmed in by the political and the economic conditions prevailing in America. Political conditions are currently such that, aside from security concerns, there is little scope for more extensive uses of big data by government for policymaking. US companies, on the other hand, will continue to be at the forefront of big data uses in targeting consumers and audiences.

Finally, Sweden has a strongly developed tradition of government record-keeping but also of strong data protection laws. Sweden furthermore has widespread use of a system of personal identifiers. This identifier – the 'person number' – is required for all those living in Sweden, and has been in continual use since before computerized records began. They are routinely used for everything from healthcare and national statistics to taxation and shopping, tying together many facets of individual behaviour and capturing the whole of the population. Sweden's data protection laws have been tested by a number of highly publicized cases where data was misused by researchers, but there is still a high level of public trust in researchers and in the government concerning the uses of data (Axelsson and Schroeder 2009). Sweden can therefore be seen as an example of how a strong state has favourable preconditions for capitalizing on big data.

Thus we can see that media systems, but also states, shape the role of big data in policymaking. Digital media companies cut across national contexts, except in the case of China, where nationally bounded commercial digital media (Baidu, Alibaba, Tencent) dominate. In addition to national data protection, the European Data Protection Regulation is likely to at least partly curb American companies' use of big data. Thus the commercial and policymaking uses of big data only partly overlap: policymakers want to make use of digital media data since it is the single most important source of big data apart from nationally collected statistics and surveys. But media companies and researchers do more – though as we have seen, within the limits of data sources and uses.

7
Futures

7.1 Media, globalization, technology

This book has given an account of how digital media bring about social change in four countries – and perhaps beyond. The account has a number of implications for social theory, and we can begin by relating these to the subtitle of the book, starting with the concept of 'media': the internet has brought more mediatization – or increasing uses of information and communication technologies (ICTs), now digital. The implication is that social theory needs a theory of media; media play a role that cannot simply be subsumed under 'ideology', 'culture' or disciplinary subfields such as 'political communication'. Media shape social change. Increasing mediatization does not, however, entail some kind of overall change or a global 'cultural thickening' of connections, nor does it entail ever-denser mediated relations within and across societies. Instead, the effects of mediatization are specifically related to the social orders or powers in which they operate. No doubt there are more 'global flows via networks', as Castells (2009) argues, but it takes only a moment's reflection on the previous chapters to recognize that communication has not made nation-states redundant. Nor has a more global culture emerged: yes, across our four countries individuals have become more 'always on' in their everyday lives, or, as I prefer to call it, more 'tethered'. They have increasingly mediated relations to each other and to information. But these 'micro'– or everyday relations – do not translate directly into general 'macro' changes.

At the macro level, too, the Web and its audience go against, for example, facile claims that information has become 'global', as we saw in chapters 5 and 6. The extent of cultural thickening across borders in terms of Web audiences is limited and the attention of these audiences continues to be fragmented along linguistic and geographical lines.

Another example is the rise of right-wing populism: does the fact that we can chart this rise in all four countries mean that cultural borders online are becoming more porous – or less so? The answer is neither: online right-wing populists form ties across borders, but as we have seen, they are still mainly interested in putting their own nation and people first, and aim their politics at their own states. And I have tied my explanation of their success to the context of the nation-bounded media systems in the four countries, even though digital media are, in different ways, a crucial part of the explanation in all four cases.

A different way to highlight this conclusion is to contrast it with the opposite argument, made by Miller et al. (2016). Their argument is that contexts inescapably shape social media uses and that their country case studies show how social media are always shaped by 'the world' rather than shaping the world. But I have found certain shaping patterns in common – at least in the four countries. For example, social media companies try to maximize their market share or their share of audience attention. And there is also a convergence in uses, as when search engines and social media add to, complement and displace traditional media. To be sure, digital media are adapted to fit into people's everyday lives, but they have also become more ubiquitous. This book has argued that some patterns are global (at least in the four countries), including tetheredness to information and to each other. And nations and their media systems also have common patterns, as when populists circumvent traditional media, albeit in different ways. Like Miller et al., I have always examined technology-in-use and never technology per se or outside of its social context. Yet this role of technology – another term in the subtitle of this book – cannot be reduced to other forces. So the role of technology or, in this case, the internet – or new media-in-use – must also be part of a theory of contemporary social change.

Does technology lead to globalization, if we think of globalization as convergence in the four countries? The answer is yes, with caveats. The processes described here can be seen as modernizing or globalizing, without putting a positive or negative valuation on these processes.[1] It is possible to speak of certain processes of social development: a drive towards more responsive government, a more intensive targeting of consumers and citizens with information and (again) a greater tetheredness to others and to information. Globalizing or modernizing also means that it is possible to speak in certain respects of 'lag': for example, inasmuch as China and India have not developed an autonomous media (sub)system and so also lack democratic accountability to media. And in America and Sweden, too (as well as in India and China), there has been a departure from autonomous media institutions inasmuch as populists have bypassed them – which could be considered a regress or departure from modernization. The same applies to a more diverse, inclusive and open (mediated) culture – and to targeting: in both respects, China and India are 'lagging', although in targeting consumers and perhaps citizens via smartphones, China may soon outpace high-income democracies.

7.2 The uses and limits of theory

With this, we can turn to some specific implications of the arguments of previous chapters. Before we do so, we can briefly ask: what role should theory play in our understanding of media and the internet, and where are the limits of theory? Does a theory of the internet influence policy or aim to intervene in social change? The answer is yes, if by this we mean that theory can identify major social problems and tensions. But social theory focuses social science knowledge on particular problems and provides only general options for remedying them, such as enhancing media (including digital media) autonomy vis-à-vis politics; or seeking to ensure that reliable, diverse and open information addresses people's needs. Does this mean that social theory therefore leaves everything as it is? The answer here is no: by pinpointing how the internet has changed the media landscape, social theory shifts the debate about the role of media in society. The debate then moves to where online mediated access matters for social support and for serious information needs, for example, or whether the digital media system systematically skews power in favour of certain groups or elites. Other areas for debate are whether it enables new groups to gain visibility, or whether targeting via digital media enables new ways to shape attention.

If it is possible to identify new routine patterns of media use, then policymakers and researchers can also pinpoint where social problems or tensions have emerged – and how to think about them. In the case of information seeking, we have seen that it is necessary to separate serious information from non-serious information. The former is a requirement for developing one's capabilities. Information use, now mediating the individual's relationship to the physical and social environment more, plays a crucial role in this task. In this respect, new divides have been created by technology-in-use, including the reliability, diversity and openness of information. Overcoming this problem is beyond the scope here – and beyond the scope of quick policy 'fixes'. It is clear, however, where research needs to be directed to address the problem, as when there are major urban–rural divides in China and India. Another tension that arises jointly from how information is accessed (the realm of culture) and how consumer attention is shaped (the economic realm) is the use of data for targeting. Here policy can address regulatory issues, including privacy and biased information, but also non-competitive practices arising from opaqueness. Other patterns, for example, whereby people have become more connected to (non-serious) information and engage in more mediated socializing, can be recognized as a new way of life, which deserves documentation.

In relation to politics, we have seen that there are new social forces (populists) that have gained political power via digital media; they have circumvented the gatekeepers of traditional media to set new agendas. As we have also seen, the unit of analysis here is the nation-state and its media system, and the change brought by digital media must be put into this context. At the same time, some effects are similar across countries and media systems; circumvention occurs in all four countries, but its effects differ. I have focused on right-wing populism, and measures to counteract new populist online forces are therefore context-specific – even if there is also the common issue of loss of media autonomy, which needs to be strengthened. But context matters: in China and Sweden, there is more of a role for public media to counteract populists, whereas in America and India, it will fall largely to commercial media and to civil society actors.

The book has also taken a rather cautious or sceptical approach to the importance of the internet, which tends to be breathlessly exaggerated on the side of both positive and negative effects. At the same time, social theory cannot do without a theory of the internet because new social forces have been enabled by it, such as right-wing populism, the seeking of serious information, and new ways of directing attention. Social theory has to take into account how the internet has increased the mediatedness of social life. But, again, some changes are not consequential and are mainly in need of documentation, as with new ways of life – or being more tethered to others and to non-serious information. Identifying where changes are mainly cultural and do not lead to social problems can also be a contribution to social theory.

Finally, and most importantly, social theory guides research, here, about digital media in society. The topics covered in this book are not lacking in data; India is a partial exception as there are both inadequate data about internet uses and too few analyses, and researchers have not yet caught up with rapid changes in smartphone use (but see O'Neill et al. 2016). Digital media represent a rapidly moving research front due to big data. Yet the availability of unprecedented amounts of data and sophisticated quantitative analyses will not, on their own, bring about a more penetrating understanding of the social implications of media, as we saw in chapter 6. Although we may see better prediction of user behaviour and more powerful targeting and tailoring of messages, the main gap in our understanding of digital media is a synthetic account of technology-(already)-in-use, and here data-driven approaches can add refinement but not fuller understandings.

One objection to some of the arguments put forward here about how people's everyday lives have changed – such as being tethered to each other and to information – is that they do not apply to everyone. There are many people in the four countries, and especially in the larger two, who do not have access to smartphones or computers, and who therefore cannot maintain social support via 'perpetual contact' and lack information about basic services such as transportation or the means for political participation. This also applies to people in Sweden (Reisdorf 2012) and in the United States (for example, Robinson 2013), but more so in China and India. At the same time, these unmet needs are best recognized when there is a sense of the extent to which tetheredness has become 'taken for granted' among the bulk of the population. Put differently, the debate has moved 'beyond access' (Donner 2015), even if enabling access is still a major task for society.

A social theory that begins with common, everyday uses can therefore pinpoint those who are excluded from common ways of life or from citizenship (that should be) enjoyed by all.[2] Further, in media-saturated societies, it is important to distinguish between non-users by choice, such as those who have unsubscribed from Facebook, versus non-users who lack access. Divides persist even as more mediatized social relations have become the norm. Finally, constantly keeping up with the latest technology (apps, search via voice, the internet of things and the like) as opposed to routine everyday uses is a challenge for social theory. But analysing the adoption of new technology is also a specialist subfield within the study of ICTs, while a theory based on routine and widespread uses requires a longer-term perspective.

7.3 Technological determinism revisited

One thread that has run through this book is technological determinism; or, in this case more specifically, the social implications of the internet. Technological determinism is often misunderstood, not least in writing about the internet. As discussed, most of the time the term is mentioned, it is only to reject it out of hand. Instead of technological determinism I have often used technological shaping (and social shaping) to make things more even-handed. The point is that technology is in certain respects the main factor leading to social change. In this book I have always tied this shaping – or the effects – of new technologies to concrete instances, to new everyday routines (culture) or new relations between elites and people (politics) or to new ways in which media companies penetrate our lives (markets). Technological shaping entails that the caging structures of technology are the same across a range of settings – here, the four countries examined as well as the specific patterns found in culture, markets and politics.

Social shaping has also been evident in this book, and entails that settings dictate how people integrate technologies into their lives rather than the other way round. This social shaping applies, for example, to where media systems lack autonomy, as in India and China, because news media are skewed insofar as they are controlled by economic and political elites. Another example is the level of infrastructural technological development, particularly in India, which puts India on a different, more smartphone-intensive, course.

But technological shaping applies not only to everyday life; macro-actors at various levels are caged too. For example, parties and leaders – parties especially in Sweden and China, leaders especially in India and the United States – cannot obtain power without relying on media campaigns, and none of them can govern without managing media relations. But media per se drive the agenda only occasionally, as when new technologies give advantages to new social forces, and with the macro-shift towards right-wing populism. I have argued that right-wing populism is the most important new political force in three countries and an important one in the fourth (China) – though what has been said here for this new force could also apply to other examples, as with social movement organizations pushing new agendas (Bennett and Segerberg 2013). Further, the public can also be seen as a caged macro-actor that relies on media to be informed and to provide inputs, just as consumers or audiences rely on a media apparatus for entertainment. Media, like other technologies, are at once cages and exoskeletons, and social science provides an understanding of the increasing caging or rationalization of social relations.[3]

Caging can also be seen from the individual's perspective: individuals are enveloped in denser, more homogeneously diverse, and more tethered relations to each other and to information. They are more tied to the realm of politics – though there are limits to the amount of attention individuals pay to politics, with some being more tethered (or engaged) than others. But people are also increasingly targeted by campaigns via social media and via tailored news sources. The same applies to access to information in the realm of culture and to mediated sociability – here too there is increasing competition for attention without a zero-sum limit. Similarly, there is 'more' and more targeted and tailored consumption and entertainment – again without a zero-sum limit. Caging is an ongoing process, but a long-term perspective can avoid exaggeration by pointing to the limits of this process, such as where it is more open-ended or less coercive or imposed: a rubber cage rather than an iron one, as discussed in chapter 1.

By pointing to specific changes, this book has taken issue with other 'wholesale' theories of media and technology. For example, constructivism or mediatization theory suggests that the whole of the social – and political – world is constructed by media (Luhmann 2000; Williams and Delli Carpini 2011). This goes too far, since it leaves nothing 'outside' of media – something I have avoided as I have argued that media are a 'subsystem'. Still, mediatization is useful insofar as it points to the fact that people are increasingly 'caged' by media, and media also give them more control over the environment – an exoskeleton rather than a cage. Mediatization is useful as long as the scope and limits of this process are acknowledged. Finally, social scientists – and the public – are afraid to entertain the idea of technological determinism or technological shaping because it is feared that this leaves little room for human 'agency' or control by people over their lives. But structures impose themselves only in limited respects. And as far as public sentiment is concerned, the fear of technological determinism is understandable since contemporary culture values individualism and free will. Yet it is odd to find this fear among social scientists since, apart from technology, the shaping or determining by social forces is what much of social science is about (Schroeder 2007, 121–40).

With this in mind, we can turn to the implications for the three areas investigated – politics, culture and markets – paying particular attention to the intersections, and lack of intersections, between them.

7.4 Mediated politics

The theory put forward here has departed from the major theories of the role of the internet (or media), and we can begin with politics. Habermas is correct in positing a public sphere where the political agenda is set, but he puts too much weight on this sphere when he argues that it cements capitalist domination – and that this domination could be counteracted with agreements arrived at through rational consensus. Media do not provide the necessary cohesion for capitalism, and the public sphere is an arena of conflict as well as consensus. Nor is there an increasing concentration of power among capitalist conglomerates, as for Castells, which is always being resisted by progressive forces. Societies that depart from capitalist economies, such as China, or that constitute a particular variety of capitalism, for instance, Sweden, do not evince capitalist media concentration. And while Castells focuses on progressive resistance to capitalism, there are regressive (right-wing populism) as well as progressive changes brought about by 'networks'. Luhmann's idea that media are a steering mechanism for society is more accurate since, as here, it is necessary to recognize that media are the conduit which translates publics (civil society and citizens) into the political apparatus and enables elites to steer this apparatus. What Luhmann, as a functionalist, leaves out of this picture (as does Habermas) is political conflict, or the idea that new social forces or counterpublics emerge in the public arena but that new powers do so too 'from above'. Luhmann also omits reference to new media changing away from mass media (digital media hardly existed when Luhmann was writing), as when they bypass gatekeepers or develop new agenda-setting modes.

Political science, with its marketplace of ideas, captures the contention or struggle for shaping society via media, but it exaggerates the openness or open-endedness of this struggle in the media: the media constitute a limited attention space where different societal groups or political elites compete for attention or visibility – but with only some dominating. Put differently, instead of a public sphere, there is a public arena, a subsystem of increasingly mediated politics. The role of media in politics is not a 'marketplace of ideas' (Neuman 2016; Åsard and Bennett 1997): first, because unlike in a market situation, there is not a large and divisible range of goods. In America, for example, during presidential elections, the choice is essentially between two options, and in other democracies, among a limited number. The attention space is limited, and dominating it gives an advantage, as during struggles for power such as elections but also routinely when legitimacy rests on prevailing ideologies.

Second, not only are political 'goods' not divisible in the same way as tangible goods or calculable in terms of costs, they have a time horizon and their function shifts slowly – the importance of issues and ideologies is stable except when new major forces redirect politics. In other words, leaders and parties offer 'package deals', and while they adjust their policies to voters or the public, they also compete for these packages to dominate the attention space.[4] The 'marketplace' idea fits with methods for studying how the public is engaged in politics, via surveys that measure individual ('rational') choices or other indicators of public opinion. But again, the public's – including counterpublics' – engagement can also be seen in terms of its inputs into the political system and how these inputs shift, via media, in structural terms (being lined up behind certain limited options) and how their 'choices' change over time – here, towards right-wing populism. It can be added that the marketplace idea does work for entertainment or consumption: here the marketplace idea entails that people choose from a wide range of choices that are divisible (or fungible), and they constantly adjust and revise them. The contrast with political 'choices' is obvious.

In a democracy or a political system that rests on democratic legitimacy, the media subsystem should reflect the inputs of elites and people as undistortedly as possible. Autonomy of the media (impartiality, objectivity and inclusiveness) is needed for this. The example that has been discussed here, online populism and how autonomy is circumvented, has skewed power towards populists and against the autonomy of media. But there are wider lessons here for the public arena and for other counterpublics: the internet could lead to greater or more direct political engagement and enable more visibility or attention, particularly for new political actors – again with pros and cons. This requires a public arena in which these actors are adequately (inclusively) reflected and, aside from impartial and objective media, the main obstacle to this added engagement is the limited attention space: only so much becomes visible when attention is scarce. Circumvention can be understood only in the light of this limited attention, and works both ways: it enables new actors, but also constrains autonomy by taking away from mainstream or traditional media or reshaping the content of the latter. It can be added that these ideas also apply to cultural diversity, though here the implication is to ensure plurality or diversity in the sense of inclusion without a zero-sum space (though not an unlimited one), while politics requires proportional or impartial representation in a zero-sum space.

The connection between the agenda-setting of elite politics and the mediatedness of everyday life is denser communication between the two. But there is also a distortion: the added density matters mainly 'from above', in how people are targeted for messages; people's engagement has not – except for groups that bypass traditional media or who mobilize informally outside of institutions – become more democratically enabled.[5] And there is a flipside: with social media, issues on the agenda can become closer to what people are interested in – more than in traditional media. Again, this results in a loss of media autonomy – or in a new shift or 'distortion'.

7.5 Information needs and an open culture of information

With this, we can turn to culture. In chapter 1 I argued that content in the cultural domain is not zero sum, unlike politics. At a fundamental level, that is because informational and communicational power or control entails power or control over the external environment, which can increase with technoscience and so adds to the sum total of power or control.[6] Political power, power of A over B or coercive power, in contrast, is zero sum insofar as it consists of domination over others rather than over the environment. This power, in democracies, needs to be legitimate, and media are the conveyor belts for legitimacy (and as we have seen, media autonomy underpins this function of the media). For information and communication in the cultural domain, on the other hand, there are different normative implications: if individuals are given more power or control over their lives by means of information or communication for serious or practical purposes, it must be reliable, open, accessible – and diverse.[7] Furthermore, these implications are only partly about access or about individuals. Even if, for example, informational needs are met for everyday practical purposes, it still remains to ensure cultural diversity and inclusiveness. This is because only a culture that is inclusive, open and plural is a well-functioning culture. And for some, particularly those who are socially isolated, the possibility of having mediated sociable relations with others can also be a serious practical need. I have not dwelled on this latter point since I have mainly stressed the cohesive sociability that digital media have intensified and extended among the bulk of the population. But tetheredness is essential for developing one's capabilities, and as such, deserves strengthening.

7.6 Big data and targeting

Big data techniques are often blackboxed for commercial reasons, but for digital media companies, they have a single aim: maximizing attention or audiences. In that sense, they are not mysterious. Whether more sophisticated targeting from above by these means – made possible by denser communication or by information seeking from below – has major effects on social change apart from an intensification of marketing, remains to be seen. But it should be remembered, first, that targeting from above and tetheredness in everyday life below are largely separate processes in terms of their dynamics, and, second, that they are extensions of existing processes. Targeting for marketing (Beniger 1986; Turow 2017) – or for persuading voters (Harding 2008; Kreiss 2016) – has been around for some time; so has ever denser mediated sociability (Licoppe and Smoreda 2006). The main departure is information seeking, which has become more extensive and reaches more deeply into everyday life with the Web.

This can be put differently: digital media companies push content towards audiences, and there is also a push from people (or audiences) to share more with others. But the density of interaction between media companies and audiences also has limits: digital media companies compete more intensively using knowledge derived from big data analytics. But after the initial creation of new infrastructures that have partly displaced traditional media, and so after the competition to dominate new services, media companies now need to encourage more 'engagement' within a not-unlimited attention space (for example, increasing time spent on a site, or shifting to video, which uses up more 'data'). Social network sites are an additional channel for consuming entertainment and information, also through sharing content, but there is competition for attention across media for audience share. For social theory, the expansion and limits here are mainly of interest in terms of the ways in which they are changing the shape of people's everyday lives. And the policy implications are mainly those arising from where there are anti-competitive (monopolistic) or discriminatory practices or infringements of privacy.

The difference with political communication is instructive: for news, targeting and tailoring content to what audiences want (what they click on or share) entails a weakening of media autonomy or of editorial or journalistic control. It is akin to tabloidization or 'infotainment' in the sense that media cater to what they think audiences want. These trends have intensified with competition among new and old media, but what is also new is that digital media targeting is based on direct measurement of user behaviour. This is a form of scientization or rationalization, yoking audiences, via measurement, to content, which at the same time lets audiences set the agenda. This competition for attention applies across media, with tailored digital media competing for attention with traditional media. So 'most shared', 'most watched' or 'most read' is one measure or indicator for audience targeting, but it can also be combined with analyses of where the content comes from and how attention is paid across all media. Attention is scarce, though its zero-sum nature matters for politics, and adding digital media does not expand the attention space except at the margins of additional time spent or bypassing existing gatekeepers.

There has been much discussion recently, in the wake of the American election of 2016, about how Google, Facebook, Twitter and others are not neutral since such a large proportion of the population receives news and information from these channels. Put differently, they are now seen as news media or gatekeepers. No doubt the influence of these new channels should be scrutinized. But it is worth bearing in mind that they do not provide content of their own. So they reshape the attention space mainly insofar as they provide a new infrastructure for content (chapter 5) and do not shape the news agenda as such – traditional media and journalists do. How advertising is shaped according to the logic of market (or audience-share) competition is less important for social theory than how media shape serious information, and here the injunction must be to ensure diversity, reliability and openness.

It may seem that the tailored push from above, and change from below in how material is shared and being tethered to online content – these two sides have become more intertwined when they used to be separate (think of the separation between offline letter writing and telephoning, or between offline news or encyclopedias). But this is a matter of perspective: it is not that our socializing has become more news- or information-centric, for example. Nor has the political agenda, say, become more infused with interpersonal issues (though it has become more yoked to 'audiences'). Digital media work differently as infrastructures for political communication, for markets and for a tethered culture. Still, as we have seen, news on social media, including items that are shared and items from online-only publications, are somewhat different from traditional media. The difference reflects how social media users share more content that is more local and aligned with being relevant within their social circle. As Miller et al. (2016) argue, content needs to reflect what is expected within one's social group, and in this sense, it is conservative. Agenda-setting, on the other hand, still takes place mainly in traditional media, oriented towards elites who are engaged with more 'abstract' issues (Neuman et al. 2014). Perhaps audiences are setting the agenda more, but that shift will reflect not just data-driven audience measurement but also a longer-term structural change in competition for audiences.

Increased targeting and tethering – and circumventing and expanding – fit into a process of ongoing rationalization: there is an advance in technological – or digital – means that is reshaping how people communicate and seek information. Tethering is a way of describing this process for the individual. In terms of the bonds in civil society or in a consumer society, the process could also be described as a 'thickening' of mediated relations.[8] There is a link between macro and micro insofar as socializing online (sharing information) and searching for information (rather than receiving broadcast messages) contribute to shaping the agenda that was previously shaped by media institutions (journalists) and elites (political, cultural and economic). But it is useful to keep this in perspective: the media subsystem is only marginally reshaped (expanded or circumvented); elite content still dominates; and new political impulses from below (here, populism) also have causes other than media. And most of how everyday life has been reshaped by increased tethering is not related to politics.

7.7 Digital versus traditional media

The differences that digital media (the internet and Web) make beyond traditional (mass and interpersonal) media are: 1. they enable new political forces; 2. they provide new sources of information; 3. they target content more closely to people. As for the first point, new political forces are enabled insofar as they overcome the autonomy of traditional media. A concrete example of the second point is Wikipedia (though as we have seen, for political reasons, and because different media companies dominate, China has a different online encyclopaedia, Baidu Baike). The first and second points share an implication: politics requires standards of impartiality and objectivity from its media subsystem, at least as far as news is concerned, and sources of serious information should also be reliable and meet the standards of science where, for example, the physical or social environment is concerned.

Regarding the third point, a more mediatized world is dominated by large new media companies that seek the largest share of attention. There is also an overlap between culture in the sense of everyday life, and commercial media, which provide much of the infrastructure for information and socializing. Cultural policies should foster diversity, openness and inclusiveness, but it is difficult to see how the dominance of consumer media could be counteracted. Where and how it is necessary to do so, in view of plural sources, is another question. Within the political realm, the public arena is autonomous, even if the main digital media are commercial. The public arena must enable counterpublics, seen here in neutral terms as forces that challenge the political status quo (just as the cultural realm must be open to new cultural forces). Again, in keeping with the theory that media are a subsystem, the sources of these challenges need to be sought among political and cultural elites and publics. Ideally, media would promote a more open, diverse and inclusive culture, as well as an autonomous media subsystem where political forces are more responsive to each other.

One way to think about the difference in the three patterns identified is to go back to the definition of power and control in different realms or orders: in politics, changes are 'vertical', exercising coercion over a population; in everyday life, they are at once diffuse and 'horizontal' (interpersonally, and across populations) and locally bounded (or micro); and finally the changes brought by digital media companies are also diffuse but extensive (global, or following the reach of these companies). The three patterns also lead in different directions: more powerful digital media companies are now able to better target audiences or consumers, shaping how people devote attention to online content. In politics, new forces have been introduced, and I have focused on right-wing populism, which is the main new force in three of the four countries examined (and a major one in China), with its success being due in large part to digital media. In culture, people have become more tethered to each other and to information via digital media. These three patterns do not reinforce each other structurally, or they do so only marginally, insofar as increased everyday uses of digital media are at the root of all three.

This leaves the question of whether there is an overall or master process that can be identified for the role of the internet. But this master process is simply an extension of the role of media technology in our everyday lives – the different types of mediatization. The role of technology on a mass scale has been ongoing since the industrial and technoscientific revolution of the nineteenth century, and the role of media infrastructures (mass print and the telephone) since the late nineteenth century, followed by radio and TV in the twentieth. This master process has intensified during the past quarter-century with digital technologies, though with quite different consequences in the three areas or realms considered here. It may seem a disappointing conclusion to a book about the internet and social theory that there is no claim that the internet has fundamentally transformed society in some one overall direction. Instead, I have pointed to more specific areas of change in three areas. But these three more concrete changes are the main ones that I could identify in my four cases. There are of course others, outside of the four countries treated here, and pertaining to different or more specialized areas of life – such as health, surveillance or telecommunications policy.

Nevertheless, locating a small but important number of changes in all four countries, it becomes possible to pinpoint where social theory needs to take the internet into account. Again, not all of social theory needs to be revised, but those parts dealing with new political forces (populism), changes in ways of life (tethering, including information seeking) and how media companies have changed their hold on our lives as consumers (targeting) – do. These changes can fit into social theory and a theory of how technology shapes society, extending its insights in particular ways. As we have seen, there are specific implications, though in terms of policy, there are, as ever, options within constraints. There are limits to how social theory guides knowledge – aside from the limits to how the internet has changed our social lives.

The theory put forward here has drawn on a number of theorists and existing theories: Meyrowitz and mediatization, Weber and Durkheim, Luhmann, domestication, and more. At the core is a theory of science, technology and social change drawing on Hacking's realist philosophy of science, Collins' idea of how technologies go from the laboratory to being consumer devices, Weber's idea of rationalization and an 'iron cage' of technology as modified by Gellner into a 'rubber cage' of user-friendly technologies. The theory has also taken as a backdrop ideas about the relation between different types of power or different social orders (Mann, Schroeder). Finally, it has taken some key ideas from the study of media, such as gatekeeping and agenda-setting – here, within a limited attention space. But I have also argued that media theory must integrate these ideas within an overall theory of the role of media in society, including other social sciences such as anthropology. These elements do not combine neatly into a simple package, but together, I claim that these elements fit together and explain the main changes in the role of media in society since the advent of the internet.[9] They are the most useful or powerful elements of theory available, though that claim is one that the reader must evaluate by comparing it to other theories and judging how well what has been presented here meshes with the evidence.

I have also argued that it is necessary to go beyond mass versus interpersonal media models. But apart from offering various accounts of the workings of digital media, no one single straightforward alternative to mass versus interpersonal has emerged. That is because in the private realm of everyday life, sociability has not so much 'scaled up', as Miller et al. (2016) argue, as become more dense and few-to-few via social media. In the public arena of politics, elites dominate the agenda, as does the content of traditional media even as it shifts online – but, importantly, new forces can bypass them via non-traditional media. And likewise in markets competing for attention, a few companies dominate, and they are able to target populations and tailor content more accurately to audiences – to penetrate not a mass audience, but the maximum reachable audience. This is not a simple picture, but it is illustrated in figure 7.1, where the arrows indicate the main changes that have been charted here (and these arrows indicate that digital media operate unlike traditional media – circumventing, tethering information seekers and socializers, and penetrating audiences and consumers). This account, I argue, captures contemporary changes more accurately than either Castells' all-pervasive networks or Chadwick's hybrids and other theories that we encountered in the introduction.

To put the changes in figure 7.1 into context, circumventing traditional media, agenda-setting and a limited attention space can be found in all four countries, but circumvention takes place via new (but different) media in each case. They set new agendas that enable populists to gain power in all four cases (though populism as a new force also arises from both similar and somewhat different sources in the four countries, as we have seen), and they all operate within the limited attention space of old and new media combined. The same applies to visibility and competition for audiences; there is a greater volume of tetheredness and targetedness, so there is also more competition within a not-unlimited space for visibility and audience share. In other words, for culture and markets too, there are winners and losers, but no single new direction of change except 'more', unlike in politics.

7.8 Separate changes and limited impact

The changes that have been charted here are interrelated but they do not promote or propel each other. Bypassing gatekeepers occurs within the bounds of national media systems and so operates in specific ways; fostering everyday cohesion and closeness to information changes everyday life, without contributing to macro-changes; and penetrating audience attention and online consumers more powerfully changes leisure and shopping – not more (again, figure 7.1 illustrates this). These three developments are orthogonal – they affect different realms of social life without intersecting with or reinforcing each other. It is true that increasing everyday tetheredness is a precondition for greater political engagement

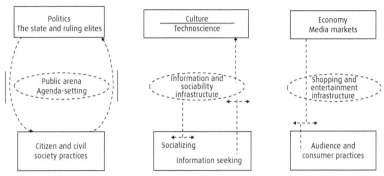

Fig. 7.1 Three spheres or powers (politics, culture, economy) and how dominant institutions and people's everyday practices are shaped by digital media technologies (dashed arrows).

and more attention devoted to online consumption – but changes in the political realm, as with greater efforts to reach publics via different media, do not change everyday life: people devote only a limited amount of energy or time to following or pursuing politics. Similarly with the economic realm: consumers are more closely monitored by advertising and marketing, but the amount of time and resources they spend on online activity in everyday life has crept up only marginally. And the same is true from the 'top down', where changes in political direction or in the intensification of the online economy have not fundamentally transformed tetheredness – though overall the change in social development is in the direction of more mediatization.

Again, increased everyday online activity is a precondition for all of the changes that have been charted here: engaging with political messages that bypass traditional media, relying more on mediated information and relations to others, and engaging in online consumption. But the political, economic and cultural mediated realms (or the media subsystems) remain separate. This rather abstract way of conceiving social change may be considered to be splitting hairs, but it is integral to theorizing the internet or the relation between technology and social change to avoid conceiving of change in a blanket way. Orthogonality is also integral to the relation between media, technology and globalization because while there is more mediation and tetheredness, this leaves the varieties of capitalism (or the economic system of markets, though marketization is also globalizing) and the political systems and their media systems, and indeed the (non-technologically mediated) parts of the four cultures, intact.

As mentioned in chapter 1, the importance of the internet for social change and so for social theory can be put in its place by noting that there are at least three more significant macro-changes in these four countries that have little or nothing to do with the internet: climate change, financialization and the limits to social citizenship.[10] Changes brought about by the internet can be seen as a fourth significant change, but which of these changes is more fundamental remains to be seen. The three main changes brought about by digital media are also on different time scales (as are the three non-internet macro-changes; see Schroeder 2013), with politics being less glacial than the other two. They also have different degrees of reversibility, again, with populism perhaps being the most reversible. Tetheredness and penetration of online markets into consumer life are less reversible, but also advance more slowly and invisibly.

Hence, too, the idea of a network society, or of an information society, being due to the internet is misleading. There are more important macro-changes, and those changes that have been attributed to the internet here are partly longer-term, linked to the rise of a consumer society in the early twentieth century (Beniger 1986; Schroeder 2007). Some changes are also more recent than the advent of the internet in the 1990s, if we think of populism in the four countries (though the timing of how populism circumvents gatekeepers roughly coincides with the spread of user-generated content in the early 2000s). And the timing of one change coincides with the diffusion of the internet – or rather the Web – in particular: information seeking.

Social theory must take the internet into account because it extends the mediatization of society. Again, mediatization is a longer-term process: it reaches back into the nineteenth and early twentieth centuries, with newspapers, then the telephone, radio and TV broadcast media. These were mass or interpersonal media, but the internet extends mediatization in three main ways: 1. traditional media can be circumvented by digital media, enabling new political forces to become more prominent; 2. people become more tethered to each other and to information; 3. consumers and audiences are being targeted more and becoming more engaged with tailored online content. Mediatization thus entails more mediation (more use of media to interact with the world), but it also results in disintermediation in the sense that mass media are displaced with more direct communication – even if this new form of communication also represents still further mediation.

There is increasing mediatization in politics and consumption, and in socializing and information seeking (the last two both part of everyday culture). In all three domains, our lives are more mediated, there is a more homogeneous diversity of mediation in all four cases, and our social cage has become tighter and more effective; it has become more rationalized. Social theory needs not just a theory of political, economic or cultural change, but also of technoscientific advance, which transforms these three realms, via increasing mediatization. But media are only a subsystem within these three realms, including within the realm of culture, where it mediates culture – though technoscience also initiates the transformation of all three realms (the arrows in figure 1.1 that issue from technoscience are also the ultimate cause of the arrows in figure 7.1). Mediatization thus extends caging from 'above' and from 'below', but the effects of an increasingly mediatized world should not be exaggerated: consumers are more targeted online, publics are engaged more directly, and people's everyday lives are more tethered. But as we have seen, all three processes are constrained in terms of the reach and depth of digital media: there are limits to mediatization whereby, for example, tetheredness to others remains circumscribed by small personal circles, or tetheredness to information is circumscribed by how new gatekeepers such as search engines shape visibility. Likewise, consumers' attention is more tightly yoked to how information is tailored to particular recipients. And finally, people's and elites' political mediation is limited by the attention space.

7.9 What is to be done?

I have argued that social theory does not lead directly to policy but clarifies the options, not just for policymakers but for the public-at-large, including citizens and journalists. As for online right-wing populism, one task is to improve public debate by strengthening media autonomy, preventing media from paying attention to direct communication from right-wing populists, and allowing them to express their views only in fora where they can be held accountable. Certain types of speech are illegal, such as calling for violence or specific types of hate speech, and need to be ferreted out. But the vast bulk of online right-wing populism is not of this type, and one step must be to acknowledge that populist ideas are for the most part the expression of genuine discontent – not the irrational emotions of people who have been misled. Another step is to put populist ideas in their place where they are deceitful (for example, Islamic terrorism is not the major threat that it is claimed to be in the four countries analysed here: this must be corrected, and there needs to be a better understanding of why so many believe this). There is also the fact-checking movement that monitors the media. Another element is more education about the benefits of tolerance, free trade and open borders.

Then there are young people who spend more time online and are (often) less inclined to right-wing populism: are there ways to mobilize them by means of digital media to counter regressive ideas? Finally, understanding the quite different mechanisms of how digital media have been used successfully is a first step to countering them: even Twitter, as used by Modi and Trump, can be counteracted in a different way in the United States (where it works mainly via mainstream media that could refuse to publicize or respond to tweets) and India (where it works mainly via rallying BJP/RSS supporters, so engaging them in conversations on Twitter directly could help). Other examples could be given, but a key point is that the same tools that give populists an advantage in the online realm also provide tools to mobilize against them (and they will be used by other political forces). And again, it is important to strengthen the institutional basis for objective and impartial journalism that reflects the totality and diversity of significant social issues.

In the realm of culture, commentaries about being alone together or information overload and the like are bound to continue. But they detract from the issue of serious information needs, access to information, and the diversity and openness of cultural content, as well as the cases of groups that lack online social support. Markets alone cannot ensure that a diverse, open and reliable online information infrastructure is provided. Markets require a level playing field, a means whereby consumers or audiences obtain what they need without, for example, information asymmetries. But a diverse, open and reliable online infrastructure also does not fall within the purview of the state – except, for example, where the role of the state is to support cultural diversity (as when minority cultures are subsidized by public-service media) or supply information for the public good (such as public safety and the like). The role of science also cannot bear this responsibility, save as part of its remit to provide reliable knowledge within the autonomous and open institution of scientific knowledge production. This, too, does not ensure an open (in the sense of pluralistic), diverse and reliable culture – except as these pertain to scientific knowledge. Provision of a suitable information infrastructure is thus partly within the purview of all of these institutions (or orders) and of other actors besides – such as third-sector organizations. How these are combined in the four media systems examined here varies, as we have seen. But again, there is a common yardstick or aim whereby the combination of all of these orders and actors should promote the diversity, reliability and openness of cultural information. And sociability also matters most in cases of social support. Otherwise, again, a more mediatized culture is neither more nor less desirable – a relativist position.

As for big data, there is a need for more transparency of data uses, which can also counteract discrimination, and for robust privacy regulation, as well as ensuring there is a level playing field in online markets. It is also important to point to areas where there are no major implications: in terms of consuming media, the fact that there is generally simply more media consumption is not a cause for concern since it is less resource-intensive than other infrastructures such as transport or energy uses. Similarly with the greater abundance of socializing and information seeking. These are general options that all have constraints; again, no detailed policy prescriptions arise from social theory. Finally, despite data abundance, which has led to a more thoroughly grounded understanding of the mediated social world, there is also a need for a more penetrating theoretical account of this world.

Notes

Chapter 1

1 The following is based in part on Schroeder (2017). It can also be noted here that I will use the term 'digital media' rather than 'social media' because the latter excludes search engines and could exclude apps as well as sites such as Wikipedia. Hence, instead, I use the more inclusive 'digital media' or 'online media' (interchangeably), which include all of these, and compare them with traditional or mainstream media ('media' is always used in the sense of information plus communication, to be distinguished and defined in chapter 5) and also with offline or non-mediated relations.

2 Neuman (2016) is a good exception.

3 See Schroeder (2013) and Mann (2013).

4 'People' and 'civil society' will be used interchangeably.

5 A different way to point to this imbalance is that two chapters (2 and 3) are devoted to politics and two chapters (4 and 5) to culture – whereas only two sections (6.4 and 6.5) are devoted to the economics of digital media, and even here the emphasis is on audiences and consumers rather than on production. But this imbalance is also somewhat artificial, since digital media companies have created the information infrastructures (chapter 5) that support new cultural practices and new ways of disseminating news and reaching citizens (chapters 2 and 3).

6 'Ideology' will be used in the sense of political belief systems, without the implication that ideology is false. There is much social science baggage attached to the term (Abercrombie et al. 1980), but here there is no implication that dominant or prevailing ideologies hold the political or social system together, though the claim is that there are prevailing beliefs or ideologies purveyed across all media, dominating and legitimating rule or challenging it – via counter-publics – within a territory.

7 Many analyses point to this – for example, Hall and Lindholm (2001) and Schroeder (2013).

8 For example, Neuman (2016, chapters 6–8), but see Åsard and Bennett (1997) for an America–Sweden comparison.

9 For social theorists who share this view, see Collins (1986), Gellner (1988), Mann (2013) and Schroeder (2013); for a realist and determinist view of technoscience, see Schroeder (2007). Scientific realism or an anti-constructivist view of science will also make a comeback against the current dominance of constructivism when questions of scientific validity, for example, concerning climate change, return to the foreground.

Chapter 2

1 Note that this 'responsiveness' yardstick allows us to examine the four country cases on the same (neutral) scale, despite the fact that democratic regimes and an authoritarian regime are being compared. This problem of finding a common yardstick will be encountered at several points

in the book. A universal or objective yardstick, or at least one that applies to the four countries and perhaps globally (and in a value-free way), here, as elsewhere below, will allow us, in the concluding chapter (7) to draw out some (normative policy) options in the second instance.

2 The following is based on Schroeder (2016a). See Schroeder (2007; 2013) for the rationale of comparing these two cases, and also India and China.

3 A third category, polarized pluralist, with countries such as Italy and Spain, falls outside the scope here, and India and China will be put into Hallin and Mancini's scheme later.

4 Online news could be said to be more polarized in the United States than in Sweden (and the Nordics generally), simply because of the two-party system, but people also use a range of sources for news, so media or news polarization would need to be put in the context of this varied diet of news (see Newman et al. 2017, 39).

5 See also Newman et al. (2017, 17), who say that Sweden has 'one of the highest levels of mobile news consumption' among advanced societies. It can be noted that domestication theory, discussed in chapter 1, helps to explain why, among young people especially, smartphones are used more than computers in the home to access news (aside from use outside the home, while commuting or similar): it is simply easier to pick up a phone to read the news anywhere in the home, such as the bedroom, than to go to the room that contains the computer or the digital TV (Newman et al. 2017, 17).

6 News (and other content) is being shared more, but not enough is known to date about how this affects overall news consumption (although see the review in Kümpel et al. 2015). To be sure, such sharing is part of the increasing differentiation of how news is accessed. But whether this leads to more diverse sources, or sources that are different from traditional media (many links that are shared are to traditional or 'legacy' media) remains a question for research since this change is still ongoing, and is a question that can be answered only by reference to which sources (shared and not shared) dominate the attention space as a whole (see also note 8 below).

7 Vilhelmsson et al. (2017, 260) say that ICT use in Sweden – overall, not just for news – is an 'elastic activity that simply "fills up" available time in daily life and quite easily adapts – increasing or decreasing – depending on current needs and constraints...the total time spent using ICTs is largely associated with free time availability', although overall 'the temporal implications of internet use are quite marginal'. It is interesting to note that some forthcoming research (on Americans) about how people obtain news on mobile phones and other devices finds a habit of 'snacking': sessions obtaining news on mobile phones are more frequent but they are also briefer than when news is obtained via computers, TV, newspapers or radio. These sessions fit, too, into otherwise 'empty' time slots. Additionally, news is formatted in distinctive ways for mobile phones as opposed to computers, which may further encourage 'snacking'. But smartphones are also used in conjunction with other devices, so it is not clear what happens as smartphone news consumption displaces other devices for news.

8 Newman et al. (2017, 10) say that in the United States, a little over half (51 per cent) of internet users get their news from social media, but just 2 per cent get their news *only* from social media in an average week. And the newness of using social media needs to be put in context: 'Even those relying more on social media would have found much of the news in their feed came from traditional media outlets' (Newman et al. 2017, 10). As mentioned earlier (see note 6), how sharing makes a difference is a question that has hardly been addressed by research to date: even if social media replace traditional news media, how much of this content is different from the content in traditional media, albeit served up in a different form? For the United States, Taneja et al. (2017 forthcoming, 18) find that despite differences such as higher Facebook use for news among a younger generation as opposed to a generation of older users, there is 'only a modest "generational gap" in online news consumption...these two generations largely consume the same sets of popular outlets'.

9 Another way to think about what journalists provide versus what audiences want, which also relates to the question of sharing news already mentioned, is in terms of what mode of consuming news is more 'active' or 'passive'. In this regard, Zúñiga et al. (2017) have documented a phenomenon among some groups (in the United States) that they label 'news-will-find-me'; that is, they will receive news via their social circles without actively seeking it out. While it may be too early to say that these groups are less knowledgeable about civic affairs, which could be one implication of these findings, they are in any event less likely to seek out traditional sources of news, and in this sense new ways of staying informed may create new divides in political knowledge (2017, 118).

Chapter 3

1   Not only did Trump's mentions in tweets translate into mainstream media mentions more than his rivals, but his tweets also became more retweeted over the course of the election and his Twitter handle was mentioned more often in mainstream media than those of his primary rivals. Trump also had more weeks when he dominated over his rivals during the primary campaign in terms of mentions on CNN, Fox News and MSNBC (and he had more mentions on CNN compared to Fox News than his rivals). And even though Hillary Clinton was ahead in the polls during the general election campaign, she too was mentioned far less on CNN than Trump (for these points, see Cowls and Schroeder 2018).
2   Cramer (2016) has documented this base of support among a population that considers itself left out by the country's media and established party elites in Wisconsin.
3   Overall, trust in Swedish journalists and Swedish media has been comparatively high and remarkably stable over several decades. However, for recent years (2014–16), Strömbäck and Karlsson (2017) found this trust to be significantly lower and declining for one group only: Sweden Democrat supporters. If they therefore turn to 'alternative media' sources, this may reinforce their lack of trust since these alternative media attack the mainstream media for their bias.
4   Indeed, some Sweden Democrats supporting 'alternative media' have begun (since 2017) to receive government subsidies that are mandated for all media because they have reached a certain audience threshold.
5   Populism in India is not confined to the national level, and it can also go hand-in-hand with pro-market policies, as Wyatt (2013) shows for Tamil Nadu. In this state, populist politicians have given away cheap rice and TV sets, among other things, in order to gain electoral support.

Chapter 4

1   The following is based on Schroeder (2016b).
2   Such usage is considered social as long as they are used for personal rather than institutional purposes, as when people make a business out of being a YouTube celebrity.
3   O'Neill et al. (2016) interviewed lower middle-class smartphone users in India, and found that they mainly use WhatsApp and Facebook for socializing and sharing – especially pictures and video – content. They are still – unlike internet users in China, Sweden and America – more careful with their data budgets, using public WiFi, having several pre-paid SIM cards and sharing files. But like smartphone users everywhere, they mainly use these devices for entertainment, socializing and passing the time rather than for instrumental, self-improvement or economically gainful purposes, and even though the cost represents a considerable part of their salary.
4   For discussions of multimodality, 'presence' and 'copresence', see Schroeder (2010a; 2010b).

Chapter 5

1   The following is based on Schroeder (2014a).
2   But see the volume edited by Aspray and Hayes (2011), which deals with aspects of mainly offline information.
3   The domestication approach has been applied to search and information behaviour only to a limited extent (Savolainen 2008).
4   There are now various sources for search engine market share, including http://returnonnow. com/internet-marketing-resources/2015-search-engine-market-share-by-country/, according to which, for the United States in 2015, Google's share was 72 per cent and Bing's 21 per cent.
5   http://www.worldinternetproject.com/, last accessed 2 September 2017.

6   See Segev and Ahituv (2010, 35), table A3: Google sites had a 77 per cent share of UK searches in 2004.

7   These lifestyle groups range from 'privileged prosperity', described as 'the most affluent families in the most desirable locations', to 'community disconnect', described as 'older blue-collar workers and retirees in country and coastal locations'.

8   See Broder (2002) on the category of 'navigational search'.

9   The authors partly use the Yahoo! search engine for the United States because Google allows analysis using its Google Zeitgeist tool (https://trends.google.com/trends/topcharts) for only a restricted period for American searches. However, the authors note that there is broad comparability between searches in Google and in Yahoo! (2010, 32, note 7). Yahoo! has been the main competitor for Google in the United States, although Yahoo! has been far less prominent outside the United States (see 2010, 35, tables A1 and A2). We see here, as in Waller's analysis, the problems of social science relying on commercial digital tools and transactional data, a problem that has been discussed by Savage and Burrows 2007, and that will be addressed in chapter 6.

10 A different but related categorization problem is evident in the diary study carried out by St Jean et al. (2012), which groups together all 'information' behaviours on the internet in contrast with communication behaviours. Yet this categorization highlights the ambiguity of 'communication' versus 'information': large parts of what they categorize as information behaviour has the 'information object'(in their table 7) as 'online course', 'TV/radio/podcast' or 'video', while 'time spent' (table 8) includes 'listen/watch/view', 'play' and 'shop' – should these be 'communication' or 'information entertainment' behaviours?

11 In relation to search engines, it is interesting to consider that this large technological system could have developed otherwise, and still may: search engines could be non-commercial, based on open-source licensing, or equally they could charge money for each result. However, at this point, the model of commercial search engines based on advertising has become overwhelmingly dominant, even in markets such as Russia or China where Google is not the main search engine.

12 I leave aside here the question of the 'dark Web', or the part of the Web that is not covered by search engines: this topic has been extensively documented, including by Introna and Nissenbaum (2000).

13 Hindman has coined the term 'Googlearchy' (2008, 38–57), a hierarchy in the link structure of political websites such that the top sites receive the most attention by far, while many sites receive little or no traffic. This idea is an important complement to those discussed here. Yet, as Hindman himself notes, political websites are a tiny fraction of the online content that is consumed, and it is unclear how the dominance of Google as described here relates to this concentration of political online content.

14 According to Google's annual investor report, http://investor.google.com/pdf/2010_google_annual_report.pdf, accessed 24 April 2012, p.29, 96 per cent of its revenue in 2010 came from advertising.

15 There is, of course, a connection between organic (non-advertising) and sponsored link (advertising) results, as Yang and Ghose (2010) have shown. Further, search engine optimization also shapes results, organic and sponsored (van Couvering 2008). Note, however, that Google and other search engines also try to counter efforts at 'gaming' its rankings; in other words, it works to counter bias and maintain neutrality.

16 http://gs.statcounter.com/search-engine-market-share

17 http://gs.statcounter.com/search-engine-market-share/all/united-states-of-america

18 http://gs.statcounter.com/search-engine-market-share/all/asia

19 NBC Bay Area News 2011: http://www.nbcbayarea.com/blogs/press-here/Schmidt-on-Antitrust-Competition-is-One-Click-Away-130300333.html, last accessed 17 April 2012.

20 It is true that this neutrality is violated by 'personalizing' results, as described by Pariser (2011), but this, too, could be seen as a 'neutral' tailoring, and this feature can also be switched off by the user.

21 https://abc.xyz/investor/other/google-code-of-conduct.html

22 https://www.google.com/intl/en/about/

23 The following is based in part on Schroeder (forthcoming).

24 See also Meyer and Schroeder (2015) for scientific knowledge.

25 This method can also be used to examine different formats and genres (Wu and Taneja 2016).

26 Mukerjee et al. (forthcoming 2017) have identified problems with this method and improve upon it in their research. It was too late for me to take into consideration how these problems affect the findings described here, but gauging audience attention on the Web is bound to be an area that will evolve quickly.

27 Again, Australia is the country for which the most detailed analysis of Wikipedia uses together with online information seeking is available.

28 Note that the aim in distinguishing between 'serious' and other information, as in previous chapters (with 'responsiveness' in politics, in chapter 2), is to provide a universal or neutral yardstick that works across the four country cases (and beyond) in the first instance – before we can draw out below, and in the concluding chapter, the policy implications (in this case, the ways to promote an infrastructure that enhances realizing a person's capabilities) in the second instance.

Chapter 6

1 The following is based on Schroeder (2014b; 2014c).

2 For an overview of using social media for sentiment analysis, see Thelwall et al. (2012), who also point to problems aside from the 'irony' problem.

3 The following is based partly on Schroeder (2016c).

4 For an example of comparative research on India and China that addresses these difficulties, see Haenssgen (2016).

5 China has an ambitious programme underway to create a 'social credit system', using big data to manage society more effectively, though there is little research on this system (published in English). While the political implications of this system are perhaps what spring to mind immediately in the Chinese context, it can be mentioned that from the point of view of the government's aims, this effort is presented as primarily directed at improving economic efficiency (see Meissner 2017).

6 It can be mentioned that the view of big data here, as in the rest of this book, in terms of its impact as scientific knowledge, departs from other approaches: new technology, rather than 'capitalism', shapes how big data is used. Online entertainment and services compete for people's attention and custom, and the main question for social science is how digital media have reshaped people's everyday habits. For Marxists (Castells 2009; McChesney 2013), capitalism is exploitative, increases divides, and corporations try to avoid regulation. For liberals and economists, capitalism and media companies generate 'value', improve lives and produce more prosperity. But there is a simpler and more accurate explanation in relation to how big data is changing media industries: media corporations that operate in competitive markets push for conditions in which they try to increase profits (including, where possible, relying on state regulation and on existing ICT infrastructures to do so) and they optimize and seek these conditions regardless of politics (including in China) and of how the varieties of markets create digital inequality or equality. Hence, again, scientific knowledge is part of an ongoing scientization or rationalization of the world, for good or ill.

7 See Wilson et al. (2012) for consent and privacy in Facebook research.

8 While new uses of data are significant, it is important, again, not to overestimate their role. As Hersh (2015) has documented, for American election campaigns at least, most of the data used by parties to identify voters or supporters is publicly available electoral register and census data rather than digital media data, even if the two are also sometimes used in combination.

9 One effect of big data targeting and tailoring is therefore (as indicated by the arrows in the right-hand column in figures 1.1 and 7.1) that this knowledge cements a culture of consumerism as it enables markets to maximize their reach and depth among audiences or consumers.

10 Qin et al. argue that this is one reason why the Chinese government does not censor social media as strongly as it could: while social media do not pose a large threat, removing social media content would 'impair the regime's ability to learn from bottom-up information and to address social problems before they become threatening' (2017, 137). They base this finding on a study of 13.2 billion posts on Sina Weibo between 2009 and 2013, from which they extracted posts on social and political topics. They also argue that social media surveillance shifts the balance of power towards the central government leadership and towards social

media users at the expense of local leaders since the former share an interest, for example, in counteracting local corruption or abuses of power (2017, 138).

11 Rao and Greenleaf (2013) find that Aadhaar is both in a state of legal limbo and that its implementation is patchy and uncertain. But this very state of uncertainty, they argue, also means that its uses and potential uses can spread unchecked. Although it would be useful to expand on the implications of this form of big data for the Indian case, there is simply not enough research (as far as I am aware) on the early implications of this system.

12 White House (2014), and https://obamawhitehouse.archives.gov/blog/2016/05/04/big-risks-big-opportunities-intersection-big-data-and-civil-rights

Chapter 7

1 On the relation between 'globalization' and 'modernization', see Mann (2013) and Schroeder (2013).

2 For citizenship as an integral part of social theory, see Schroeder (2013) and Mann (2013). 'Citizenship' can also be tied to 'capabilities'. One argument has been made to the effect that there has been a shift away from political (civic, political and social) citizenship towards 'consumer citizenship' (Mann 2016) or a 'managed', 'privatized' citizenship, also with digital media (Howard 2005). But as I have argued here, and elsewhere (Schroeder 2016d), political and consumer citizenship are 'orthogonal' to each other.

3 Indeed, the tools for social science analysis also cage researchers, as when they use computational tools and data as a 'machine' for knowledge production (Meyer and Schroeder 2015).

4 It may be true that money, rather than ideologies, plays a role in campaigning and political influence, and the United States is exceptional in this respect (though in India it plays an even more outsized role, unlike in China and Sweden) but, again, this is a 'market' with limited options. It can also be mentioned that money does not determine outcomes: for instance, in the 2016 US presidential election, the primary rivals to the winner for the Republican nomination and the losing candidate in the general election far outspent the winning one.

5 This argument tallies with the 'connective' mode or logic of Bennett and Segerberg (2013).

6 See Mann (2013) and Schroeder (2007; 2013).

7 An obvious example here is climate change, but another could be the harmful effects of smoking, still on the rise in Asia.

8 Other processes have not been discussed here that are not directly media-related, as when digital data are collected from purchases.

9 It is interesting to reflect at this point on the role of disciplinary specialization, which was discussed at the outset and on several occasions: many disciplines do not address the theories of the role of the media and the internet in society as a whole, except perhaps sociology, which should do so (and the few examples here include Castells 2009, Luhmann 2000 and Habermas 1982 – although these three do not address the level of everyday uses or base their evidence on these uses). On the other hand, many theories, such as in media and communications, or in anthropology or political science, do not have theories of the role of media in society, or if so, they are more limited in scope. They also do not address the relations between the three orders or powers, or how (sub)systems fit into these orders or interrelate, or how media relate to social change generally.

10 Only the last of these is linked to the changes discussed here, since there is an (albeit tangential) link to (online) populism inasmuch as right-wing populism is partly caused by the welfare chauvinism that can, in turn, be attributed to limits to social citizenship.

References

Aalberg, T. & J. Curran. 2012. Conclusion. In *How Media Inform Democracy: A Comparative Approach*, edited by T. Aalberg & J. Curran, 189–200. New York: Routledge.

Aalberg, T., Z. Strabac & T. Brekken. 2012. Research Design. In *How Media Inform Democracy: A Comparative Approach*, edited by T. Aalberg & J. Curran, 15–29. New York: Routledge.

Abercrombie, N., S. Hill & B. Turner. 1980. *The Dominant Ideology Thesis*. London: George Allen & Unwin.

Ahmed, S., K. Jaidka & J. Cho. 2016. The 2014 Indian Elections on Twitter: A Comparison of Campaign Strategies of Political Parties. *Telematics and Informatics* 33: 1071–87.

Anderegg, W.R. & G.R. Goldsmith. 2014. Public Interest in Climate Change over the Past Decade and the Effects of the 'Climategate' Media Event. *Environmental Research Letters* 9(5), 054005.

Arnold, D. 2013. *Everyday Technology: Machines and the Making of India's Modernity*. Chicago: University of Chicago Press.

Arsène, S. 2011. De l'autocensure aux mobilisations. *Revue française de science politique* 5(61): 893–915.

Arthur, B. 1989. Competing Technologies, Increasing Returns, and Lock-in by Historical Events. *The Economic Journal* 99: 116–31.

Åsard, E. & L. Bennett. 1997. *Democracy and the Marketplace of Ideas: Communication and Government in Sweden and the United States*. Cambridge: Cambridge University Press.

Aspray, W. & B. Hayes. 2011. *Everyday Information: The Evolution of Information Seeking in America*. Cambridge, MA: MIT Press.

Athique, A. 2012. *Indian Media*. Cambridge: Polity Press.

Axelsson, A.-S. & R. Schroeder. 2009. Making it Open and Keeping It Safe: e-Enabled Data Sharing in Sweden, *Acta Sociologica* 52(3): 213–26.

Baas, D. 2014 (2nd ed.). *Bevara Sverige Svenskt. Ett Reportage om Sverigedemokraterna*. Stockholm: Bonniers.

Bakshy, E., S. Messing & L.A. Adamic. 2015. Exposure to Ideologically Diverse News and Opinion on Facebook. *Science* 348(6239), 1130–2.

Barberá, P. & G. Rivero. 2015. Understanding the Political Representativeness of Twitter Users. *Social Science Computer Review*, 33(6): 712–29.

Bar-Ilan, J. & N. Aharony. 2014. Twelve Years of Wikipedia Research. *Proceedings of WebSci'14* (June 23–26, 2014). Bloomington, Indiana. DOI: 10.1145/2615569.2615643

Barnett, G. & H.-W. Park. 2014. Examining the International Internet Using Multiple Measures: New Methods for Measuring the Communication Base of Globalised Cyberspace. *Quality and Quantity* 48: 563–75.

Baron, N. 2008. *Always On: Language in an Online and Mobile World*. New York: Oxford University Press.

Barzilai-Nahon, K. 2008. Toward a Theory of Network Gatekeeping. *Journal of the American Society for Information Science and Technology* 59(9): 1493–1512.

Baum, M. & T. Groeling. 2008. New Media and the Polarization of American Political Discourse. *Political Communication* 25: 345–65.

Bayly, C. 2009. The Indian Ecumene: An Indigenous Public Sphere. In *The Indian Public Sphere: Readings in Media History*, edited by A. Rajagopal, 49–64. New Delhi: Oxford University Press.

Baym, N. 2015 (2nd ed.). *Personal Connections in the Digital Age*. Cambridge: Polity Press.

Belair-Gagnon, V., S. Mishra & C. Agur. 2014. Reconstructing the Indian Public Sphere: Newswork and Social Media in the Delhi Gang Rape Case. *Journalism* 15(8): 1059–75.

Beniger, J. 1986. *The Control Revolution: Technological and Economic Origins of the Information Society*. Cambridge, MA: Harvard University Press.

Benkler, Y. 2006. *The Wealth of Networks: How Social Production Transforms Markets and Freedom*. New Haven: Yale University Press.

Bennett, W.L. & S. Iyengar. 2008. A New Era of Minimal Effects? The Changing Foundations of Political Communication. *Journal of Communication* 58: 707–31.

Bennett, W.L. & A. Segerberg. 2013. *The Logic of Connective Action: Digitalization and the Personalization of Contentious Politics*. Cambridge: Cambridge University Press.

Bimber, B. 2003. *Information and American Democracy*. Cambridge: Cambridge University Press.

Bimber, B. 2014. Digital Media in the Obama Campaigns of 2008 and 2012: Adaptation to the Personalized Political Communication Environment, *Journal of Information Technology & Politics* 11(2): 130–50.

Boczkowski, P. & E. Mitchelstein. 2013. *The News Gap: When the Information Preferences of the Media and the Public Diverge*. Cambridge, MA: MIT Press.

Bolsover, G. 2017. *Technology and Political Speech: Commercialisation, Authoritarianism and the Supposed Death of the Internet's Democratic Potential*. DPhil thesis, Oxford Internet Institute, University of Oxford.

Bond, R., C.J. Fariss, J.J. Jones, A.D. Kramer, C. Marlow, J.E. Settle & J.H. Fowler. 2012. A 61-Million-Person Experiment in Social Influence and Political Mobilization. *Nature* 489: 295–8.

Bonikowski, B. & N. Gidron. 2016. The Populist Style in American Politics: Presidential Campaign Rhetoric, 1952–1996. *Social Forces* 94(4): 1593–1621.

Borgman, C. 2015. *Big Data, Little Data, No Data*. Cambridge, MA: MIT Press.

boyd, D. 2014. *It's Complicated: The Social Lives of Networked Teens*. New Haven: Yale University Press.

Brady, A.-M. 2008. *Marketing Dictatorship: Propaganda and Thought Work in Contemporary China*. Lanham, MD: Rowman & Littlefield Publishers.

Brady, A.-M. 2016. Plus ca change? Media Control under Xi Jinping. *Problems of Post-Communism*. DOI: 10.1080/10758216.2016.1197779

Brandtzæg, P.B. 2012. Social Networking Sites: Their Users and Social Implications – a Longitudinal Study. *Journal of Computer-Mediated Communication* 17(4): 467–88.

Bright, J. 2016a. The Social News Gap: How News Reading and News Sharing Diverge. *Journal of Communication* 66(3): 343–65.

Bright, J. 2016b. 'Big Social Science': Doing Big Data in the Social Sciences. In *Handbook of Online Research Methods*, edited by R. Lee, N. Fielding & G. Blank, chapter 8. London: Sage.

Bright, J. & T. Nicholls. 2014. The Life and Death of Political News: Measuring the Impact of the Audience Agenda Using Online Data. *Social Science Computer Review* 32: 170–81.

Brin, S. & L. Page. 1998. The Anatomy of a Large-Scale Hypertextual Search Engine. *Proceedings of the Seventh International World Wide Web Conference*, April, Brisbane, Australia: 107–17, accessed 16 April 2012, http://infolab.stanford.edu/~backrub/google.html

Broder, A. 2002. A Taxonomy of Web Search. *SIGIR Forum* 36(2): 3–10.

Burchell, K. 2015. Tasking the Everyday: Where Mobile and Online Communication Take Time. *Mobile Media & Communication* 3(1): 36–52.

Carey, J. 1989. *Communication as Culture*. London: Routledge.

Carlson, A.R., A. Costa, P. Duara, J. Leibold, K. Carrico, P.H. Gries, N. Eto, S. Zhao & J.C. Weiss. 2016. Nations and Nationalism Roundtable Discussion on Chinese Nationalism and National Identity. *Nations and Nationalism* 22: 415–46. DOI: 10.1111/nana.12232

Castells, M. 2009. *Communication Power*. Oxford: Oxford University Press.

Chadwick, A. 2013. *The Hybrid Media System: Politics and Power*. New York: Oxford University Press.

Chakravarty, P. 2004. Telecom, National Development and the Indian State: A Postcolonial Critique, *Media, Culture and Society* 26(2): 227–49.

Chakravarty, P. & S. Roy. 2015. Mr. Modi Goes to Delhi: Mediated Populism and the 2014 Indian Elections. *Television & New Media* 16(4): 311–22.

Chen, J., J. Pan & Y. Xu. 2016. Sources of Authoritarian Responsiveness: A Field Experiment in China. *American Journal of Political Science* 60(2): 383–400.

Cherubini, F. & R. Nielsen. 2016. *Editorial Analytics: How News Media Are Developing and Using Audience Data and Metrics: Digital News Reports*, accessed 27 March 2017, http://reutersinstitute.politics.ox.ac.uk/publication/editorial-analytics-how-news-media-are-developing-and-using-audience-data-and-metrics

Claggett, W.J., P.J. Engle & B.E. Shafer. 2014. The Evolution of Mass Ideologies in Modern American Politics. *The Forum* 12(2): 223–56.

Cohen, M., D. Karol, H. Noel & J. Zaller. 2016. Party Versus Faction in the Reformed Presidential Nominating System. *PS: Political Science & Politics* 49(4): 701–08. DOI: 10.1017/S1049096516001682

Collins, R. 1986. *Weberian Sociological Theory*. Cambridge: Cambridge University Press.

Collins, R. 1994. Why the Social Sciences Won't Become High-Consensus, Rapid-Discovery Science. *Sociological Forum* 9(2): 155–77.

Collins, R. 1999. *The Sociology of Philosophies*. Cambridge, MA: Harvard University Press.

Conover, M., J. Ratkiewicz, M.R. Francisco, B. Gonçalves, F. Menczer & A. Flammini. 2011. Political Polarization on Twitter. *ICWSM* 133: 89–96.

Cook, T. 2005 (2nd ed.). *Governing with the News: The News Media as a Political Institution*. Chicago: University of Chicago Press.

Couldry, N. 2012. *Media, Society, World: Social Theory and Digital Media Practice*. Cambridge: Polity Press.

Cowls, J. & R. Schroeder. 2018. Tweeting All the Way to the White House. In *Trump and the Media*, edited by P. Boczkowski & Z. Papacharissi. Cambridge, MA: MIT Press.

Cramer, K. 2016. The Politics of Resentment: Rural Consciousness in Wisconsin and the Rise of Scott Walker. Chicago: University of Chicago Press.

Crawford, K. 2009. Following You: Disciplines of Listening in Social Media. *Continuum: Journal of Media and Cultural Studies* 23(4): 525–35.

Cunningham, C., D. Craig and J. Silver. 2016. YouTube, Multichannel Networks and the Accelerated Evolution of the New Screen Ecology. *Convergence* 22(4): 376–91.

Curran, J., S. Iyengar, A. Brink Lund & I. Salovaara-Moring. 2009. Media System, Public Knowledge and Democracy: A Comparative Study. *European Journal of Communication* 24(1): 5–26.

Dahl, R. 1998. *On Democracy*. New Haven: Yale University Press.

Demker, M. & S. van der Meiden. 2016. Allt starkare polarisering och allt lägre flyktingmotstånd. In *Ekvilibrium*, edited by J. Ohlsson, H. Oscarsson & M. Solevid, 197–214. Gothenburg: Göteborgs Universitet: SOM-Institutet.

de Reuver, M., S. Nikou & H. Bouwman. 2016. Domestication of Smartphones and Mobile Applications: A Quantitative Mixed-Method Study. *Mobile Media & Communication* 4(3): 347–70. DOI: 10.1177/2050157916649989

Dikötter, F. 1994. Racial Identities in China: Context and Meaning. *The China Quarterly* 138: 404–12.

Dimitrova, D. & J. Strömbäck. 2011. Election News in Sweden and the United States: A Comparative Study of Sources and Media Frames. *Journalism* 13(5): 604–19.

Donner, J. 2015. *After Access: Inclusion, Development, and a More Mobile Internet*. Cambridge, MA: MIT Press.

Doron, A. & R. Jeffrey. 2013. *The Great Indian Phone Book: How the Mass Mobile Changes Business, Politics and Daily Life*. Harvard: Harvard University Press.

Duggan, M. 2013. Photo and Video Sharing Grow Online. Pew Research Internet Project, accessed 21 August 2017, http://www.pewinternet.org/files/old-media/Files/Reports/2013/PIP_Photos%20and%20videos%20online_102813.pdf

Duggan, M., N.B. Ellison, C. Lampe, A. Lenhart & M. Madden. 2015. Social Media Update 2014, Pew Research Center, accessed 21 August 2017, http://www.pewinternet.org/2015/01/09/social-media-update-2014/

Dunbar, R. 2012. Social Cognition on the Internet: Testing Constraints on Social Network Size. *Philosophical Transactions of the Royal Society of London B: Biological Sciences* 367(1599): 2192–201.

Dutton, W.H. 2009. The Fifth Estate Emerging through the Network of Networks. *Prometheus* 27(1): 1–15.

Dutton, W. & G. Blank. 2011. *Next Generation Users: The Internet in Britain. Oxford Internet Survey 2011*. Oxford Internet Institute, University of Oxford, accessed 16 April 2012, http://www.oii.ox.ac.uk/events/?id=453

Eagle, N. & K. Greene. 2014. *Reality Mining: Using Big Data to Engineer a Better World*. Cambridge, MA: MIT Press.

Earl, J. & K. Kimport. 2011. *Digitally Enabled Social Change: Activism in the Internet Age*. Cambridge, MA: MIT Press.

Eisenstein, E.L. 2005. *The Printing Revolution in Early Modern Europe*. Cambridge: Cambridge University Press.

Ekbia, H., M. Mattioli, I. Kouper, G. Arave, A. Ghazinejad, T. Bowman & C.R. Sugimoto. 2015. Big Data, Bigger Dilemmas: A Critical Review. *Journal of the Association for Information Science and Technology* 66(8): 1523–45.

Engesser, S., N. Ernst, F. Esser & F. Büchel. 2016. Populism and Social Media: How Politicians Spread a Fragmented Ideology. *Information, Communication & Society*. DOI: 10.1080/1369118X.2016.1207697

Eslami, M., K. Karahalios, C. Sandvig, K. Vaccaro, A. Rickman, K. Hamilton & A. Kirlik. 2016. First I "Like" It, then I Hide It: Folk Theories of Social Feeds. *Human Factors in Computing Systems Conference (CHI)*.

Eslami, M., A. Rickman, K. Vaccaro, A. Aleyasen, A. Vuong, K. Karahalios, K. Hamilton & C. Sandvig. 2015. "I Always Assumed that I Wasn't Really that Close to [Her]:" Reasoning about Invisible Algorithms in the News Feed. *Proceedings of the 33rd Annual SIGCHI Conference on Human Factors in Computing Systems*, Association for Computing Machinery (ACM): 153–62.

Esser, F. & B. Pfetsch. 2004. *Comparing Political Communication: Theories, Cases, and Challenges*. Cambridge: Cambridge University Press.

Fewsmith, J. 2001. *China since Tiananmen: The Politics of Transition*. Cambridge: Cambridge University Press.

Findahl, O. 2014. *Swedes and the Internet*, accessed 21 August 2017, http://en.soi2014.se/

Findahl, O. & P. Davidsson. 2015. *Svenskarna och Internet* [Swedes and the Internet], accessed 21 August 2017, https://www.iis.se/docs/Svenskarna_och_internet_2015.pdf

Fischer, C. 1992. *America Calling: A Social History of the Telephone to 1940*. Berkeley and Los Angeles: University of California Press.

Fischer, C. 2011. *Still Connected: Family and Friends in America Since 1970*. New York: Russell Sage Foundation.

Fischer, C. 2014. *Lurching toward Happiness in America*. Cambridge, MA: MIT Press.

Fraser, N. 1990. Rethinking the Public Sphere: A Contribution to the Critique of Actually Existing Democracy. *Social Text* 25/26: 56–80.

Gans, H. 1999. *Popular Culture and High Culture: An Analysis and Evaluation of Taste*. New York: Basic Books.

Gans, H. 2004. *Deciding What's News: A Study of CBS Evening News, NBC Nightly News, Newsweek, and Time*. Evanston, IL: Northwestern University Press.

Gellner, E. 1987. *Culture, Identity and Politics*. Cambridge: Cambridge University Press.

Gellner, E. 1988. *Plough, Sword and Book: The Structure of Human History*. London: Collins Harvill.

Gellner, E. 1992. *Postmodernism, Reason and Religion*. London: Routledge.

George, C. 2016. *Hate Spin: The Manufacture of Religious Offense and its Threat to Democracy*. Cambridge, MA: MIT Press.

Gidron, N. & B. Bonikowski. 2013. Varieties of Populism: Literature Review and Research Agenda, *Weatherhead Working Paper Series*, No. 13-0004; accessed 7 November 2016, http://scholar.harvard.edu/gidron/publications/varieties-populism-literature-review-and-research-agenda

Gleick, J. 2011. *The Information*. London: Harper Collins.

Golbeck, J., J.M. Grimes & A. Rogers. 2010, Twitter Use by the U.S. Congress. *Journal of the Association for Information Science and Technology* 61: 1612–21.

Granka, L. 2010. The Politics of Search: A Decade Retrospective, *The Information Society Journal* 26(5): 364–74.

Graves. L. 2016. *Deciding What's True: The Rise of Political Fact-Checking in American Journalism*. New York: Columbia University Press.

Gries, P. 2004. *China's New Nationalism: Pride, Politics, and Diplomacy*. Berkeley: University of California Press.

Grimmelman, J. 2014. Personal website, with sources for the Facebook Emotional Manipulation Study, accessed 21 August 2017, http://laboratorium.net/archive/2014/06/30/the_facebook_emotional_manipulation_study_source

Groeling, T., J. Joo, W. Lie & F. Steen. 2016. Visualizing Presidential Elections. Presented at the *Annual Meeting of the American Political Science Association*, Philadelphia.

Gulati, G. & C. Williams. 2013. Social Media and Campaign 2012: Developments and Trends for Facebook Adoption. *Social Science Computer Review* 31: 577–88.

Gustafsson, N. 2012. The Subtle Nature of Facebook Politics: Swedish Social Network Site Users and Political Participation. *New Media & Society* 14(7): 1111–27.

Guy, I. 2016. Searching by Talking: Analysis of Voice Queries on Mobile Web Search. In *Proceedings of the 39th International ACM SIGIR Conference on Research and Development in Information Retrieval*, ACM, 35–44.

Habermas, J. 1982. *Theorie des kommunikativen Handelns*. Frankfurt: Suhrkamp.

Hacking, I. 1983. *Representing and Intervening*. Cambridge: Cambridge University Press.

Hacking, I. 1992. The Self-Vindication of the Laboratory Sciences. In *Science as Practice and Culture*, edited by A. Pickering, 29–64. Chicago: University of Chicago Press.

Haddon, L. 2004. *Information and Communication Technologies in Everyday Life*. Oxford: Berg.

Haddon, L. 2011. Domestication Analysis, Objects of Study, and the Centrality of Technologies in Everyday Life. *Canadian Journal of Communication* 36(2): 311–23.

Haenssgen, M. 2016. *Mobile Phone Diffusion and Rural Healthcare Access in India and China*. DPhil, University of Oxford.

Halavais, A. 2008. *Search Engine Society*. Cambridge: Polity Press.

Hall, J.A. & C. Lindholm. 2001. *Is America Breaking Apart?*. Princeton: Princeton University Press.

Hallin, D. & P. Mancini. 2004. *Comparing Media Systems: Three Models of Media and Politics*. Cambridge: Cambridge University Press.

Hallin, D. & P. Mancini (eds). 2012. *Comparing Media Systems Beyond the Western World*. Cambridge: Cambridge University Press.

Hamby, C. (2013). Did Twitter Kill the Boys on the Bus? Searching for a Better Way to Cover a Campaign. *Shorenstein Center Report*, accessed 7 November 2016, http://shorensteincenter.org/d80-hamby/

Hampton, K., L.S. Goulet, L. Rainie & K. Purcell. 2011. Social Networking Sites and Our Lives, Pew Research Center, accessed 21 August 2017, http://www.pewinternet.org/2011/06/16/social-networking-sites-and-our-lives/

Harding, J. 2008. *Alpha Dogs: How Political Spin Became a Global Business*. New York: Farrar, Straus and Giroux.

Hargittai, E. & Y.P. Hsieh. 2013. Digital Inequality. In *Oxford Handbook of Internet Studies*, edited by W. Dutton, 129–50. Oxford, UK: Oxford University Press.

Hargittai, E., W.R. Neuman & O. Curry. 2012. Taming the Information Tide: Perceptions of Information Overload in the American Home. *The Information Society* 28(3): 161–73.

Hassid, J. 2016. *China's Unruly Journalists: How Committed Professionals Are Changing the People's Republic*. Abingdon: Routledge.

Hedman, U. & M. Djerf-Pierre. 2013, The Social Journalist. *Digital Journalism* 1(3).

Heilman, J. & A. West. 2015. Wikipedia and Medicine: Quantifying Readership, Editors, and the Significance of Natural Language, *Journal of Medical Internet Research* 17(3): e62.

Hektor, A. 2001. *What's the Use? Internet and Information Behaviour in Everyday Life*. Linköping: Department of Technology and Social Change (PhD thesis). Linköpings Universitet.

Hellström, A., T. Nilsson & P. Stoltz. 2012. Nationalism vs. Nationalism: The Challenge of the Sweden Democrats in the Swedish Public Debate. *Government and Opposition* 47(2): 186–205.

Hersh, E. (2015). *Hacking the Electorate: How Campaigns Perceive Voters*. Cambridge: Cambridge University Press.

Hilbert, M. & P. López. 2011. The World's Technological Capacity to Store, Communicate, and Compute Information. *Science* 332(6025): 60–5.

Hindman, M. 2008. *The Myth of Digital Democracy*. Princeton: Princeton University Press.

Hjarvard, S. 2008. The Mediatization of Society: A Theory of the Media as Agents of Social and Cultural Change. *Nordicom Review* 29(2): 105–34.

Hockx, M. 2015. *Internet Literature in China*. New York: Columbia University Press.

Holmqvist, M. 2015. *Djursholm: Sveriges Ledarsamhaelle*.[Djursholm: Sweden's Leadership Community]. Stockholm: Atlantis.

Holt, K. 2016a. 'Alternativmedier'? En Intervjustudie om mediekritik och mediemisstro. *Migrationen i medierna: Men det får en väl inte prata om?* Stockholm, Institutet för mediestudier, 111–47.

Holt, K. 2016b. Skilda Verkligheter? 'Internets undervegetation' vs 'PK maffian', *Migrationen i medierna: Men det får en väl inte prata om?*. Stockholm, Institutet för mediestudier, 148–71.

Howard, P. 2005. *New Media Campaigns and the Managed Citizen*. Cambridge: Cambridge University Press.

Howard, P. 2010. *The Digital Origins of Dictatorship and Democracy: Information Technology and Political Islam*. Oxford: Oxford University Press.

Hu, Y., L. Manikonda & S. Kambhampati. 2014. What We Instagram: A First Analysis of Instagram Photo Content and User Types. In *Proceedings of ICWSM* (June).

Hughes, T. 1987. The Evolution of Large Technological Systems. In *The Social Construction of Technological System*, edited by W. Bijker, T. Hughes & T. Pinch, 51–82. Cambridge, MA: MIT Press.

Hughes, T. 1994. Technological Momentum. In *Does Technology Drive History? The Dilemma of Technological Determinism*, edited by L. Marx and M. Roe Smith, 101–13. Cambridge, MA: MIT Press.

Introna, L. & H. Nissenbaum. 2000. Shaping the Web: Why the Politics of Search Engines Matters. *The Information Society* 16: 169–85.

Ito, M. & D. Okabe. 2005. Intimate Visual Co-presence. In *Proceedings of 2005 Ubiquitous Computing Conference*, Tokyo.

Jaffrelot, C. 2015a. Narendra Modi and the Power of Television in Gujarat. *Television and New Media*, April. http://journals.sagepub.com/doi/10.1177/1527476415575499

Jaffrelot, C. 2015b. The Modi-centric BJP 2014 Election Campaign: New Techniques and Old Tactics. *Contemporary South Asia* 23(2): 155–61.

Jansen, B. & S.J. Rieh. 2010. The Seventeen Theoretical Constructs of Information Searching and Information Retrieval. *Journal of the American Society for Information Science and Technology* 61: 1517–34.

Jeffrey, R. 2000. *India's Newspaper Revolution: Capitalism, Technology and the Indian-language Press, 1977–1997*. London: C. Hurst.

Jeffrey, R. 2002. Communications and Capitalism in India, 1750–2010. *South Asia – Journal of South Asian Studies*, 25(2): 61–75.

Judis, J. 2016. *The Populist Explosion: How the Great Recession Transformed American and European Politics*. New York: Columbia University Press.

Karpf, D. 2015. *Analytic Activism: Digital Listening and the New Political Strategy*. Oxford: Oxford University Press.

Karpf, D. 2016. Schrodinger's Audience: How News Analytics handed America Trump. *Civicist*, 4 May, accessed 7 November 2016, http://civichall.org/civicist/schrodingers-audience-how-news-analytics-gave-america-trump/

Kazin, M. 1998. *The Populist Persuasion: An American History*. Ithaca: Cornell University Press.

King, G., J. Pan & M. Roberts. 2013. How Censorship in China Allows Government Criticism but Silences Collective Expression. *American Political Science Review* 107(2): 1–18.

Kirk, D.S., A. Sellen & X. Cao. 2010. Home Video Communication: Mediating 'Closeness'. In *Proceedings of the 2010 ACM Conference on Computer Supported Cooperative Work*, ACM, 135–44.

Kramer, A., J. Guillory & J. Hancock. 2014. Experimental Evidence of Massive-Scale Emotional Contagion through Social Networks. *Proceedings of the National Academy of Sciences* 111(24): 8788–90.

Kreiss, D. 2016. *Prototype Politics: Technology-Intensive Campaigning and the Data of Democracy*. Oxford: Oxford University Press.

Kumar, N. 2014. Facebook for Self-Empowerment? A Study of Facebook Adoption in Urban India. *New Media & Society* 16(7): 1122–37.

Kümpel, A.S., V. Karnowski & T. Keyling. 2015. News Sharing in Social Media: A Review of Current Research on News Sharing Users, Content, and Networks. *Social Media + Society* 1(2). DOI: 10.1177/2056305115610141

Lange, P.G. 2007. Publicly Private and Privately Public: Social Networking on YouTube. *Journal of Computer-Mediated Communication* 13(1): 361–80.

Larsson, A.O. 2013. Tweeting the Viewer—Use of Twitter in a Talk Show Context. *Journal of Broadcasting & Electronic Media* 57(2): 135–52.

Larsson, A.O. 2014. Online, All the Time? A Quantitative Assessment of the Permanent Campaign on Facebook. *New Media & Society* 18(2): 274–92. DOI: 10.1177/1461444814538798

Larsson, A.O. 2015. Going Viral? Comparing Parties on Social Media during the 2014 Swedish Election. *Convergence: The International Journal of Research into New Media Technologies* 23(2): 117–31. DOI: 10.1177/1354856515577891

Larsson, A.O. & B. Kalsnes. 2014. 'Of Course We Are on Facebook': Use and Non-Use of Social Media among Swedish and Norwegian Politicians. *European Journal of Communication* (29)6: 653–67.

Larsson, A.O. & H. Moe. 2012. Studying Political Microblogging: Twitter Users in the 2010 Swedish Election Campaign. *New Media & Society* 14: 729–47.

Leibold, J. 2010. More than a Category: Han Racial Nationalism on the Chinese Internet. *The China Quarterly* 203: 539–59.

Leibold, J. 2011. Blogging Alone: China, the Internet, and the Democratic Illusion? *The Journal of Asian Studies* 70(04): 1023–41.

Leibold, J. 2016. Han Cybernationalism and State Territorialization in the People's Republic of China. *China Information* 30(1): 3–28.

Levy, S. 2011. *In The Plex: How Google Thinks, Works, and Shapes Our Lives.* New York: Simon and Schuster.

Lewis, K., J. Kaufman, M. Gonzalez, A. Wimmer & N. Christakis 2008. Tastes, Ties, and Time: A New Social Network Dataset Using Facebook.com. *Social Networks* 30(4): 330–42.

Liao, H.-T. 2009. Conflict and Consensus in the Chinese version of Wikipedia. *IEEE Technology and Society Magazine* 28(2): 49–56.

Licoppe, C. 2004. 'Connected' Presence: The Emergence of a New Repertoire for Managing Social Relationships in a Changing Communication Technoscape. *Environment and Planning D: Society and Space* 22(1): 135–56.

Licoppe, C. & Z. Smoreda. 2006. Rhythms and Ties: Towards a Pragmatics of Technologically-Mediated Sociability. In *Computers, Phones, and the Internet: Domesticating Information Technologies*, edited by R. Kraut, M. Brynin & S. Kiesler, 296–314. Oxford and New York: Oxford University Press.

Lindroth, B. 2016. *Vaeljarnas Haemnd. Populism och nationalism i Norden.* Stockholm: Carlsson.

Ling, R. 2012. *Taken for Grantedness: The Embedding of Mobile Communication into Society.* Cambridge, MA: MIT Press.

Ling, R., J. Bjelland, P.R. Sundsøy & S.W. Campbell. 2014. Small Circles: Mobile Telephony and the Cultivation of the Private Sphere. *The Information Society* 30(4): 282–91.

Litt, E. & E. Hargittai. 2016. The Imagined Audience on Social Network Sites. *Social Media + Society* (January–March): 1–12.

Lomborg, S. 2015. The Internet in My Pocket. In *The Ubiquitous Internet: User and Industry Perspectives*, edited by A. Bechmann & S. Lomborg, 35–53. New York: Routledge.

Luhmann, N. 2000. *The Reality of the Mass Media.* Cambridge: Polity Press.

Malik, A., A. Dhir & M. Nieminen. 2016. Uses and Gratifications of Digital Photo Sharing on Facebook. *Telematics and Informatics* 33: 129–38.

Mann, M. 2013. *The Sources of Social Power Vol. 4: Globalizations 1945–2011.* Cambridge: Cambridge University Press.

Mann, M. 2016. Response to the Critics. In *Global Powers: Mann's Anatomy of the 20th Century and Beyond*, edited by R. Schroeder, 281–322. Cambridge: Cambridge University Press.

Marwick, A. E. 2013. *Status Update: Celebrity, Publicity, and Branding in the Social Media Age.* New Haven: Yale University Press.

Mayer-Schoenberger, V. & K. Cukier. 2013. *Big Data: A Revolution that Will Transform How We Live, Work and Think.* London: John Murray.

McChesney, R.W. 2013. *Digital Disconnect: How Capitalism Is Turning the Internet Against Democracy.* New York: The New Press.

McCombs, M. 2013. *Setting the Agenda: The Mass Media and Public Opinion.* London: John Wiley & Sons.

Mehta, N. 2015. *Behind a Billion Screens: What Television Tells Us about Modern India.* New Delhi: Harper Collins.

Meissner, M. 2017. China's Social Credit System: A Big-Data Enabled Approach to Market Regulation with Broad Implications for Doing Business in China, accessed 23 July 2017, https://www.merics.org/en/redirect/pdf-china-monitor-nummer-39-en/

Messing, S. & S. Westwood. 2014. Selective Exposure in the Age of Social Media. *Communication Research* 41(8): 1042–63.

Meyer, M. 2014. Misjudgements Will Drive Social Trials Underground. *Nature* 511(265), 17 July.

Meyer, E.T. & R. Schroeder. 2015. *Knowledge Machines: Digital Transformations of the Sciences and Humanities.* Cambridge, MA: MIT Press.

Meyrowitz, J. 1985. *No Sense of Place: The Impact of Electronic Media on Social Behavior.* Oxford: Oxford University Press.

Miller, D. 2016. *Social Media in an English Village.* London: UCL Press.

Miller, D., E. Costa, N. Haynes, T. McDonald, R. Nicolescu, J. Sinanan, J. Spyer, S. Venkatraman & X. Wang. 2016. *How the World Changed Social Media.* London: UCL Press.

Miller, D. & J. Sinanan (2017). *Visualizing Facebook: A Comparative Perspective.* London: UCL Press.

Mudde, C. 2016. Europe's Populist Surge: A Long Time in the Making. *Foreign Affairs*, November 7, accessed 7 November 2016, https://www.foreignaffairs.com/articles/europe/2016-10-17/europe-s-populist-surge

Mudde, C. & C.R. Kaltwasser. 2013. Populism. In *The Oxford Handbook of Political Ideologies*, edited by M. Freeden & M. Stears. DOI: 10.1093/oxfordhb/9780199585977.013.0026

Mueller, J.W. 2016. *Was ist Populismus? Ein Essay*. Frankfurt: Suhrkamp.

Mukerjee, S., S. Majó-Vázquez & S. González-Bailón. (forthcoming 2017). Networks of Audience Overlap in the Consumption of Digital News. *Journal of Communication*.

Naaman, M., J. Boase & C.H. Lai. 2010. Is It Really about Me?: Message Content in Social Awareness Streams. In *Proceedings of the 2010 ACM Conference on Computer Supported Cooperative Work*, 189–92.

Napoli, P. & J. Obar. 2015. The Emerging Mobile Internet Underclass: A Critique of Mobile Internet Access. *The Information Society: An International Journal* 30(5): 323–34.

NBC Bay Area News. 2011, September 21. Schmidt on Antitrust: Competition is One Click Away, accessed 21 August 2017, http://www.nbcbayarea.com/blogs/press-here/Schmidt-on-Antitrust-Competition-is-One-Click-Away-130300333.html

Neuman, W.R. 2016. *The Digital Difference: Media Technology and the Theory of Communication Effects*. Cambridge, MA: Harvard University Press.

Neuman, W.R., L. Guggenheim, S. Mo Jang & S.Y. Bae. 2014. The Dynamics of Public Attention: Agenda-Setting Theory Meets Big Data. *Journal of Communication* 64: 193–214.

Neuman, W.R., Y.J. Park & E. Panek. 2012. Info Capacity: Tracking the Flow of Information into the Home: An Empirical Assessment of the Digital Revolution in the US from 1960–2005. *International Journal of Communication*, 6(20): 1022–41.

New York Times. 2014, February 15. The Plus in Google Plus? It's Mostly for Google. P. A1.

Newman, N., R. Fletcher, A. Kalogeropoulos, D. Levy & R. Nielsen. 2017. *Reuters Institute Digital News Report 2017*. Oxford: Reuters Institute for the Study of Journalism.

Neyazi, T.A., A. Kumar & H. Semetko. 2016. Campaigns, Digital Media, and Mobilization in India. *The International Journal of Press/Politics* 21(3): 398–416.

Ng, J. 2015. Politics, Rumors, and Ambiguity: Tracking Censorship on WeChat's Public Accounts Platform, accessed 14 July 2016, https://citizenlab.org/2015/07/tracking-censorship-on-wechat-public-accounts-platform/

Nielsen, R.K. & K. Schrøder. 2014. The Relative Importance of Social Media for Accessing, Finding, and Engaging with News, *Digital Journalism* 2(4): 472–89.

Ninan, S. 2007. *Headlines from the Heartland: Reinventing the Hindi Public Sphere*. New Delhi: Sage.

Nippert-Eng, C.E. 2010. *Islands of Privacy*. Chicago: University of Chicago Press.

Noam, E. 2016. *Who Owns the World's Media?: Media Concentration and Ownership around the World*. New York: Oxford University Press.

Norris, P. 2000. *A Virtuous Circle: Political Communication in Post-Industrial Societies*. Cambridge: Cambridge University Press.

Norris, P. & R. Inglehart. 2009. *Cosmopolitan Communication: Cultural Diversity in a Globalized World*. Cambridge: Cambridge University Press.

O'Hara, K., M. Massimi, R. Harper, S. Rubens & J. Morris. 2014. Everyday Dwelling with WhatsApp. In *Proceedings of the 17th ACM Conference on Computer Supported Cooperative Work & Social Computing*, ACM, New York, 1131–43. DOI: 10.1145/2531602.2531679

Oldenburg, R. 1989. *The Great Good Place*. New York: Marlowe and Co.

Oliver, J.E. & W.M. Rahn. 2016. Rise of the Trumpenvolk Populism in the 2016 Election. *The Annals of the American Academy of Political and Social Science* 667(1): 189–206.

O'Neil, C. 2016. *Weapons of Math Destruction: How Big Data Increases Inequality and Threatens Democracy*. London: Allen Lane.

O'Neill, J., K. Toyama, J. Chen, B. Tate & A. Siddique. 2016. The Increasing Sophistication of Mobile Media Sharing in Lower-Middle-Class Bangalore. In *Proceedings of the Eighth International Conference on Information and Communication Technologies and Development (ICTD 16)*, ACM, New York, Article 17. DOI: 10.1145/2909609.2909656

Oreglia, E. 2013. *From Farm to Farmville: Circulation, Adoption and Use of ICT between Urban and Rural China*. PhD thesis, University of California Berkeley.

Osnos, E. 2016. *Age of Ambition: Chasing Fortune, Truth and Faith in the New China*. London: Allen Lane.

Pal, J., P. Chandra & V. Vydiswaran. 2016. Twitter and the Rebranding of Narendra Modi. *Economic & Political Weekly* 51(8): 52–60.

Palshikar, S. 2016. Who is Delhi's Common Man?. *New Left Review* 98: 113–28.

Pan, J. 2016. How Market Dynamics of Domestic and Foreign Social Media Firms Shape Strategies of Internet Censorship. *Problems of Post-Communism*. DOI: 10.1080/10758216.2016.1181525

Pan, J. & Y. Xu. (forthcoming). China's Ideological Spectrum. *Journal of Politics*, accessed 2 September 2017, http://jenpan.com/

Pariser, E. 2011. *The Filter Bubble: What the Internet Is Hiding from You*. Harmondsworth: Penguin.

Pasquale, F. 2015. *The Black Box Society: The Secret Algorithms that Control Money and Information*. Cambridge, MA: Harvard University Press.

Perry, E.J. 2015. The Populist Dream of Chinese Democracy. *Journal of Asian Studies* 74(04): 903–15.

Petrie, C. 2015. *The Traffic Factories: Metrics at Chartbeat, Gawker Media, and The New York Times*, accessed 27 March 2017, http://towcenter.org/research/traffic-factories/

Pew Research Center. 2015 (June). Millennials & Political News, accessed 21 August 2017, http://www.journalism.org/files/2015/06/Millennials-and-News-FINAL-7-27-15.pdf

Pollock, R. 2010. Is Google the Next Microsoft: Competition, Welfare and Regulation in Online Search. *Review of Network Economics* 9(4): 1446–9022. DOI: 10.2202/1446-9022.1240

Porter, T. 2008. Statistics and Statistical Methods. In *The Modern Social* Sciences, edited by T. Porter and D. Ross, 238–50. Cambridge: Cambridge University Press.

Postigo, H. 2014. The Socio-technical Architecture of Digital Labor: Converting Play into YouTube Money. *New Media & Society* 18(2): 332–49. DOI: 10.1177/1461444814541527

Price, L. 2016 (2nd ed.). *The Modi Effect: Inside Narendra Modi's Campaign to Transform India*. London: Hodder.

Prior, M. 2007. *Post-Broadcast Democracy: How Media Choice Increases Inequality in Political Involvement and Polarizes Elections*. Cambridge: Cambridge University Press.

Purcell, K., J. Brenner & L. Rainie. 2012. Search Engine Use 2012. *Pew Internet and American Life Project, Pew Research Center*, accessed 2 September 2017, http://pewinternet.org/Reports/2012/Search-Engine-Use-2012.aspx

Putnam, R.D. 2001. *Bowling Alone: The Collapse and Revival of American Community*. New York: Simon and Schuster.

Qin, B., D. Stroemberg & Y. Wu. 2017. Why Does China Allow Freer Social Media? Protests versus Surveillance versus Propaganda. *Journal of Economic Perspectives* 31(1): 117–40.

Qiu, J. 2009. *Working-Class Network Society: Communication Technology and the Information Have-Less in Urban China*. Cambridge, MA: MIT Press.

Qiu, J. & W. Bu. 2013. China ICT Studies: A Review of the Field, 1989–2012. *China Review* 13(2): 123–52.

Rainie, L., A. Smith, K.L. Schlozman, H. Brady & S. Verba. 2012. Social Media and Political Engagement. *Pew Internet & American Life Project*, accessed 21 August 2017, http://www.pewinternet.org/2012/10/19/social-media-and-political-engagement/

Rainie, L. & B. Wellman. 2012. *Networked: The New Social Operating System*. Cambridge, MA: MIT Press.

Rajagopal, A. 2016. The Rise of Hindu Populism in India's Public Sphere. *Current History* (April): 123–9.

Rangaswamy, N. & P. Arora. 2015. The Mobile Internet in the Wild and Every Day: Digital Leisure in the Slums of Urban India. *International Journal of Cultural Studies* (April): 1–16.

Rangaswamy, N. & J. Benny. 2015. Social Media – China and India Compared. In *Media at Work in China and India: Discovering and Dissecting*, edited by R. Jeffrey & R. Sen, 295–326. New Delhi: Sage.

Rangaswamy, N., G. Challugulla, M. Young & E. Cutrell. 2013. Local Pocket Internet and Global Social Media. Bridging the Digital Gap: Facebook and Youth Sub-Stratum in Urban India. *International Conference on Social Implications of Computers in Developing Countries*.

Rantanen, T. 2004. *The Media and Globalization*. London: Sage.

Rao, U. & G. Greenleaf. 2013. Subverting ID from Above and Below: The Uncertain Shaping of India's New Instrument of e-Governance. *Surveillance and Society* 11(3): 287–300.

Rauchfleisch, A. & M. Schäfer. 2015. Multiple Public Spheres of Weibo: A Typology of Forms and Potentials of Online Public Spheres in China. *Information, Communication & Society* 18(2): 139–55.

Reisdorf, B. 2012. *Internet Non-Use: A Comparative Study of Great Britain and Sweden*. DPhil, Oxford Internet Institute, University of Oxford.

Rieh, S.Y. 2004. On the Web At Home: Information Seeking and Web Searching in the Home Environment. *Journal of the American Society for Information Science and Technology* 55: 743–53.

Robinson, L. 2013. Freeways, Detours, and Dead Ends: Search Journeys among Disadvantaged Youth. *New Media & Society* 16(2): 234–51.

Rothenbuhler, E.W. 1998. *Ritual Communication: From Everyday Conversation to Mediated Ceremony.* London: Sage.

Rule, J. 1997. *Theory and Progress in Social Science.* Cambridge: Cambridge University Press.

Rule, J. 2007. *Privacy in Peril: How We Are Sacrificing a Fundamental Right in Exchange for Security and Convenience.* New York: Oxford University Press.

Rydgren, J. & S. van der Meiden. 2016. Sweden, Now a Country Like All the Others? The Radical Right and the End of Swedish Exceptionalism. *Stockholm: Department of Sociology Working Paper Series.*

Sannerstedt, A. 2016. Sverigedemokraternas sympatisoerer: fler an nagonsin. In *Ekvilibrium*, edited by J. Ohlsson, H. Oscarsson & M. Solevid, 161–78. Gothenburg: Gothenburg University: SOM Institute.

Savage, M. & R. Burrows. 2007. The Coming Crisis of Empirical Sociology. *Sociology* 41(5): 885–99.

Savolainen, R. 2008. *Everyday Information Practices: A Social Phenomenological Perspective.* Lanham, MD: Scarecrow Press.

Schall, C.E. 2016. *The Rise and Fall of the Miraculous Welfare Machine: Immigration and Social Democracy in 20ᵗʰ Century Sweden.* Ithaca: Cornell University Press.

Schlozman, K.L., S. Verba & H.E. Brady. 2010. Weapon of the Strong? Participatory Inequality and the Internet. *Perspectives on Politics* 8(2): 487–509.

Schrøder, K. 2015. News Media Old and New: Fluctuating audiences, News Repertoires and Locations of Consumption. *Journalism Studies* 16(1): 60–78.

Schroeder, R. 2007. *Rethinking Science, Technology and Social Change.* Stanford: Stanford University Press.

Schroeder, R. 2010a. Mobile Phones and the Inexorable Advance of Multimodal Connectedness. *New Media and Society* 12(1): 75–90.

Schroeder, R. 2010b. *Being There Together: Social Interaction in Virtual Environments.* Oxford: Oxford University Press.

Schroeder, R. 2013. *An Age of Limits: Social Theory for the 21st Century.* Basingstoke, Palgrave Macmillan.

Schroeder, R. 2014a. Does Google Shape What We Know?. *Prometheus: Critical Studies in Innovation* 32(2): 145–60.

Schroeder, R. 2014b. Big Data and the Brave New World of Social Media Research. *Big Data and Society* (July–December): 1–11.

Schroeder, R. 2014c. Big Data: Towards a More Scientific Social Science and Humanities?. In *Society and the Internet*, edited by M. Graham & W.H. Dutton, 164–76. Oxford: Oxford University Press.

Schroeder, R. 2015. A Weberian Analysis of Global Digital Divides. *International Journal of Communication* 9: 2819–37, accessed 25 July 2016, http://ijoc.org/index.php/ijoc/article/view/3062/1456

Schroeder, R. 2016a. Rethinking Digital Media and Political Change. *Convergence: The International Journal of Research into New Media Technologies*, accessed 21 August 2017, http://journals.sagepub.com/doi/full/10.1177/1354856516660666

Schroeder, R. 2016b. The Globalization of Onscreen Sociability: Social Media and Tethered Togetherness. *International Journal of Communication*, accessed 21 August 2017, http://ijoc.org/index.php/ijoc/article/view/5729

Schroeder, R. 2016c. Big Data and Communication Research. *Oxford Research Encyclopedia of Communication*, accessed 21 August 2017, http://communication.oxfordre.com/

Schroeder, R. 2016d. Mann's Globalizations and their Limits. In *Global Powers: Mann's Anatomy of the 20th Century and Beyond*, edited by R. Schroeder, 164–82. Cambridge: Cambridge University Press.

Schroeder, R. 2017. Towards a Theory of Digital Media, *Information, Communication & Society*. DOI: 10.1080/1369118X.2017.1289231

Schroeder, R. (forthcoming). Theorizing the Uses of the Web. In *Handbook of Web Studies*, edited by N. Bruegger. London: Routledge.

Schroeder, R. & R. Ling. 2014. Durkheim and Weber on the Social Implications of New Information and Communication Technologies. *New Media and Society* 16: 789–805.

Schroeder, R. & L. Taylor. 2015. Big Data and Wikipedia Research: Social Science Knowledge across Disciplinary Divides. *Information, Communication and Society* 18(9): 1039–56.

Schudson, M. 2011 (2nd ed.). The Sociology of the News. New York: W.W. Norton.

Segev, E. & N. Ahituv. 2010. Popular Searches in Google and Yahoo!: A "Digital Divide" in Information Uses?. *The Information Society* 26 (1): 17–37.

Sen, A. 2009. *The Idea of Justice*. London: Allen Lane.

Settle, J., C.J. Fariss, R.M. Bond, J.J. Jones, J.H. Fowler, L. Coviello, A.D.I. Kramer & C. Marlow. 2016 forthcoming. Quantifying Political Discussion from the Universe of Facebook Status Updates, accessed 21 August 2017, http://papers.ssrn.com/sol3/papers.cfm?abstract_id=2307685

Silverstone, R. & E. Hirsch (eds). 1992. *Consuming Technologies: Media and Information in Domestic Spaces*. London: Routledge.

Sonnenwald, D. (ed). 2016. *Theory Development in the Information Sciences*. Austin: University of Texas Press.

Stanyer, J., S. Salgado & J. Strömbäck. 2016. Populist Actors as Communicators or Political Actors as Populist Communicators: Cross-National Findings and Perspectives. In *Populist Political Communication in Europe*, edited by T. Aalberg, F. Esser, C. Reinemann, J. Strömbäck & C. de Vreese, 353–64. London: Routledge.

Stehr, N. 1994. *Knowledge Societies*. London: Sage Publications.

Stern, R. & J. Hassid. 2012. Amplifying Silence Uncertainty and Control Parables in Contemporary China. *Comparative Political Studies* 45(10): 1230–54.

St Jean, B., S.J. Rieh, Y.M. Kim & J.Y. Yang. 2012. An Analysis of the Information Behaviors, Goals, and Intentions of Frequent Internet Users: Findings from Online Activity Diaries. *First Monday* 17(2), accessed 5 May 2013, http://journals.uic.edu/ojs/index.php/fm/article/viewArticle/3870/3143

Stockmann, D. 2013. *Media Commercialization and Authoritarian Rule in China*. Cambridge: Cambridge University Press.

Stockmann, D. 2015a. Chinese Online Publics: Who Seeks Political Information Online?. In *Urban Mobilization and New Media in Contemporary China*, edited by H. Kriesi, D. Kübler & L. Dong, 19–32. London: Ashgate.

Stockmann, D. 2015b. Big Data from China and its Implications for the Chinese State: A Research Report on the 2014 Hong Kong Protests on Weibo. *Paper presented at the Annual Meeting of the American Association of Asian Studies*, Chicago, 26–29 March 2015, Chicago, accessed 2 September 2017, http://www.authoritarianism.net/publications/

Stockmann, D. & T. Luo. 2015. Which Social Media Facilitate Online Public Opinion in China?, accessed 21 August 2017, https://papers.ssrn.com/sol3/papers.cfm?abstract_id=2663018

Strömbäck, J. & D. Dimitrova. 2011. Mediatization and Media Interventionism: A Comparative Analysis of Sweden and the United States. *International Journal of Press/Politics* 16(1): 30–49.

Strömbäck, J., A.-C. Jungar & S. Dahlberg. 2016. Sweden: No Longer a European Exception. In *Populist Political Communication in Europe*, edited by T. Aalberg, F. Esser, C. Reinemann, J. Strömbäck & C. de Vreese, 68–81. London: Routledge.

Strömbäck, J. and M. Karlsson. 2017. Sjunkande förtroende för svenska medier? En analys av hur medborgarnas medieförtroende och betydelsen av partisympati har förändrats mellan 2014 och 2016. In *Misstron mot medier*, edited by L. Truedson, 84–99, Stockholm: Institutet för mediestudier.

Subramanian, N. 2007. Populism in India. *SAIS Review of International Affairs* 27(1): 81–91.

Svensson, M. 2014. Voice, Power and Connectivity in China's Microblogosphere: Digital Divides on SinaWeibo. *China Information* 28(2): 168–88.

Tai, Z. 2015. Networked Resistance: Digital Populism, Online Activism, and Mass Dissent in China. *Popular Communication* 13(2): 120–31.

Taneja, H. 2016. Mapping an Audience-Centric World Wide Web: A Departure from Hyperlink Analysis. *New Media and Society*. DOI: 10.1177/1461444816642172

Taneja. H & J.G. Webster. 2016. How Do Global Audiences Take Shape? The Role of Institutions and Culture in Shaping Patterns of Web Use. *Journal of Communication* 66(2): 161–82.

Taneja, H. & A.X. Wu. 2014. Does the Great Firewall Really Isolate the Chinese? Integrating Access Blockage with Cultural Factors to Explain Web User Behavior. *The Information Society* 30(5): 297–309.

Taneja, H., A.X. Wu. & S. Edgerly. 2017 forthcoming. Rethinking the Generational Gap in Online News Use: An Infrastructural Perspective. *New Media and Society*.

Tang, W. 2016. *Populist Authoritarianism: Chinese Political Culture and Regime Stability*. New York: Oxford University Press.

Tencent (2016, March). "微信"影响力报告 [The Influence of WeChat], accessed 21 August 2017, http://tech.qq.com/a/20160321/007049.htm#p=14

Thelwall, M., K. Buckley & G. Paltoglou. 2012. Sentiment Strength Detection for the Social Web. *Journal of the American Society for Information Science and Technology* 63(1): 163–73.

Thompson, J. 1995. *The Media and Modernity: A Social Theory of the Media*. Cambridge: Polity Press.

Thomson, D. 2016. *Television: A Biography*. New York: Thames & Hudson.

Thornton, P. 2007. *Disciplining the State. Virtue, Violence and State-Making in Modern China*. Cambridge, MA: Harvard University Press.

Tomasky, M. 2016. Can He Be Stopped? *New York Review of Books*, April 21st, accessed 21 August 2017, http://www.nybooks.com/articles/2016/04/21/can-donald-trump-be-stopped/

Tomlinson, J. 1999. *Globalization and Culture*. Chicago: University of Chicago Press.

Trentmann, F. 2016. *Empire of Things: How We became a World of Consumers, from the Fifteenth Century to the Twenty-First*. London: Allen Lane.

Turkle, S. 2012. *Alone Together: Why We Expect More from Technology and Less from Each Other*. New York: Basic Books.

Turow, J. 2017. *The Aisles Have Eyes: How Retailers Track Your Shopping, Strip Your Privacy, and Define Your Power*. New Haven: Yale University Press.

Udupa, S. 2015. Internet Hindus: New India's Ideological Warriors. In *Handbook of Religion and the Asian City: Aspiration and Urbanization in the Twenty-First Century*, edited by P. van der Veer, 432–49. Berkeley: University of California Press.

Udupa, S. 2016. Archiving as History-Making: Religious Politics of Social Media in India. *Communication, Culture & Critique* 9: 212–30.

Vaidhyanathan, S. 2011. *The Googlization of Everything: (And Why We Should Worry)*. Berkeley: University of California Press.

van Couvering, E. 2008. The History of the Internet Search Engine: Navigational Media and the Traffic Commodity. In *Web Search: Interdisciplinary Perspectives*, edited by A. Spink & M. Zimmer, 177–206. Berlin: Springer.

Vilhelmsson, B., E. Thulin & E. Ellder. 2017. Where Does Time Spent on The Internet Come From? Tracing the Influence of Information and Communications Technology Use on Daily Activities. *Information, Communication and Society* 20(2): 250–63.

Waller, V. 2011a. Not Just Information: Who Searches for What on the Search Engine Google? *Journal of the American Society for Information Science and Technology* 62(4): 761–75.

Waller, V. 2011b. The Search Queries that Took Australian Internet Users to Wikipedia. *Information Research*, 16(2), accessed 21 August 2017, http://search.ebscohost.com/login.aspx?direct=true&db=lxh&AN=62852994&site=ehost-live

Waller, V. 2013. Diverse Everyday Information Practices in Australian Households. *Library and Information Research* 37(115): 58–79.

Walther, J.B. 1996. Computer-Mediated Communication: Impersonal, Interpersonal, and Hyperpersonal Interaction. *Communication Research* 23(1): 3–43.

Wang, X. 2016. *Social Media in Industrial China*. London: UCL Press.

Watts, D.J. 2017. Should Social Science Be More Solution-Oriented? *Nature Human Behaviour* 1. DOI: 10.1038/s41562-016-0015

Webster, J.G. 2005. Beneath the Veneer of Fragmentation: Television Audience Polarization in a Multichannel World. *Journal of Communication* 55(2): 366–82.

Webster, J.G. 2014. *The Marketplace of Attention: How Audiences Take Shape in a Digital Age*. Cambridge, MA: MIT Press.

Weibull, L. & I. Wadbring. 2014. *Mass Medier: Nya villkor för press, radio och tv i det digitala medialandskapet*. Stockholm: Ekerlids.

Westlund, O. & L. Weibull. 2013. Generation, Life Course and News Media Use in Sweden 1986–2011. *Northern Lights* 11: 147–73.

White House. 2014. The Big Data and Privacy Review, accessed 21 August 2017, http://www.whitehouse.gov/issues/technology/big-data-review

Whitley, R. 2000 (2nd ed.). *The Intellectual and Social Organization of the Sciences*. Oxford: Oxford University Press.

Williams, B. & M. Delli Carpini. 2011. *After Broadcast News: Media Regimes, Democracy, and the New Information Environment*. Cambridge: Cambridge University Press.

Wilson, R., S. Gosling & L. Graham. 2012. A Review of Facebook Research in the Social Sciences. *Perspectives on Psychological Science* 7(3): 203–20.

Wu, A.X. & H. Taneja. 2016. Reimagining Internet Geographies: A User-Centric Ethnological Mapping of the World Wide Web. *Journal of Computer-Mediated Communication* 21(3), 230–46.

Wu, L. & R. Ackland. 2014. How Web 1.0 Fails: The Mismatch between Hyperlinks and Clickstreams. *Social Network Analysis and Mining* 4(1): 1–7.

Wu, X. 2007. *Chinese Cybernationalism: Evolution, Characteristics, and Implications*. Lanham, MD: Lexington Books.

Wyatt, A. 2013. Populism and Politics in Contemporary Tamil Nadu. *Contemporary South Asia* 21(4): 365–81.

Yang, G. 2009. *The Power of the Internet in China: Citizen Activism Online*. New York: Columbia University Press.

Yang, G. 2014. Internet Activism & the Party-State in China. *Daedalus* 143(2): 110–23.

Yang, S. & A. Ghose. 2010. Analyzing the Relationship Between Organic and Sponsored Search Advertising: Positive, Negative, or Zero Interdependence? *Marketing Science* 29: 602–23.

Yongming, Z. 2006. *Historicizing Online Politics: Telegraphy, the Internet, and Political Participation in China*. Stanford: Stanford University Press.

Zeng, J. 2016. China's Date with Big Data: Will It Strengthen or Threaten Authoritarian Rule?. *International Affairs* 92(6): 1443–62.

Zhao, Y. 2012. Understanding China's Media System in a World Historical context. In *Comparing Media Systems Beyond the Western World*, edited by D. Hallin & P. Mancini, 143–76. Cambridge: Cambridge University Press.

Zhu, Y. 2012. *Two Billion Eyes: The Story of China Central Television*. New York: The New Press.

Zúñiga, G., B. Weeks & A. Ardèvol-Abreu. 2017. Effects of the News-Finds-Me Perception in Communication: Social Media Use Implications for News Seeking and Learning about Politics. *Journal of Computer-Mediated Communication* 22(3): 105–23.

Index

Bold page numbers indicate figures.

Lomborg, S. 96
Luhmann, N. 41, 156
Lunarstorm, Sweden 86
Luo, T. 75, 145

Mancini, P. 10, 32
market model. *see* commercial media
markets, digital media 6
Marwick, A.E. 89
Marxist theory 10
mass media, theories of as now misleading
1–2, 30
Mayawati 55–6
Mayer-Schoenberger, V. 137
media systems
autonomy of 10–13, **13**, 29–30, 42–3, 47,
157–8, 167–8
policymaking and big data 146–8
as subsystems 11–13, **13**
Sweden 33–4
United States 32–3, 34
mediatization
attention, limits of as constraining 7–8
and cultural, economic and political
power 2–3
defined 2–3
extension of via technoscience 20
increased 166–7
internet as intensifying 7–8, 166
of politics, economics and culture 12–13, **13**
social orders/powers, effects on 149–50
usefulness as theory 155
medical content 123
Messing, S. 37
metrics, use of 142–6
Meyrowitz, J. 7, 84, 163
microblogs, China 53
middle range, theories of 3–4
Miller, D. 82, 86, 88, 90, 91, 92, 94, 97–8,
150, 160
mobile phones
big data research 132–3
gendered use of 90
geographical reach 95
home usage 171n5
India, use of in elections 55–7
smartphones in India 55, 58
'snacking' on news 171n7
urban/rural populations 132
modernization
arguments against 46
technology and 150–1
Modi, Narendra 70–4
Mueller, J.W. 61
mutuality of sociability 95

Naaman, M. 96
Napoli, P. 88, 119, 132
national media systems
differences as still important 4
and network power, theory of 2, 30
see also media systems
national newshole 15–16
nationalism
China 74–8, 79
Hindu nationalism, India 71–3

network power, theory of 2, 30
Neuman, W.R. 16–17, 43
Newman, N. 171n5, 171n8
'news-will-find-me' phenomenon 171n9
newshole, national 15–16
newspapers
generational effects and media
consumption 34
India 48
Nicholls, T. 42
Nielsen, R.K. 38
Nippert-Eng, C.E. 90
Nissenbaum, H. 110–11

Obar, J. 88, 119, 132
Okabe, D. 92
Oliver, J.E. 67
Oreglia, E. 89, 91
Orkut, India 86
orthogonality 164–5
Oxford Internet Survey (OxIS) 104

Page, L. 110
Pal, J. 71, 72
Pan, J. 52, 54, 76
people. *see* civil society
Perry, E.J. 74–5
personal action frames 39
Pew Internet and American Life Project 104
photo sharing on social media 91–3
polarization in the US 32–3, 37, 171n4
policymaking and big data 146–8
politics
activism, digital media use of 39–40, 57
agenda-setting theory 31
attention space, struggle to dominate 5
big data analytics, use of 142–3
changes in as separate to culture and
economics 164–7
China 46–7, 51–5, 57–9
choice in media, impact of 33
and culture and economics, media's role in
compared 13–15
dangers of digital media 43–4
delimiting relevant media 30
demands, managing 41
digital media 6
elections 37–8, 55–7, 63–7, 68–9, 70–4
Facebook, sharing of views on 131–2
gatekeepers, circumventing traditional 5
holistic traditional/digital contrast,
lack of 30
hybrid media system 30
ideology, political, in China 54, 76
India 47–9, 55–9
inequality in political involvement 33
legitimacy, responsiveness as enhancing 41
limited attention space 15–17, 31, 41–2, 131
mediated 155–8
mediatization of 12–13, **13**, 20
mobile phones, use of in elections 55–7
opportunities of digital media 44
polarization in the US 32–3
presidential campaigns 37–8
responsiveness to civil society 29
as separated from culture and economics 29

28

21·14

Printed in the USA
CPSIA information can be obtained
at www.ICGtesting.com
CBHW071552080424
6567CB00005B/12